Upgrade & Repair Your PC

on a **Shoestring**

Maximum Technology at Minimum Cost

Wayne N. Kawamoto

D0140597

VENTANA

Upgrade & Repair Your PC on a Shoestring
Copyright ©1997 by Wayne N. Kawamoto

Library of Congress Cataloging-in-Publication Data

Kawamoto, Wayne N.
    Upgrade & Repair Your PC on a Shoestring / Wayne N.
Kawamoto. — 1st ed.
      p. cm.
    Includes index.
    ISBN 1-56604-529-0
    1. Microcomputers—Upgrading. 2. Microcomputers—Maintenance and
repair. I. Title.
    TK7887.K39 1996
    621.39'16—dc20   96-35964
                                        CIP

First Edition 9 8 7 6 5 4 3

Printed in the United States of America

Ventana Communications Group, Inc.
P.O. Box 13964
Research Triangle Park, NC 27709-3964
919.544.9404
FAX 919.544.9472
http://www.vmedia.com

Chief Executive Officer
Josef Woodman

**Vice President of
Content Development**
Karen A. Bluestein

Managing Editor
Lois J. Principe

Production Manager
John Cotterman

Technology Operations Manager
Kerry L. B. Foster

Product Marketing Manager
Jamie Jaeger Fiocco

Creative Services Manager
Diane Lennox

Art Director
Marcia Webb

Acquisitions Editor
Neweleen A. Trebnik

Project Editor
Jessica A. Ryan

Developmental Editor
Linda Orlando

Copy Editor
Norma Emory

CD-ROM Specialist
Ginny Phelps

Technical Reviewer
Robert H. Nichols

Desktop Publisher
Lance Kozlowski

Proofreader
Ron Ferrell

Indexer
Sherry Massey

Cover Illustrator
Elena Skrinak

About the Author

Wayne Kawamoto is an established freelance writer in the field of computing, with hundreds of published articles, columns, and reviews in a variety of national publications. Wayne has worked as an engineer, market analyst, and program manager at different points in his career. When he's not evaluating the latest software and hardware, upgrading or repairing computers, or writing about them, he enjoys spending time with his wife and three children. Wayne lives in La Verne, California.

Acknowledgments

I could never take on the daunting task of writing a book on my own. I have lots of people to thank for helping make this book a reality.

To the pros at Ventana who reviewed drafts, provided technical suggestions and advice, laid out the pages, and caught my mistakes, especially, Jessica Ryan, Norma Emory, and Linda Orlando.

To Martha Kaufman, my agent, who made this book happen and who didn't get mad at me when I accidentally called her at 3:00 A.M.

To Diamond Multimedia, Nanao, Creative Labs, and Intel for providing me with timely background information.

More thanks, a little closer to home:

To Mark Kurtz, friend and network guru, who provided advice over lunches of cheap burritos and let me borrow his equipment.

To Wayne Reinecke and the owners of Computer Village in San Dimas for lending me equipment.

To Gregg Keizer, writer extraordinaire, who lent advice, gave me pep talks, and—in the early days—helped boost my fledgling writing career.

To Serge Handchin, lunch partner and teriyaki chicken expert, who boosted my spirits by telling me he wanted an autographed copy of the book when it was done.

To Janet Kawamoto, my wife, who read drafts, provided suggestions on making the text more approachable, and generally backed me up throughout this project.

Contents

Introduction xvii

Section I Time for an Upgrade

1 Why Upgrade? 1

The Solution 3
When Is a Good Time to Upgrade? 4
Can I Really Do it Myself? 5
Where Do I Begin? 6

2 What Do You Want to Do With Your System? 9

Do You Want to Run Windows 95? 10
Do You Want to Run Windows 3.1? 14
Do You Want to Connect to the Internet &
  Other Services? 15
Do You Want Multimedia? 17
Do You Want to Work With Specialties?................................. 21
  Desktop Publishing • Image Editing • Video Editing
The All-Around System 26

3 What Upgrades Will You Need? 29

If You Own an 8088, Original IBM PC, or XT 30
If You Own an AT or 286 30
If You Own a 386SX or 386DX 31
If You Own a 486SX or 486DX 33
If You Own a Pentium 34

Section II The Components

4 The CPU & the Mother of All Boards 39

Why Replace Your CPU? 43
When the Chips Are Down 44
Who's Driving the Bus? 50
Other Things Mother Never Told You About 53
How to Buy a Motherboard 55

5 Thanks for the Memory 57

Expand Your Memory 59
Extend Out 60
Shopping for RAM 61

6 Video Cards 67

Upgrading Video 72
The Video Card 72
Bottom Line 80

7 Hard Drives 81

Storage Space: A Final Frontier 82
The Need for Speed 85
Hard Drive Nuts & Bolts 87
Buying a New Hard Drive 88
Don't Forget the Floppy 90
More Storage & Backups 91
   Get It On Tape • Recordable CD-ROM • Removable Drives
   • Re-writable Optical Disk Drives

8 Monitor This 99

Upgrading a Monitor 101
Bigger Is Better 103
The Rest of the Story 105
The Intangibles 107
Buying a Monitor 108

9 CD-ROMs 111

What to Look For 113
Making the Connection 115
Buying the CD-ROM 116
Innie or Outey 117

10 Sound Cards.. 119

Which One Sounds Best? 120
Games People Play... 121
    Catch a Wave • MIDI (Musical Instrument Digital Interface)
    • Audio CD • Hearing Voices

Sound Shopping Advice 126

11 Modems 129

A World of Information 130
Just the Fax 132
Hearing Voices 135
Remote Computing 137
Modem Considerations 139
    Playing the Numbers • Fax Considerations • Voice
    Considerations • Internal vs. External

12 Bargain Basement 147

Specialty Computer Stores 148
Warehouse Stores 149
Computer Superstores 150
Mail Order 151
Computer Swap Meets 152
Where to Buy 154
General Buying Tips 154

Section III Nuts & Bolts

13 The Tools & Work Area 159

Tools for All Your Needs 160
    A Basic Set of Screwdrivers • Needle-nose Pliers • Tweezers
    • Three-prong Extractor • Flashlight • Fine-point Permanent
    Marker • DOS Boot Disk • Foam Padding • Small Adhesive
    Labels • Antistatic Wrist Strap • Work Space

Additional Tools You Might Need 166
    Nut or Hex Drivers • Torx Screwdriver • Chip Puller

14   Opening Up Your PC & Adding Expansion Cards 173

Opening Up Your Computer 173
   To Open Your Case

Installing Expansion Boards 177
   Installing a New Expansion Board • Just a Few More Tips
   Before You Begin Working

15   Upgrading Your CPU 183

Overdrive Chip Installation 186
   Replacing Your ZIF-socketed CPU • Replacing Your Non-ZIF-
   socketed CPU • Installing the Chip in a Socket Near Your CPU
   • Now, Test the System

Troubleshooting 188

16   Replacing the Motherboard 191

RAM for Your Motherboard 192
Opening Your PC 192
Removing the Motherboard (Bye, Mom!) 193
Putting It All Back Together (Hi, Mom!) 198
Troubleshooting 201
This Is It 202

17   Replacing or Adding RAM 203

Adding a SIMM to Your Motherboard 205
To Remove Existing SIMMs 207
Inserting New SIMMs 208
SIMM Troubleshooting 211

18   Replacing the Video Card 213

Replacing a Video Card 214
   If You Have to Remove an Existing Video Board • To Install
   Your New Video Board • Problems & Solutions

19 Installing a Modem 229

Installing an External Modem 230
Configuring Your Internal Modem 237
If you're Running Windows 95 & Have Installed a Plug-&-Play Modem • If You Have Installed a Non-Plug-&-Play Modem • If You Have Installed a Non-Plug-&-Play Card With Windows 95 • If You're Running Windows 3.1
Setting Up Communications Software 239
Troubleshooting 240

20 Installing an IDE Hard Drive & Floppy 241

Adding a New IDE Hard Drive 242
Removing the Old Hard Drive • Installing Your New Drive • Troubleshooting
Replacing Your Floppy Drive 258
Removing the Existing Floppy Drive • Installing a New Floppy Drive • Floppy Troubleshooting

21 Installing Multimedia: The CD-ROM Drive & Sound Card 265

To Install the Sound Card 267
If You Are Running Windows 95 & Have Installed a Plug-&-Play Video Card • If You Are Running Windows 95 & Have Installed a Non-Plug-&-Play Video Card
Installing the CD-ROM Drive 272
Powering Up Your Multimedia System 276
Test Your New Multimedia System
Troubleshooting 277

22 You've Got Trouble, My Friend: Repairing Your PC 279

General Troubleshooting 280
Isolating a Faulty Component 282
More Specific Troubleshooting 283
If Your Computer Doesn't Turn on at All • If Your Hard Drive Is Failing • If You Can't Read a Floppy • If Your System Locks Up • If Screens Don't Look Right • If You're Having CD-ROM Problems • If You're Hearing the Sounds of Silence • If You Have Printing Problems • Lack of Communications—Modem Problems • Keyboard Problems • Mouse Traps

23 Maintenance **295**

Computer Placement 295
Power 298
Periodic Maintenance 299
Other Maintenance (or, Defending Your System From Children &
    Other Gremlins) 300
Other System Considerations 301

Section IV Appendices

A About the Companion CD-ROM **307**

B Removing Unwanted Windows 3.x Files **313**

C Those Pesky General Protection Faults **317**

D Upgrade-Related Vendors **321**

E Upgrade Vendors by Category **363**

Glossary **375**

Index **383**

Introduction

What is *Upgrade & Repair Your PC on a Shoestring?* Perhaps it's easier to tell you first what it's not. You won't find suggestions on giving your old jeans new life as inexpensive mouse pads or tips on recycling old floppy disks as coasters.

What you will find is solid advice and pretty much all the information you need to figure out what you can do to make your computer run faster and do the things you want it to do. This book will tell you how to make the best and most worthwhile upgrades at the lowest possible cost. First, you will use this information to decide what components to upgrade. Then I will show you, step-by-step, how to perform the upgrade yourself, with your own two hands. This may sound like a stretch for some of you, but you can do it. Trust me.

Of course, before you can upgrade, you must have an idea what you want to do with your computer. *Upgrade & Repair Your PC on a Shoestring* is perhaps the only book that dedicates a chapter to discussing your computer needs (multimedia, educational programs, Internet, etc.) and what type of computer you will require. This way, you'll make only the absolutely necessary upgrades, without wasting money on unneeded horsepower.

Even if you get cold feet and decide to have someone else make the upgrades, you'll find that this book still provides an excellent introduction to computers and their components and can help you decide what upgrades your system will need. Armed with this knowledge, you'll be able to talk with technicians at your local computer repair store and not be intimidated by them and their technical jargon.

You'll end up with a system that you're happy with and get extra mileage out of your investment. You'll also find related troubleshooting advice that will help get you through almost any computer catastrophe. The Companion CD-ROM included with this book contains diagnostic tools and utilities to assist you with troubleshooting and upgrading.

Who Can Use This Book?

Most computer upgrade books are geared toward those who already know a lot about computers. Such books discuss in endless and laborious detail the workings, principles, and background of each and every component. *Upgrade & Repair Your PC on a Shoestring* takes the simple and easy route for beginner and intermediate computer users. Whether you're new to upgrading computers or fairly confident of your upgrading ability, this is a book for you.

This book never assumes that you are a technical whiz. For this reason, you'll find definitions of virtually all computer terms when they first appear, under the heading "Definition, Please." Also, to help you save money during your upgrades, you'll find specific "Cost" tips throughout the chapters.

While this book features in-depth discussions of computer components, the emphasis is on what they do, how you might upgrade them to improve your system, and what to look for when buying them. What you won't find are boring details on how each component works at a technical level.

I hope that this book will open the possibilities of upgrading a computer to a much wider audience—even to people who may never have considered upgrading before.

What's Inside

This book is divided into three sections: "Time for an Upgrade," "The Components," and "Nuts & Bolts." The "Time for an Upgrade" section features chapters that discuss what you might want to do with your computer and help you determine what type of system you will need. "The Components" chapters explain the major components in detail: what they do, how they fit into your system, how they can improve your system's performance, and what to look for when you buy them. Finally, the "Nuts & Bolts" section provides step-by-step instructions for performing the upgrade yourself.

Here's a chapter-by-chapter rundown:

Section I: Time for an Upgrade

Chapter 1: Why Upgrade?

This chapter talks about upgrading as a viable option: advantages and disadvantages, what's involved, how you can perform your own upgrades and repairs by following the instructions in the book, and how to build up a more powerful system at minimum cost.

Chapter 2: What Do You Want to Do With Your System?

Before you can upgrade your system, you have to understand what you want to do with it—so you can determine the necessary and cost-effective upgrades. This chapter talks about what you'll need to run Windows, Windows 95, and multimedia and recommends system upgrades for tasks such as image editing, desktop publishing, video editing, and 3D graphics.

Chapter 3: What Upgrades Will You Need?

After you have determined what you want to do with your system, this chapter will help you decide what upgrades you'll need. Here you'll find charts to help you describe your current system and show you upgrade options. I offer recommendations on getting the most value for your hard-earned dollars and outline the upgrades that are absolutely necessary, as well as those that will provide the greatest performance gains.

Section II: The Components

In this section, I discuss the various components of the system—
what they are, what they do, how they affect your computer's
performance, cost-vs.-performance trade-offs, where to buy components, and what to look for. I conclude this section with Chapter
12, "Bargain Basement," where I talk about finding the best buys
on the components you need.

Chapter 4: The CPU & the Mother of All Boards

This chapter talks about the evolution of the central processing
unit (CPU) over the years, and the various types that you can
consider for your upgrade. There's also a discussion on the different ways you can upgrade your CPU by either buying an
OverDrive chip or replacing the motherboard.

Chapter 5: Thanks for the Memory

Here I talk about how adding memory to your system can improve significantly the performance of your PC, the different types
of memory available, the types that you should consider for your
upgrade, and issues you need to think about before adding
memory to your motherboard.

Chapter 6: Video Cards

This chapter covers what a video card is—how it improves the
performance of your system and when you should consider a
video card upgrade. You'll also find definitions of the various
terms you need to understand in order to buy the best video card
for your system and needs.

Chapter 7: Hard Drives

When you keep running out of space to store your data and applications, you can turn to this chapter for explanations on what hard
drives are, the different types that you should consider for your
upgrade, the terms that define a hard drive's performance, and
what to look for.

Chapter 8: Monitor This

What you see isn't always what you get. Chapter 8 tells you what
a monitor is, how it works, what types of monitors have been

available through the years, and which ones you should consider for your upgrade. This chapter also talks about issues such as picture quality and size, how to match your monitor with your video card, and electromagnetic emissions.

Chapter 9: CD-ROMs

To bring multimedia to your system, you'll want to consider a CD-ROM drive. In this chapter, I talk about the issues that you need to understand to purchase a drive, including raw speed, how fast a drive can transfer data, and the different types that you can buy. We'll take a close look at your system to see which is right for your PC.

Chapter 10: Sound Cards

So you can have sound that complements your multimedia, I talk about what sound cards do, the different types of sound cards (including those that can play audio effects in Windows and compose and play music like a real-life orchestra) and what you need to play the latest games and educational titles.

Chapter 11: Modems

If you want to cruise the information superhighway and go online to discover continents of data, I explain what a modem is and what it does. I talk about how you can use a modem to go online, send and receive faxes from your computer, answer your phone and record messages, and control other PCs across telephone lines. Last, I define for you the terms and concepts associated with modems and tell you what to look for when shopping for one.

Chapter 12: Bargain Basement

Where can you get the best prices on upgrade components? Refer to this chapter for the pros and cons of buying at your neighborhood mom and pop computer store, from the general warehouse/price saving stores, at computer superstores, through mail order, and at computer swap meets. With the advice here, you can reduce that bottom line. I'll also present strategies to protect yourself when making purchases so you don't get burned.

Section III: Nuts & Bolts

In this section, I describe the tools and work area you'll need and precautions to take before actually opening your computer. The following chapters give step-by-step instructions, with photographs, on how to install your new components and discuss possible problems and solutions. The last chapters offer a complete troubleshooting guide plus maintenance tips.

Chapter 13: The Tools & Work Area

To work on your computer, you must have the right tools. Here I discuss the various items that make up a computer tool kit including screwdrivers, pliers, chip pullers, and more. I also talk about how to organize your work area. Even if you're performing the upgrade on your kitchen table, you'll learn how to set it up so the upgrade is smooth and the table is cleared before dinnertime.

Chapter 14: Opening Up Your PC & Adding Expansion Cards

Here's where we dive in and begin performing upgrades. In this chapter, I provide you with step-by-step instructions on how to open your PC and change expansion cards. Included here are suggestions for making the task easier and precautions to help keep it safe.

Chapter 15: Upgrading Your CPU

In this chapter, I show you how to perform an upgrade by replacing the CPU. I talk about the different types of motherboards that you might encounter and then show you the steps to perform this upgrade. And should anything go wrong, there's troubleshooting advice to help you through.

Chapter 16: Replacing the Motherboard

Here's where I provide detailed instructions on how to replace your motherboard. I cover removing the various components, connectors, and the motherboard itself and show you how to tell if a motherboard fits in your case. Then there are instructions for securing the motherboard into the case, reconnecting the cables, reinstalling the components, and then testing the system. Of course, I also include plenty of precautions and tips plus a troubleshooting guide.

Chapter 17: Replacing or Adding RAM

In this chapter, I show you how to add random access memory (RAM) to your PC—from pushing the tiny levers on a memory slot to seating a new board in its place. You can follow the step-by-step instructions and photographs to add RAM quickly, and if you run into problems, there's troubleshooting advice to help you solve almost any problem.

Chapter 18: Replacing the Video Card

When your system is ready for a new look, you can follow the instructions in this chapter to change your video card. The step-by-step directions consider whether you're running Windows 3.1 or Windows 95 and include a comprehensive array of tips, precautions, and problem-solving suggestions. You'll find that in almost no time, your system will be looking good.

Chapter 19: Installing a Modem

If you're itching to surf the Web, you can turn to this chapter, which will show you the necessary steps to install an external or internal modem, make connections, and get it running under Windows 3.1 or Windows 95. We'll also cover your communications, fax, or other software, plus how to solve any problems you may run into.

Chapter 20: Installing an IDE Hard Drive & Floppy

To seriously increase your PC's real estate and storage space, you can use this chapter to learn how to install a controller board, hook up cables, secure a drive in the case, set up and configure the hard drive, and get it running. And just in case things don't go smoothly, there's a helpful list of potential problems and suggestions on how to solve them. If you're adding a floppy drive, here's where you find instructions on installing that as well.

Chapter 21: Installing Multimedia: The CD-ROM Drive & Sound Card

If you've gone out and bought a new sound card and CD-ROM drive, you can follow the instructions in this chapter to learn how to install and connect them. The chapter also shows you the steps to take to configure them. There are also suggestions to get you through any problems you may encounter.

Chapter 22: You've Got Trouble, My Friend

I hope that you never have to refer to this chapter, but if you do, you'll find strategies for figuring out what's wrong with your PC. First I give you general strategies that you can perform to isolate a problem part. Later on in the chapter, I talk about specific conditions and their probable causes.

Chapter 23: Maintenance

To keep your PC running, you can follow the suggestions in this chapter about factors in your own home or office that can affect your PC's life, along with suggestions on periodic maintenance steps that you can perform to significantly increase the life of your computer and its parts.

About the Companion Disk

To help you with your system diagnostics, this book comes with a Companion CD-ROM disk full of software utilities and other helpful programs. You'll find that the utilities will be invaluable as you go about the process of evaluating your system, upgrading it by installing new components, and troubleshooting any problems that you may encounter. Throughout the book, you'll be referred to the appropriate part of the CD-ROM to help you at that particular moment.

I hope that you find this book useful and that it helps you get more enjoyment and productivity from your computer. Enough of this introductory stuff. Let's get on with it so you can get on with your computing!

Wayne N. Kawamoto

SECTION I

Time for an Upgrade

Why Upgrade?

You can't be too rich or too thin. Your computer can't be too fast or your hard drive too big. You've probably noticed that PC technology keeps evolving at an incredible pace: The term "cutting edge" usually includes only systems that are less than three months old. After that, the newest CD-ROMs, the latest games, and the most recent operating systems change everything and require newer, higher, and faster hardware.

When you buy a new car and drive it off the lot, its value immediately drops. Likewise, once you buy a personal computer with your hard-earned money, your investment is suddenly worth less. But computer systems become outdated a lot faster than cars, so a system's resale value is a fraction of its original cost just a year or two after it was the latest and greatest on the market. If cars were like PCs, there would be faster, sleeker car models every six months, and you could buy a used car that was only a year old for less than half its original price. As you can see in Figure 1-1, computers have vastly increased their speed and performance over the years.

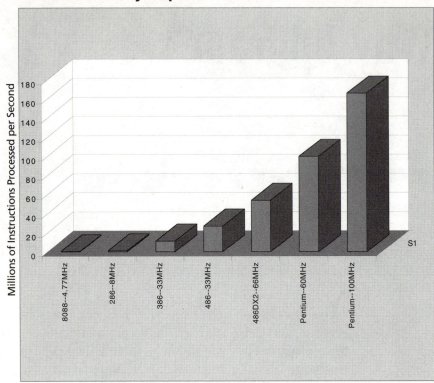

PC Performance by Chip

Figure 1-1: Chip speeds in history.

I learned the hard way about the useful life of computers. Years ago, before I started writing about computers, my wife and I were buying our first 8088 PC. (Actually, my wife was the one who wanted to buy the computer, and I was the one who got hooked.) After mulling over the considerable expense, we finally justified the purchase with the idea that our baby could use the system when she went to college.

The baby is now 10 years old and has two siblings, and I've gone through at least eight systems. My current computer runs more than two hundred times faster than the one that our daughter won't be taking to college.

The Solution

There's no shortage of computer owners who paid thousands of dollars a few years ago for what were then state-of-the-art systems. Today, those computers can't run any of the newer programs and are worth only a few hundred dollars. For anyone buying a computer, the rapid changes in price and technology are overwhelming.

So what's a computer owner to do? The answer is to upgrade your computer to keep your system current.

While upgrading isn't a magic answer—no application of smoke and mirrors will instantly make your computer run faster, brew coffee, and solve all of humanity's problems—upgrading is a viable and very cost-effective alternative to watching your system's capabilities fade.

Upgrading means that you replace key components in your system to increase its speed and give it more storage capacity. By buying only select components, you can get much of the benefit of a newer and faster PC. This book will show you the key components and help you decide which ones to buy.

Upgrading has another advantage. As you go through the process, you'll gain a far better understanding of your system, and it won't intimidate you if something should go wrong. We'll get to the matter of repairs in Section III, "Nuts & Bolts."

Finally, of course, you can save money by upgrading your current system instead of buying a new one. It costs less to replace a few components than to buy an entire new system, even though the industry continually introduces better computers at lower prices. In later chapters, we will give you tips on where to shop to find low prices on components.

On the downside—to be frank—there's a point at which a system becomes so outdated that upgrading isn't feasible. You'll know that's happened when you update one component, but it's so much faster than the rest of the system that you find yourself changing almost everything else. Before you know it, you have built an entire new computer and you have a box full of unusable spare parts. In that case, you'll be financially and emotionally better off if you buy an entire new computer (unless you *want* to build a system of your own from the ground up, which is an interesting and educational challenge).

When Is a Good Time to Upgrade?

Obviously, it's not necessary to upgrade just to have the latest and fastest system (although I know people who do—it makes for great party and office conversation). If you're thinking about upgrading, there's usually a reason. The most common impetus is that you want to use certain software or a new operating system that won't run on your current machine. Or it may be that your computer is too slow when running multimedia, graphic-intensive programs, or new games. In either case, it's definitely time to upgrade, if only to minimize your frustration. Of course, if you're happy with your current system and it does everything you could possibly want it to do, enjoy it and forget upgrading for the moment!

Ask yourself the following questions to know when it's time to upgrade:

○ Do your applications load without causing delays or frustrations?

○ Can your applications handle your data? For example, can you quickly scroll from one part of a document to another part?

○ Does your computer often keep you waiting?

○ Have you avoided purchasing new software or a new operating system because your computer can't run it?

○ Do you feel when reading the latest computer magazines that there isn't much information in them that applies to your system?

Can I Really Do it Myself?

At this point, you're probably saying to yourself, "Well this all sounds fine on paper, but can I really do my own upgrades?" If you're having second thoughts, read on for some advice and encouragement. I asked myself these very same questions when I upgraded my first system years ago.

○ *Can I really perform an upgrade myself?*
  Yes, absolutely. There are some tricks and some knowledge involved, but I'll try to explain everything you need to know. Just by buying this book, you've taken the first step toward upgrading your computer's performance. You *will* be able to do it.

○ *Doesn't upgrading mean that I actually have to open the computer case and replace components?*
  Yes, you will have to get your hands dirty, but I'll walk you through each step and discuss the tools that you will need. As you'll see, changing components isn't that difficult. A computer is a simple box that houses a bunch of components. Not that it's as easy as changing a light bulb. If that were the case, you wouldn't need this book.

○ *But how do I know which parts to buy for my computer?*
  In upcoming chapters, you'll find explanations and charts that tell what upgrades you should make, based on your current system and what you'd like to be able to run on it. I'll talk about each of the components in detail so you can gain an understanding of what they do and what to look for when you go shopping. I'll suggest where to shop for the lowest prices. Finally, I'll walk you through the installation process.

○ *What if I mess something else up when I change a component?*
  Unfortunately, this is a possibility, and it's natural to be nervous. (You should have seen me the first time I opened a computer case.) I'll do my best to help you and provide warnings and precautions along the way, along with troubleshooting tips in each chapter. Some computers are very sensitive and seem to go crazy at the slightest provocation, but you can usually undo any mistakes that you make.

Where Do I Begin?

To give you a starting point, it will help if you write down the key facts about your current system in the following form. Don't worry if you don't know some of the answers. You can fill them in after you've read the chapters that define and explain components.

CPU _____

Speed _____

Amount of memory _____

Type of memory _____

Motherboard slots _____

Hard drive size _____

Hard drive speed _____

Floppy drive sizes (list all)_____

_____

Video card memory _____

Video card type (number of bits/memory) _____

CD-ROM (yes/no) _____

    CD-ROM speed _____

Modem (yes/no)_____

    Modem speed_____

Sound card (yes/no) _____

    16-bit (yes/no) _____

    Wave table (yes/no)_____

Form 1-1: Your current system.

Moving On

By purchasing this book, you've already taken the first step in upgrading your computer. You've learned the advantages of upgrading—how it saves you money and gives you a system that can run the latest applications.

Now you've begun making notes about your current system, which will help you decide exactly what upgrades you will need to make. With this information in hand, we're ready to move to Chapter 2 and the next step: deciding what you want to do with your computer.

What Do You Want to Do With Your System?

Before you upgrade your computer, before you figure out what low-priced components you'll need to buy, before you determine what capabilities your computer needs, you must decide what you want to do with your computer system.

This chapter will describe some key types of computing and present some of the basic technology that you will need to know about each one. To show you what kind of system you will need to do the tasks or play the games you want, the following charts list information about *processors*, *hard drives*, *video cards*, *memory*, *CD-ROMs*, and *sound cards*. Using these guidelines, you can determine what changes you want to make to your system.

If you're new to computers, or at least to the technical aspects, some of the terms will sound foreign to you. Don't panic. I'll briefly explain some key terms as we go along and give you more details in later chapters.

Definition, Please

There are several important terms that will help you understand the way your computer works, and you'll come across them often in this book. Briefly, the processor is at the center of your computer's hardware and controls all of the functions of your computer. The processor is what you are referring to when you call a computer a 386, 486, or Pentium. The hard drive is where your computer stores applications (software) and your data. The video card outputs (translates) video from your computer onto your computer's screen. Memory is your computer's work space, where it actually does all the things it's supposed to do. You'll learn more about all of these terms later.

So here's your chance to do some real dreaming and window-shopping. With a faster, more powerful computer you might be able to finish your work so quickly you'll have time to lie in your hammock and contemplate baseball scores, decide what movies you want to see, or watch the grass grow. That's probably not very realistic, but we *are* dreaming.

Do You Want to Run Windows 95?

Never in the history of computing has there been a product with a rollout and prehype like Windows 95. Even my mother asked me what this "Windows 95 stuff" was all about. If she, who has barely ever used a computer, is asking about Windows 95, I know that the advertising has reached almost everyone in America.

Windows 95 has been the subject of a lot of criticism, but I have to say that it has generally succeeded. Windows 95 is the next-generation graphical *operating system* for the PC.

Definition, Please

An *operating system* is the program on a computer that performs basic memory, disk, and file management. In other words, it's the core program that defines how your computer works, so it can run software programs and accept what you type in on a keyboard or click with a mouse. You can see in Figure 2-1 that the operating system lies at the center of your computer's operations, taking inputs from your keyboard and mouse and providing a platform on which software can run. Well-known operating systems include Windows, Windows 95, Windows NT, DOS, OS/2, and UNIX. A *graphical operating system* is one in which you can communicate with the computer by using a mouse to select *icons*, tiny pictures that represent many commands you would ordinarily type in on a keyboard.

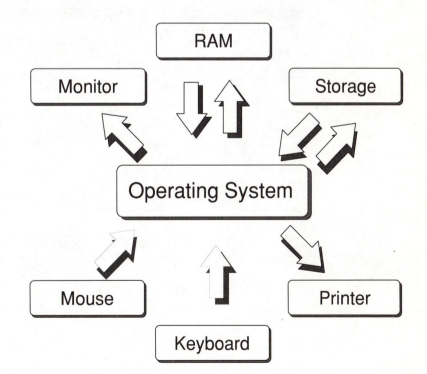

Figure 2-1: The operating system is at the heart of your computer's operations.

Windows 95 is generally easy to understand and use. It can recognize certain hardware, so you don't have to go through complicated installation processes. It can identify files with names that are longer than the eight characters allowed by DOS and earlier versions of Windows. Windows 95 can run several programs at the same time, a process called *multitasking* (see Figure 2-2). This way, you can perform two things at the same time—for example, download files from the Internet while you work in your word processing program. Of course, to take advantage of these features, the software you run has to be specifically designed to use them.

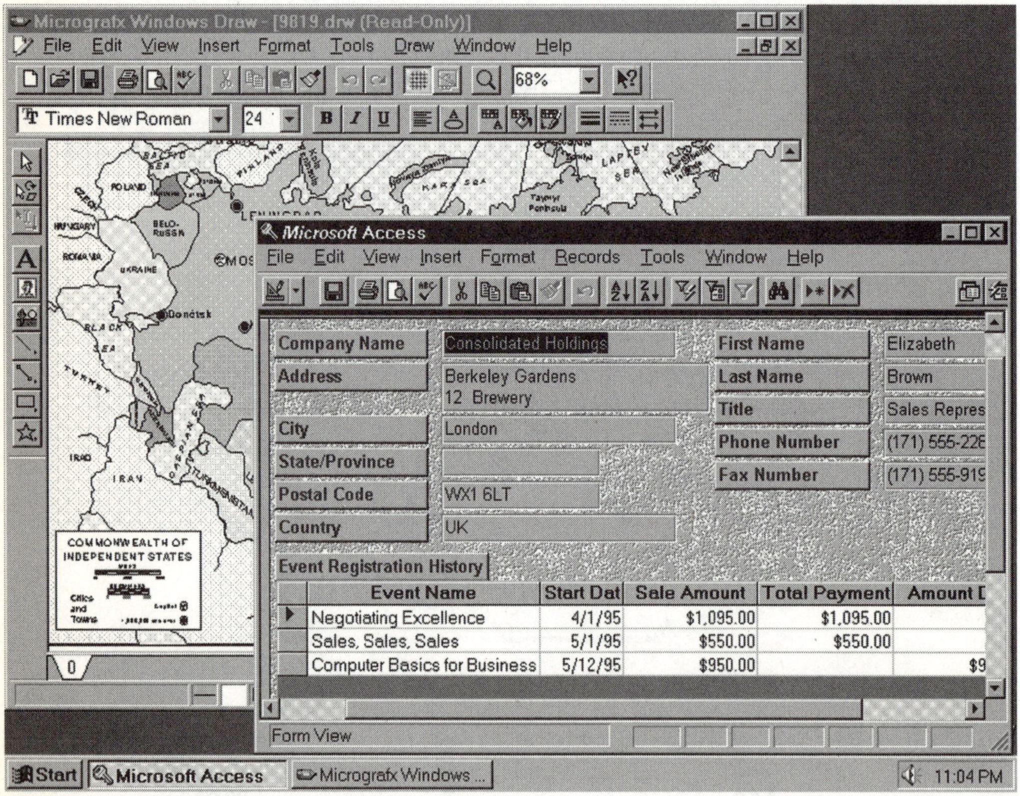

Figure 2-2: Windows 95 lets you open several software programs at the same time.

Because Windows 95 is so popular, many well-known programs now come in Windows 95 versions. Microsoft's ads claim that everything runs faster under Windows 95, but my own experience suggests otherwise. However, now that lots of popular software programs are geared toward Windows 95 and include new "gotta have" features, you're probably going to have to use Windows 95 to run the latest programs and keep up with the Joneses. You'll find that all major programs are available for Windows 95 and Windows 3.x, but you probably won't find dedicated versions of most programs for other operating systems such as OS/2 Warp.

Of course, Windows 95 makes enormous demands on computer systems. Suddenly, a host of computer owners who could adequately run older versions of Windows on their systems have found that their PCs are too slow and don't have enough memory to run Windows 95.

If your goal is to run Windows 95 on your computer, you'll want a fast system, a large hard drive, and lots of memory. Keep in mind that Microsoft's stated minimum requirements will run Windows 95 but will run it so slowly that it's virtually unusable. You really will need more capacity.

Table 2-1 will help you determine the requirements for your system to run Windows 95. These figures are not those supplied by the software publishers. Rather, they are my recommended systems, based on my experience using them.

	Processor	Hard Drive	Memory	Video	CD-ROM	Sound
Min	486	500MB	8MB	SVGA	4X	Yes
Good	Pentium	1GB	16MB	SVGA/1MB	4X+	Yes
Great	Pentium (155+)	2GB+	16MB+	SVGA/2MB+	4X+	Yes

Table 2-1: Requirements for Windows 95.

Do You Want to Run Windows 3.1?

Windows 95 has hogged much of the spotlight lately, but many businesses and home computer owners don't use it. Furthermore, many software publishers still write programs that will run under either Windows 3.1 or Windows 95. (In practice, most programs that run under Windows 3.1 and even DOS should run under Windows 95.) Bottom line: Despite the fact that Windows 95 is the latest and greatest operating system, Windows 3.1, as shown in Figure 2-3, is still very popular.

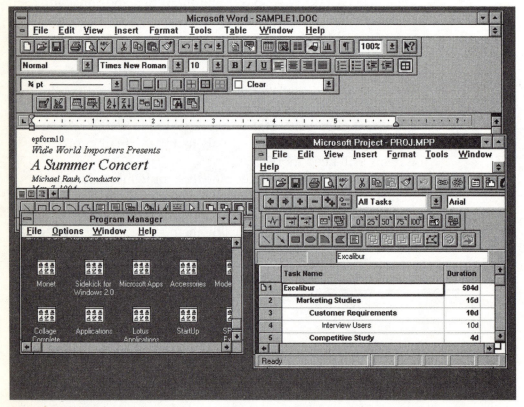

Figure 2-3: Lots of users still rely on Windows 3.1, and many software publishers continue to support it.

If your goal is to run Windows 3.1, some guidelines are shown in Table 2-2. (You'll notice that the requirements are lower than those for Windows 95.)

	Processor	Hard Drive	Memory	Video	CD-ROM	Sound
Min	486	100MB	4MB	VGA	4X	Yes
Good	Pentium	500MB	8MB	SVGA/1MB	4X+	Yes
Great	Pentium (133+)	1 GB+	16MB	SVGA/1MB	4X+	Yes

Table 2-2: Requirements for Windows 3.1.

Do You Want to Connect to the Internet & Other Services?

The information superhighway that politicians like to tout and newscasters love to babble about may be overhyped, but it is fast becoming reality. Today, business cards usually have an *e-mail* address, companies advertise their electronic addresses on television, and marriages are breaking up over cyberspace romances (just ask Ann Landers).

Definition, Please

Electronic mail (e-mail) is a way to communicate through computers. It's similar to writing a letter or fax, but you don't send any paper. The message appears electronically on the recipient's computer screen.

At its most basic level, the Internet is a huge network that connects thousands of commercial, academic, private, and government computers and networks in almost a hundred countries. Originally developed by the military, the Internet has grown to be used by millions of users to exchange and share information.

Of most interest now is the *World Wide Web*, a part of the Internet that displays graphics and is easy enough for just about anyone to use. On the Web, you'll find an endless amount of information in pages that are created by companies, educational organizations, clubs, and individuals, as shown in Figure 2-4. Mail-order catalogs, information on fly-fishing, movie ads and reviews, Star Trek fan clubs—they're all available on the Web.

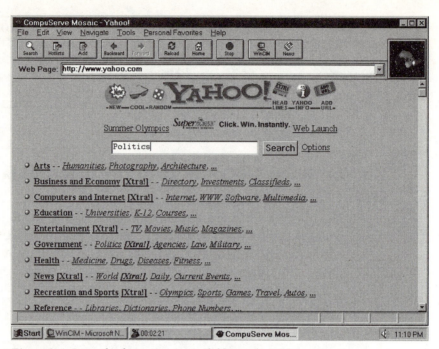

Figure 2-4: Lots of information is available on the Web.

Of course, the Internet isn't the only game in town, and long-time information providers such as CompuServe, America Online, and Prodigy offer other online services. However, they have all resigned themselves to offering Internet access, too.

To get on and ride the superhighway, you'll need the right equipment. (Table 2-3 outlines the minimum requirements.) Fortunately, the limiting factor in using a computer online isn't its processing power. Most bottlenecks occur in transmitting information over phone lines, which are used for most Internet connections. To access the Internet, you don't need an ultrapowerful computer like that needed to run multimedia programs. What you do need is a *modem*—the fastest you can get (28.8 bps).

Definition, Please

A *modem* is a device that converts computer signals into a form that may be transmitted across a telephone line and back again. This way, your computer can communicate with other computers through the phone. Modems come in internal and external versions. The internal ones go inside of your computer, while the external ones sit outside. For more on modems, refer to Chapter 11, "Modems." Modems are rated by speed in *bits per second* (bps).

Cost: 14.4 Versus 28.8 bps

A 28.8-bps modem is basically twice as fast as a 14.4-bps modem. As you would expect, you can purchase a slower modem for less, but I believe the 28.8-bps modem is well worth the extra cost.

	Processor	Hard Drive	Memory	CD-ROM	Sound
Min	486	500MB	4MB	Opt.	Yes
Good	Anything above the minimum				

Table 2-3: Requirements for online connections.

Do You Want Multimedia?

On paper, *multimedia*—usually defined as applications (software) that make use of text, video, animation, and sound—almost sounds boring. But while the definition is hardly inspiring, multimedia has become the basis for almost all of the nonbusiness software on the market. If you want to run games, reference works (encyclopedias and so on), or educational titles for kids and grown-ups, your system will need some heavy-duty multimedia capabilities.

If you're not familiar with children's programs, you might think that they're less sophisticated than those for adults and that kids can therefore get by with a less-sophisticated system. In fact, many business programs need less speed and memory than some of the newer children's programs, which are full of video, animation, and sound—a veritable Disneyland-on-the-desk. So if you have children and want to be able to run programs for them, you'll need a heavy-duty multimedia machine. Some popular programs include those by Davidson (Math Blaster 2 and Grammar Games), Broderbund (Carmen San Diego) and Math Workshop, as shown in Figure 2-5, Sierra (The Lost Mind of Dr. Brain), The Learning Company (Interactive Reading Journey), and Creative Wonders (Grammar House Rock).

Figure 2-5: With a more powerful computer, you can run the latest educational programs for your kids.

Game publishers traditionally have written programs that push the available technology, using features found only on the latest and greatest computer systems. Gamers (a computerese term for people who play games) can make do with decent multimedia machines. But many of the flashiest new games include full-screen animation and video sequences and require fast response—especially games like flight simulators that make you think you're a pilot—and you'll need a powerful machine to run them. Recent examples of high-requirement games are Id's Quake (shown in Figure 2-6 in all its 3D and texture-mapped glory), Activision's SpyCraft: The Great Game and MechWarrior 2, VR Sport's VR Soccer, Sierra's IndyCar Racing and Gabriel Knight: The Beast Within and Origin's Wing Commander IV.

Figure 2-6: To run the latest games such as Id's Quake, an intense 3D shoot 'em up, serious players have to own high-performance hardware.

Another place you'll find plenty of multimedia is in reference titles, including interactive encyclopedias such as Grolier Multimedia Encyclopedia, Softkey's Comptons Interactive Encyclopedia, and Microsoft's Encarta 96 Encyclopedia (see Figure 2-7). Also in this category are exploratory multimedia titles that concentrate on a particular topic. These include programs as diverse as Discovery Channel's The Beer Hunter and Entrepreneur Magazine's Small Business Encyclopedia. Even titles such as Intuit's Quicken, a personal finance program, offer multimedia features with sound and video.

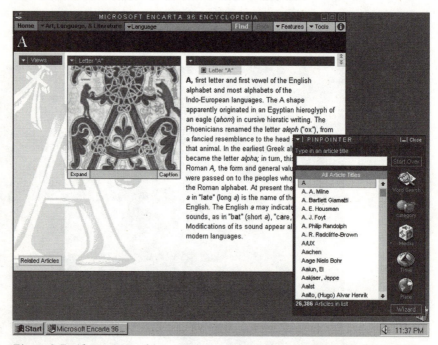

Figure 2-7: Almost everything you want to know is on multimedia CD-ROMs. This is Microsoft's Encarta, a comprehensive encyclopedia reference.

If you want to run multimedia titles, you'll have to have a *CD-ROM drive*. These days, a multimedia title on floppy disk is a rarity. Of course, the more powerful the CD-ROM drive, the better the program will run. The other major requirement is a *sound board* (or *sound card*). If your computer doesn't have one, you'll be missing a major component of your multimedia programs. For more on CD-ROM drives and sound boards, refer to Chapter 9, "CD-ROM," and Chapter 10, "Sound Cards."

Definition, Please
A computer's CD-ROM drive is much like the stereo device that plays music CDs. A computer CD-ROM drive has the same basic function as a floppy drive, but reads CD-ROMs (this is the term for CDs that store computer information) instead.

Definition, Please
A sound board is hardware that makes it possible for your PC to play the sound track on your software.

If you upgrade your machine for either playing games or using reference and educational titles, you'll have enough multimedia power to run virtually any business application.

For a summary of multimedia requirements, please refer to Table 2-4.

	Processor	Hard Drive	Memory	Video	CD-ROM	Sound
Min	486 DX4	500MB	8MB	SVGA	4X	Yes
Good	Pentium	1GB	16MB	SVGA/1MB	4X+	Yes
Great	Pentium (166+)	1GB+	16MB+	SVGA/1MB+	4X+	Yes

Table 2-4: Requirements for multimedia.

Do You Want to Work With Specialties?

Some special applications require hardware that is not part of most home and small office computers. The following sections list guidelines for these specialties. If you plan to perform these, you can start with the system requirements for multimedia and Windows 95 and add more *random access memory* (RAM) and specialized components.

Desktop Publishing

Desktop publishing (DTP) programs are used to create layouts for newsletters, advertisements, and anything else that can be put on paper. You can use them to arrange text and graphics on your computer's screen, eschewing the old-fashioned and tedious glue-and-scissors pasteup methods of the past. But DTP programs do more than just line up your text neatly. They can wrap text around graphics, resize objects, use different *fonts* (typefaces), and create special effects. Popular programs include Adobe PageMaker 6.0, QuarkXPress for Windows, and Microsoft Publisher, as shown in Figure 2-8, for entry level users.

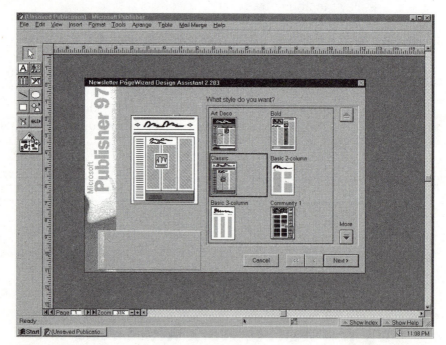

Figure 2-8: Desktop publishing programs such as Microsoft Publisher let you create fliers, newsletters, and other documents.

Because desktop publishing files tend to be large and because they work with graphics as well as text, the computer used for these programs has to be fast and have a lot of storage capacity. As a rule, you can't have too much memory and hard drive space if you're going to do this kind of work.

	Processor	Hard Drive	Memory	Video	CD-ROM	Sound
Min	486 DX4	1GB	16MB	SVGA	4X	Opt.
Good	Pentium	1GB+	16MB+	SVGA/1MB	4X+	Yes
Great	Pentium (166+)	2GB+	16MB+	SVGA/1MB+	4X+	Yes

Table 2-5: Requirements for desktop publishing.

Image Editing

Image-editing software uses electronic techniques to alter photographs. It mimics processes used in photographic darkrooms to sharpen areas in a photo, darken or lighten pictures, and apply various special effects and filters. As you'd expect, business users who need basic image editing are the target market for the lower cost products, while the high-end editors are aimed at professionals and offer sophisticated editing and prepress processes. All of these programs have special effects filters that make images look like engravings, water color paintings, and other art media. They can even merge photos together. Two popular image editors are Adobe Photoshop and Micrografx Picture Publisher, as displayed in Figure 2-9.

Figure 2-9: Image editors such as Picture Publisher let you manipulate photographs electronically.

Like desktop-publishing software, image editors perform a lot of graphics processing, requiring huge files. Therefore, to run these, you'll want a fast system with lots of memory and hard drive space for storage. For a summary of system requirements for image editing, please refer to Table 2-6.

	Processor	Hard Drive	Memory	Video	CD-ROM	Sound
Min	486 DX4	1GB	16MB	SVGA/1MB	4X	Opt.
Good	Pentium	1GB+	16MB+	SVGA/2MB	4X+	Opt.
Great	Pentium (166+)	2GB+	16MB+	SVGA/2MB+	4X+	Opt.

Table 2-6: Requirements for image editing.

Video Editing

Videos can appear on your PC as well as on MTV and "America's Funniest." With the right hardware and software—notably Adobe's Premiere—your PC becomes a Hollywood-style production studio that can manipulate, enhance, and display video images.

After you get the video onto your system, usually using a device called a *video capture board*, you can use video-editing software to combine, rearrange, and enhance the video segments. Finally, when your masterpiece is done, you can display it on your computer to show your clients how good your product is or show Aunt Eller your kid's dance recital. If you have another kind of board in your system, you can re-record your creation on videotape, using a separate VCR.

By far, the best thing about PC-based video is that you can edit and apply special effects through software. After you put your video clips together in different sequences, you can create movie-style transitions, add titles, and create stunning special effects: You can show your child flying through the Grand Canyon, change Uncle Herbert into a harp seal, or make it snow in Hawaii or rain in Death Valley. George Lucas has nothing on you and your PC.

Again, video editing involves large files and lots of data and requires a fast processor and plenty of storage. There's also specialized video hardware. On the editing side, you'll want a fast *video card* that has at least 2MB of memory, a wider *bus* (64-bit or 128-bit), and built-in *compression/decompression schemes* (*Codecs*) that help to process and display the video

For a summary of system requirements to perform video editing, please refer to Table 2-7.

	Processor	Hard Drive	Memory	Video	CD-ROM	Sound
Min	486 DX4	1GB	16MB	SVGA/2MB+	4X	Yes
Good	Pentium	1GB+	16MB+	Specialized	4X+	Yes
Great	Pentium (166+)	2GB+	16MB+	Specialized	4X+	Yes

Table 2-7: Requirements for video editing.

> **Definition, Please**
>
> *Codecs*, which stands for compression/decompression schemes, define some means for a computer to store massive quantities of video data in less space (compressing it) and quickly process and display it. Basically, you can think of codecs as high-tech software, hardware, or combination software and hardware short-cuts that help a computer show and play video. Popular codecs include MPEG and INDEO.

The All-Around System

Because you may want to do more than one thing, we have consolidated all of the "good" systems in a single table (Table 2-8). As you can see, there is some crossover. Using this chart, you can mix and match upgrades to get the system you want. Now, instead of building a winning system in one event, you can see what you need to make your system rule in the all-around category.

	Processor	Hard Drive	Memory	Video	CD-ROM	Sound
Windows 95	Pentium	1GB	16MB	SVGA/1MB	4X+	Yes
Windows 3.1	Pentium	500MB	8MB	SVGA/1MB	4X	Yes
Going Online	486	500MB	4MB	SVGA	Opt.	Yes
Multimedia	Pentium	1GB	16MB	SVGA/1MB	4X+	Yes
Desktop Pub.	Pentium	1GB+	16MB+	SVGA/1MB	4X+	Yes
Image Editing	Pentium	1GB+	16MB+	SVGA/2MB	4X+	Opt.
Video Editing	Pentium	1GB+	16MB+	Specialized	4X+	Yes

Table 2-8: Requirements for what you want to do with your computer.

Moving On

In this chapter, we looked at the various things you may want to do with your computer and the hardware you will need to perform them. At this point, you probably have a pretty good idea of the system that you want, which leads us to the next step.

In the following chapter, we'll consider the type of system that you currently have and describe the upgrades you'll need to make it do what you want to do.

What Upgrades Will You Need?

After reading the last chapter, you should have some idea of what you would like to do with your computer. This chapter will help you look at your existing system and determine what upgrades will get it to do what you want and what aspects of your current computer you probably can live with. In addition to preparing you for upgrading, this information will be useful for fending off salespeople at the computer store.

The easiest systems to upgrade are the generic *clones*—systems built with general computer parts.

Definition, Please

A *clone* is an IBM-compatible computer that is not made by IBM. This definition has evolved over the years. These days, a clone implies a machine not manufactured by a major vendor. The big manufacturers are known for building machines with non-standard parts that can make them tricky to upgrade.

A computer purchased from a name-brand manufacturer can have peculiarities that make it difficult to upgrade. If you have one of these, be sure to contact the manufacturer to find out about any potential pitfalls. And be sure to take precautions when you buy components so you can get your money back if a part doesn't work for you. We'll discuss that further in Chapter 12, "Bargain Basement."

Without going into detail on each type of system and each component, we'll talk about your current system and explain your options for upgrading. For more details on the individual components, please refer to the respective chapters later in the book. Along the way, you'll find charts that summarize everything we discuss here.

If You Own an 8088, Original IBM PC, or XT

If all you do is simple word processing, and your PC does everything you need it to do, that's great. You are fortunate.

On the other hand, if you want to do more, upgrading probably is not feasible. If you have one of the earliest PCs, you're better off donating the system to a church or charitable organization or giving it to a friend or relative and buying an entire new system of your choice. That's because you would have to upgrade almost every component in your system, which are all out of date, including the power supply. Furthermore, because of the age of the system, there's no guarantee that any new parts that you purchase would readily fit. Eventually, you'd end up spending more money than if you bought a new system. It's time to take that big step.

If You Own an AT or 286

The 286 is just one step up from the 8088 in terms of its upgrade potential. For many of the same reasons, it's probably best to scrap the system or give it away instead of trying to upgrade it. If you are determined to perform the upgrade, be prepared to replace a lot of components. You'll want a new hard drive to replace those slow, small-capacity MFM or RLL drives (older-style hard drives). Trying to locate an outdated MFM or RLL drive is fruitless. Even if you found one, you'd pay a premium price for a small drive.

By the time you add memory, you'll still be stuck with a slow video card (if the system has VGA), and you'll still want a CD-ROM drive and sound card. If you already have a sound card (one of those original 8-bit ones), it will probably work in an upgraded system. Another issue is the power supply, which may not be able to handle all of the components necessary for today's systems.

For a summary of necessary 286 upgrades for various applications, refer to Table 3-1. From a cost standpoint, upgrading a 286 doesn't make sense, even if you *were* planning to send it to college with your firstborn.

	CPU/Mother-board	Hard drive	CD-ROM	Sound	Memory	Video
Win 95	Upgrade	New controller/ larger hard drive	Add	Add	16MB	Upgrade
Win 3.1	Upgrade	New controller/ larger hard drive	Add	Add	8MB	Upgrade
Internet	Upgrade	New controller/ larger hard drive	Optional	Add	8MB	Upgrade
Multimedia	Upgrade	New controller/ larger hard drive	Add	Add	16MB	Upgrade
High Graphics	Upgrade	New controller/ larger hard drive	Add	Add	16MB+	Upgrade

Table 3-1: General 286 upgrades for different applications.

Note: An existing sound board may work.

If You Own a 386SX or 386DX

With the 386, we're starting to move toward a computer that can't realistically run today's latest applications but does a decent job of running older DOS software and even Windows 3.1. It all depends on what you would like to do. If you have a 40Mhz 386DX, you'll have performance that's close to that of a low-end 486, which might be enough for your needs.

Microsoft specifies a 386 as the minimum requirement for running Windows 95, but that's barely enough to run the operating system, and your software will run at frustratingly slow speeds. For this reason, even with extra memory, a 386 just isn't a Windows 95 machine. However, you might do all right running Windows 3.1. In this case, a little extra memory (8MB) will help you run a little faster. I'm not necessarily recommending that you invest in more memory if you own a 386. A better approach is to upgrade the *motherboard*.

Definition, Please

The motherboard is your computer's main board. It holds the *CPU*, memory, and expansion cards. CPU stands for central processing unit and is a term that is usually interchangeable with "processor" or "chip."

The 386 platform will respond fairly well to a 486 or Pentium motherboard. First, with the 386, there's a chance that you have IDE drives, and you can easily find and buy upgrades for these. The power supply might be a problem but should be adequate. On the other hand, you'll probably have to start over with the memory, as new boards may not be able to accommodate older memory chips; in later chapters we'll discuss ways to salvage the original chips. With most 386 systems, you'll be close to a new system by the time you add CD-ROM capability (if the system has a CD-ROM drive, it's probably a slow, single speed drive that won't work with today's multimedia), sound boards, and a new video card (although you might be able to use your existing one, in spite of its inherent limitations). For a summary of upgrade options for your 386, please refer to Table 3-2.

	CPU/ Mother- board	Hard drive	CD-ROM	Sound	Memory	Video
Win 95	Upgrade	New controller/ larger hard drive	Add	Add	16MB	Upgrade
Win 3.1	OK	OK	Add	Add	8MB	OK
Internet	OK	OK	Optional	Add	8MB	OK
Multimedia	Upgrade	New controller/ larger hard drive	Add	Add	16MB	Upgrade
High Graphics	Upgrade	New controller/ larger hard drive	Add	Add	16MB+	Upgrade

Table 3-2: General 386 upgrades for different applications.

Note: An existing sound board may work. You can definitely increase performance by adding a new, higher-performing video card. If you already own a 4X CD-ROM, don't bother upgrading it.

If You Own a 486SX or 486DX

If you own a 486, you have a system that adequately runs many of the latest applications, but you're probably hankering for more speed. As a rule, 486s are excellent candidates for upgrading into a Pentium machine, since the system's components—the power supply, fairly large hard drives and controllers, video card (unless it's a proprietary local bus; more on that in Chapter 4 on motherboards), and system memory—probably can be used.

Many 486 systems have fairly fast four-speed (4X) CD-ROM drives and sound cards that will work in an upgraded machine. To get up to Pentium level, you can swap the motherboard, or you may have the option of inserting Intel's Overdrive chip. To take advantage of the Overdrive, of course, your motherboard has to specifically support it. Contact your system's manufacturer for more information. For an overview of 486 upgrades for various applications, please refer to Table 3-3.

	CPU/ Mother- board	Hard drive	CD-ROM	Sound	Memory	Video
Win 95	OK	OK	Add	Add	16MB	OK
Win 3.1	OK	OK	Add	Add	8MB	OK
Internet	OK	OK	Optional	Add	8MB	OK
Multimedia	OK	New controller/ larger hard drive	Add	Add	16MB	Upgrade
High Graphics	Upgrade	New controller/ larger hard drive	Add	Add	16MB+	Upgrade

Table 3-3: General 486 upgrades for different applications.

Note: An existing sound board should be just fine. You can increase performance by adding a higher-performance video card. If you already own a 4X CD-ROM don't bother upgrading it.

If You Own a Pentium

Next is the Pentium Pro. You can upgrade it by replacing the motherboard, but you also should consider the performance issues. The Pentium Pro doesn't offer many performance enhancements for those running Windows 95. In other words, to anyone running Windows 95, a Pentium Pro and Pentium will deliver almost the same performance at the same clock speed (see Chapter 4, "The Central Processing Unit & the Mother of All Boards," for more information). Since the Pro costs much more (although the price is likely to come down eventually), the upgrade probably is not worth the expense, unless you want to run Windows NT (a true 32-bit operating system).

Moving On

Based on the information presented in this chapter, you should now have a pretty good idea of what upgrades you will want to make. Now you can read Section II, which explains the various components and improvements. Finally, in Section III, you'll find out how to actually perform the upgrades yourself.

SECTION II

The Components

The CPU & the Mother of All Boards

The heart and soul of your PC is its *central processing unit (CPU)*. When you purchased your PC, the CPU was the basic technology that you were buying. In the old days, the technology may have been based around an 8088 or a 80286 CPU chip. Today, it's far more likely to be a 486 or Pentium.

The CPU is the brains of your computer system. The CPU lies at the center of those vast substrates of silicon, transistors, and switches that make up the computer. It routes information and processes instructions between the various functions of your computer. The CPU has a significant impact on the ultimate speed of your computer. As we'll see in later chapters, areas like *random-access memory (RAM)* and the overall speed of your hard drive also play crucial and interrelated roles, but the CPU and its motherboard are the major factors.

Think of your computer as if it were a high-performance car. You can have high-performance tires, but if you don't have an engine to match, you're not going to go anywhere very fast. On the other hand, you might have a heavy horsepower engine, but cheap retread wheels will limit your pace to a crawl. In the same way, your computer contains many interrelated factors that influence its performance. We'll look at the CPU and motherboard first.

CPUs run at different speeds, which are measured in *megahertz (MHZ)*. The computer's actual speed is called *clockspeed*. You can think of clockspeed as the fellow on the galley in a movie like *Ben-Hur*, who beats a drum to keep the oarsmen rowing together. The faster he pounds the drum, the faster the oarsmen row. If the fast drum isn't enough, the mean-looking guy with the whip is called in. (Unfortunately, there's no computer equivalent for the whip when you're on a tight deadline.)

Definition, Please

A megahertz (MHZ) is one million cycles or occurrences in a second.

The original IBM PC ran at a then-impressive 4.77 MHZ. Today, some Pentium systems scream along at 200 MHZ. As you've already figured out, the faster the clockspeed, the more instructions a CPU can process in a given time. But there are other considerations: You also have to consider the type of CPU.

As we'll discuss later in this chapter, CPUs come in different generations, which started with the 8088 and evolved through the 80286, 80386, 80486, and finally the Pentium and Pentium Pro processors of today. Just remember that the higher the generation, the more powerful the chip. If all of these chips were running at the same clockspeed, the more powerful chips would turn in a faster performance, as shown in Table 4-1.

First Year	Processor	Speed	Millions of Instructions/Second
1981	8088	4.77 MHZ	.33
	8088	8 MHZ	.66
1984	80286	6 MHZ	.90
	80286	10 MHZ	1.5
1985	80386	16 MHZ	5.00
1987	80386	20 MHZ	6.00
1988	80386	25 MHZ	8.50
1989	80386	33 MHZ	11.40
1989	80486	25 MHZ	20
1990	80486	33 MHZ	27
1991	80486	50 MHZ	41
1992	486DX2	66 MHZ	54
1994	486DX4	100 MHZ	70
1993	Pentium	60 MHZ	100
1994	Pentium	75 MHZ	126
	Pentium	100 MHZ	150
1995	Pentium	120 MHZ	203
	Pentium	133 MHZ	219

Table 4-1: The new levels of performance achieved by succeeding generations of CPUs.

The motherboard is your computer's main board. It holds the CPU, memory, and *expansion cards*, as shown in Figure 4-1.

CPU
Socket

Expansion
Slots

Memory
Slots

Figure 4-1: The motherboard holds your computer's key components.

Definition, Please

An expansion card is a panel containing microchips that you can install in an *expansion card slot* to add memory or special features. Some of the functions provided by expansion cards are essential to the computer's operation—like a board to control your hard and floppy drives and a video card that sends video to your monitor. Internal modems and sound boards are also expansion cards. For the most part, motherboards are built to be used with specific processors and certain types of memory or configurations of RAM and offer different ways to accept expansion cards. Expansion cards are also called *expansion boards*.

This leads us to a major motherboard factor, the *bus*, which determines the kind of expansion cards you can install. Motherboards come with different bus styles that accommodate different expansion cards. We'll look at buses a little later in this chapter.

Definition, Please

You can think of a bus as a highway. The more lanes on this data highway, the more data may be transferred smoothly. The bus defines the internal data highways on the board, thus how much data can be relayed. It also defines the data path in an expansion card slot, which accepts expansion cards.

Why Replace Your CPU?

For the same reasons that you want to upgrade your computer, you'll want to consider upgrading your CPU and motherboard. The newest processors let you run the latest applications, offer fast performance, and take advantage of the newest features in operating systems, such as *multitasking*—running several programs at the same time.

Generally, you should replace the CPU when you are using your computer for tasks that require a lot from the CPU. These tasks include high-performance games, multimedia titles, intense graphics such as video and image editing, and desktop publishing. Of course, depending on your application, you'll want to upgrade other components as well.

Cost

Not surprisingly, the faster or more powerful the CPU, the higher the price. Looking toward the future, the Pentium is probably the best goal—it will keep you up-to-date for a while. The 80486, however, is beginning to fade. Even if you don't necessarily need a Pentium now, it will be worth the extra money you spend on it in the long run.

When you upgrade your CPU and/or motherboard, you have a couple of basic choices: (1) replacing the CPU or adding a performance-enhancing "overdrive" chip—some specialized motherboards let you do this—or (2) replacing the entire motherboard with a new one that is based around a newer and faster CPU. For the most part, you'll want to upgrade to a 486 at a minimum—a Pentium processor is even better. For a summary of options, refer to Table 4-2.

Option	Perform on	Result
Replace the CPU	Certain motherboards	Better performance
Add an overdrive chip	Certain 486 boards	Pentium capability
Replace the motherboard	Any system, depends on case	A 486 or Pentium

Table 4-2: CPU options.

When the Chips Are Down

If you got into computing in the very beginning (the early 1980s), you might recall the Intel 8088 (that's "eighty eighty-eight"). This chip originally ran at 4.77 MHZ on the original IBM PC and faster on the next-generation XT. The 8088, as shown in Figure 4-2, was an 8-bit chip, which means that internally it processed its instructions in 8-bit chunks.

Definition, Please
All CPUs process information in certain size chunks. The greater this chunk (8 bits, 16 bits, etc.), the more information the CPU can process or handle at a time.

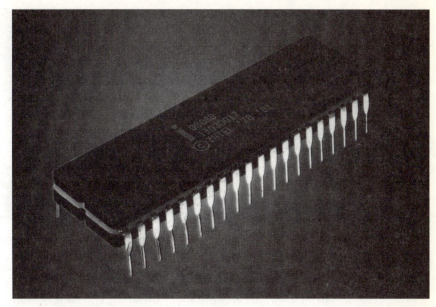

Figure 4-2: The lowly 8088.

Compared to today's Pentium-based PCs, the 8088 is a dinosaur that runs only the most basic nongraphic software of its era. An 8088 system is just not worth upgrading. Even if you could replace the motherboard, you still would be stuck with ancient and slow hard drives (if the system has them), an inadequate power supply, and prehistoric video cards that would slow your work to a crawl. In this case, it's better (and cheaper) to buy an entire new system and start over.

In 1984 IBM introduced the AT, which was based on the new 80286 (or "two eighty-six"), as shown in Figure 4-3. The AT brought in a new era of 16-bit processors that could process data 16 bits at a time and work with a whopping 16MB of memory (the 8088 was limited to 1MB). Running at the same clockspeed as an 8088, it was inherently faster. But like the 8088, the AT is obsolete and not worth upgrading. Again, it's best to buy a new computer because of the slow surrounding components.

Figure 4-3: The 80286.

Intel's 386 processor, also known as the 386DX, was the next major evolutionary step. This 32-bit processor raised the computing curve, was faster than a 286, and remained popular for years.

An offshoot of the 386 was the 386SX, a stripped-down chip that was a 32-bit 386 internally but talked to the computer as if it were a 16-bit processor, like a 286. People who bought the 386SX didn't have quite the computing power of a full 386DX, but it was reasonably inexpensive.

If you have anything less than a 386, you could upgrade your computer to reach that goal, but it would barely run any of the latest applications. For this reason, the 386DX and 386SX are not suitable for upgrading (if you can even find the components). On the other hand, depending on the hard drive and the other components in your system, your 386 is a decent candidate for an upgrade to either a 486 or Pentium motherboard.

The Intel 64-bit 486 was the next step in chip history. Until early in 1996, you could buy many different 486 systems. The various incarnations of the 486, as displayed in Figure 4-4, were based on doublers, triplers, and quads that multiplied the chip's speed. While these don't fully double or triple the performance of a 486, they come fairly close.

Figure 4-4: The 80486.

Not only could a 486 handle more instructions at a time than a 386, but the 486 came with a built-in *numeric coprocessor,* something that was never included with prior chips and always had to be purchased separately.

Definition, Please

A *numeric coprocessor* is a special chip that crunches numbers. If you're working with lots of mathematical functions—spreadsheets, for example—a numeric coprocessor will speed up your operations.

When the 486 was popular, Intel introduced the badly conceived and ill-received 486SX, which was a full 486 but did not have the built-in numeric coprocessor. Unfortunately, while Intel sold the 486SX at a lower price than the standard 486, it was actually more expensive to manufacture. Intel was taking perfectly good 486 chips and running them through an additional manufacturing process to disable the numeric coprocessor.

To add further insult, users who wanted a numeric coprocessor could purchase a 487SX chip, which was a fully functional 486 with a numeric coprocessor. After the buyer installed this chip, the original 486SX chip effectively dropped out of the system, never to be heard from again.

For most upgrading purposes, the 486 is a decent goal, but you should definitely set your sights on the fastest versions. AMD, Cyrix, and Intel make speedy versions that run at double or triple the clockspeed. These fit into a 486 motherboard, but you have to be careful—they don't work with all boards. Be sure to first check with your board's manufacturer.

If you can double the speed, you can typically expect about a 70 percent increase in performance, and by tripling, about a 250 percent increase. If you add lots of RAM—say, at least 16MB—the system will run many of the most current applications.

Today, the chip of choice is the Pentium, shown in Figure 4-5. It would have been named the "586," but Intel changed the name so that other companies couldn't copy the chips and use the same name when marketing them. This 64-bit chip is the recommended upgrade goal, and you'll want to go with a 100 MHZ, at a minimum. Even if you already own a 486, moving up to a Pentium will give you much better performance, and you should be able to use most of your existing components. Combined with a RAM upgrade to at least 16MB, you'll have a powerful and fast machine.

Figure 4-5: The Pentium.

For 486 computers, Intel sells a Pentium Overdrive chip that almost converts a 486 into a Pentium. However, you have to already own a special motherboard with an extra-large Pentium socket. While you won't get quite the performance of a Pentium, this chip can just about double the speed of your system. If you shop for the Overdrive chip, be sure to base your purchase on the speed of your present system, verify the voltage in your CPU socket, and check with the board manufacturer to make sure that the upgrade will work. There are several known incompatibility problems. For more information, you should consult the manual that came with your motherboard, or call the manufacturer to see what type of Overdrive chip you can use. Also, Intel has a list of approved systems that can accept the upgrade.

As I write this, Intel is ready to release a Pentium Overdrive chip to double the speed of a Pentium system. If you already own a Pentium, this might provide an easy upgrade option.

The Intel Pentium Pro chip is emerging as a new powerhouse. While this chip features enhancements and speed improvements, it shows increased performance only when running a true 32-bit operating system, such as Windows NT. So, if you're running Windows 95, you won't see much increased performance between a Pentium and a Pentium Pro running at the same clockspeed.

Who's Driving the Bus?

To communicate with expansion cards—things like the video card, hard drive controller, and internal modem—your motherboard features expansion slots or a bus to connect with them. As I mentioned before, a bus is like a highway for transferring data. Just as on a real-life highway, the more lanes you have, the better the traffic flow and the more cars the highway can handle. In a bus, the number of bits (like highway lanes) it can carry at a time determines its performance.

The first PC and XT buses could transfer only 8 bits of data at a time. With the AT 286 machines, IBM introduced a more powerful 16-bit bus. For a comparison of the two buses, refer to Figure 4-6. It complemented the increased power of the 80286 chip by transferring more data, and it could accept older 8-bit cards. This bus was originally called the AT bus, but is now more commonly known as the ISA. While there are many boards that use ISA buses, you'll get far better performance using what's known as a VESA or PCI style bus, which I'll discuss shortly.

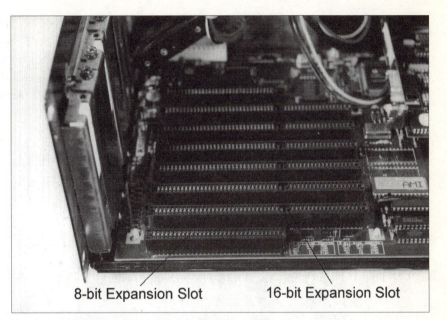

8-bit Expansion Slot   16-bit Expansion Slot

Figure 4-6: The 8-bit versus the 16-bit ISA bus.

Other standards have come and gone. For example, IBM's MicroChannel Architecture (MCA) offered improvements in speed and configuration but was not backward compatible— that is, it couldn't be used with older boards. The other problem was that IBM charged royalties that made the other computer manufacturers cringe.

As a result, the other manufacturers—Compaq, AST, and Hewlett-Packard, among others—banded together to create a bus of their own, called the Extended Industry Standard Architecture bus. It offered backward compatibility, a wider data path, and easier configuration. These buses are not upgrade goals, so I'll mostly ignore them here.

For a time, some manufacturers created higher-performance and faster "local" buses that could work only with certain motherboards. In other words, a certain card, usually a video card, would work with only one type of motherboard. While these were popular for a while and yielded improved performance, they were replaced as the industry began to establish new standards. Again, for our upgrading purposes, we'll steer clear of local buses.

When a local bus standard was created, it was known as the VESA. While VESA offers solid performance, you'll probably be happier with the latest PCI bus, as shown in Figure 4-7, which is the clear standard with its wider 64-bit data path and ability to run at higher speeds. Best of all, PCI supports Windows 95's Plug and Play, which recognizes your hardware and works with Windows 95 to set it up conveniently.

Figure 4-7: The PCI bus.

PCI is popular enough that most of the newest motherboards feature it, and it's best to upgrade to a motherboard that has it (usually in combination with ISA). Also, be sure that the motherboard works with Windows 95, particularly with Plug and Play.

Another bus-related issue is the raw number of physical slots available on the board. You'll find that some motherboards have up to seven slots, while some give you only a few. For the most part, the more expansion slots, the better. After all, you never know what you might want to add to your system in the future, and it's always best to have options.

Some motherboards come with the built-in *input/output ports* to handle your serial and parallel communications, while others rely on expansion cards.

Definition, Please
Input/output, or I/O, ports provide ways for your computer to connect to printers, external modems, a mouse, and other accessories.

If a motherboard comes with these already in place, it will save an expansion slot for another use. On the other hand, be sure that the ports will fit into your case—an important consideration.

Other Things Mother Never Told You About

Another thing to consider about your motherboard is the *basic input/output system (BIOS)*, the internal instructions of a system, which comes with every board. This is a time when you can feel confident about any of the big names, such as AMI, Award, and Phoenix.

Definition, Please
The BIOS (basic input/output system) is internal built-in software that determines the compatibilities of your system. (It does more, but that's enough for our purposes.)

Also, don't forget to consider *caches*, which help to speed performance by providing a place to store needed information so it's readily available. For most purposes, get a cache of at least 256 *kilobytes* (256K). A kilobyte is a thousand bytes.

Definition, Please

The *cache* is a system of memory that works closely with the processor to hold important data so they are immediately available. This speeds up the performance of your system.

If you upgrade your motherboard, you'll want to consider the type of RAM chips that your current motherboard uses. If the new board is compatible with the old chips, you can save money by reusing these chips in your new motherboard.

If you have older memory chips, you probably won't be able to use them. In that case, you'll have to purchase new RAM, although there are special boards—called *daughterboards*—that let you install different types of RAM and use them on boards that aren't meant to accept them.

If you would like to use your current memory, be sure to check the type you have and determine how you can use it on a new board. For more on this, see Chapter 5, "Thanks for the Memory." When buying a new board, look for one that accepts 72-pin *single in-line memory modules (SIMMs),* and you'll find that boards that accept eight SIMMs are better than those that accept only four.

Definition, Please

SIMM stands for single in-line memory module, which refers to a common configuration that memory comes in, and installs onto your motherboard.

Cost

When you buy anything, you need to seek out manufacturers that have good reputations in the computer industry. Reputable motherboard manufacturers include AMI, Muylex, and Micronics. If you purchase one of these, you probably won't go wrong. They may cost more, but the potential for fewer problems means it is money well spent.

A final note that may sound outrageous in our electronic age: You have to consider the physical size of your case and motherboard. In general, motherboards come in two basic sizes. It never hurts to go over the measurements and double-check the size of your case when you make a purchase. You also might check with the motherboard manufacturer to make sure that a board will work in your case.

How to Buy a Motherboard

Generally, if you want to install a new CPU, you'll want to purchase an entire new motherboard, although you can buy them separately. So, to reiterate, here's what you need to consider before you buy (refer to Table 4-3 for a summary of what we recommend):

Processor	Pentium
Bus	PCI
BIOS	AMI, Award, Phoenix
Cache	256K external
Input/output	Your choice
Physical size	To fit your case
Type of memory	Depends on your existing RAM
Number of slots	At least seven

Table 4-3: Summary of what to buy in a motherboard.

You can buy motherboards from a variety of places—your local computer store, mail order outlets, and even warehouse stores. From the list in Table 4-3 you should have a fairly good idea of what you will need. When shopping, don't be afraid to ask questions. You're spending a lot of money, and you have every right to know. For tips on shopping and finding the best prices, refer to Chapter 12, "Bargain Basement." After you buy your motherboard and are ready to install it, refer to Chapter 16, "Replacing the Motherboard." If it's a CPU on a specialized motherboard, go to Chapter 15, "Replacing the Central Processing Unit."

Moving On

In this chapter, we discussed the evolution of PC processors over the years, and the various motherboard and CPU upgrade options that are available for your system. In the next chapter, we will discuss memory—the different types available through the years and issues to think about when adding more memory to an existing board or using existing memory in a new board.

Thanks for the Memory

Like the other major components in your PC, memory plays a key role. In the most basic sense, you can think of memory as a work area your computer uses to hold and process your data.

In some ways, it's like a desk. A desk usually has drawers to hold your tools (pencil, calculator, etc.) and a file drawer to store data and records. To work with your tools and data, you bring them up out of the drawers and onto your desktop where they're handy. Of course, the more data or equipment that you have to use, the more room it will take on your desk. In the same way, memory—or *RAM* (which stands for *random access memory* and is pronounced just like a male sheep)—is your computer's work space.

Adding memory to your system is one of the best performance-enhancing upgrades that you can make. If you're working with lots of large applications with equally large data files, the more memory you can provide, the better. In particular, if you need to *multitask*—that is, to switch between programs running simultaneously under Windows—you'll want to have a lot of RAM on your system. The more of your application that you can load into memory, the less your computer will have to rely on the much slower hard drive to take care of any spillover.

The CPU has to manage how it uses RAM—a process sometimes called *addressing*—and different units have different capabilities. The more RAM a CPU can address or work with, the more powerful the CPU.

The 8088 used in the original IBM PC could only work with up to 1MB of data. This is shown in Figure 5-1. During this time, DOS was saddled, by decree, with the now-infamous 640K memory limitation. In other words, DOS can only use 640K of memory in anything that it does (without using some special tricks). At the time the first IBM PC was released, the makers decided that the operating system would reserve the upper 360K of memory for controller use, leaving 640K (a whopping amount in those days) for use by applications. Until recently, the mainstream memory approaches were intended to get past this limitation.

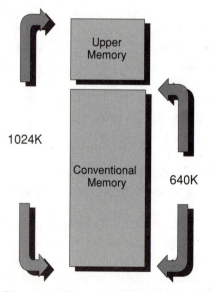

1024K

Upper Memory

Conventional Memory   640K

Figure 5-1: The original IBM PC could address only up to 640K of the 1MB that it was capable of using.

Expand Your Memory

While 640K at first seemed like endless memory, many users—particularly those who worked with large spreadsheets—found themselves running out of memory. As a result, Lotus Corporation (as in Lotus 1-2-3) worked with Intel and IBM to create what became known as *expanded memory*, as shown in Figure 5-2. This is a special way of using upper memory so an application can work with files beyond 640K.

Definition, Please
Expanded memory is additional memory in a system that can be used by special applications.

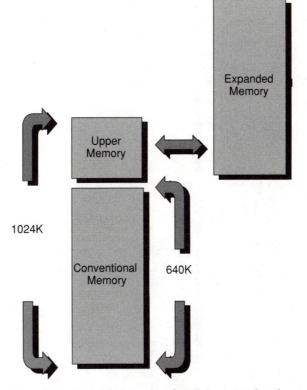

Figure 5-2: Expanded memory lets PC users take advantage of more than the standard 640K.

Adding expanded memory to XTs and 80286 machines requires a combination of hardware and software. For our upgrade purposes, expanded memory is more of a DOS issue and not really an upgrade goal.

Extend Out

With the introduction of the 286, a PC could work with up to 16MB of RAM but was still saddled with the 640K DOS limitation. From then on, all memory beyond the first megabyte of RAM became known as *extended memory,* as shown in Figure 5-3. After that, all CPUs—starting with the 386 and moving to 486s and Pentiums—were able to address 4 *gigabytes (GB)* of RAM (a gigabyte is a thousand megabytes). With these chips, extended memory takes on a lot of importance and is the only type of memory that we will consider for our upgrades.

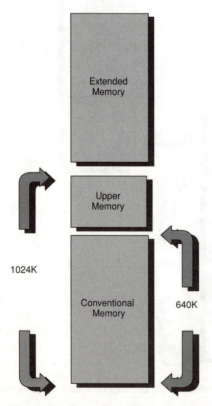

Figure 5-3: Extended memory is memory beyond 1MB.

Operating systems, such as Windows 95, work with all of your system's memory to load programs and data. The more RAM your system has, the more programs and data that can be loaded and the faster your computer can run. If the applications and data that you load go beyond the capacity of your system's RAM, Windows will use the hard drive as memory. Unfortunately, because a hard drive is so much slower than RAM, your computing slows down immensely. So, to run Windows, all you need to add is extended memory.

These days, most new computers come with a minimum of 8MB of RAM to run Windows 95, but it's far better to have 16MB or even 32MB. For memory-intensive applications—such as desktop publishing, video editing, and image editing—the memory sky is the limit. For these specialized applications, it's not unusual to see systems with 64MB RAM or more.

Generally, if you will be running Windows 95, a good goal is to get 8–16MB RAM onto your system. Obviously, if you plan to run some of the more specialized applications, you need to plan your RAM requirements accordingly.

To see how much RAM you have in your system, you can run the "Mem" command that should exist in your DOS directory if you're running Windows 3.1. Or, in any Microsoft application, click on System Info under the Help | About menu. With this information, you can call the manufacturer of your system or motherboard and find out how much more RAM you can add and how much the board can hold.

Shopping for RAM

Memory comes on chips that are mounted on tiny boards. These memory configurations have changed and evolved over the years.

The first major RAM consideration is speed. You might upgrade a system with a blazing fast processor, yet with slow RAM or not enough of it, you'll still have poor performance. Memory speed is rated in *nanoseconds (ns),* which is one-billionth of a second. The lower the number, the faster the memory. The older memory could run as slow as 120 ns. Today, the most popular RAM comes in 70- and 60-ns configurations.

Memory also comes in different forms. The most common is called *DRAM*. Other types of memory go by the names *EDO RAM* and *synchronous DRAM*. These kinds of memory are for higher performance, and you will always want to match types. It's unlikely that the system you're upgrading will have EDO or synchronous DRAM.

While it might be tempting to purchase the fastest RAM you can buy and add it to slower RAM, it's not a good idea to mix speeds. Also, computer systems usually are rated to work with memory of a certain speed. While you can buy faster memory, it won't help the performance of your system, and you will have spent extra money unnecessarily.

The other major consideration is the physical configuration of your RAM. If you're upgrading, the type of memory configuration you already have may or may not work with your upgraded system. Right now, memory on SIMMs is the most popular, as shown in Figures 5-4 and 5-5.

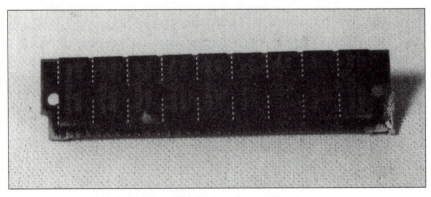

Figure 5-4: Memory in a 30-pin SIMM configuration.

Figure 5-5: Memory in a 72-pin SIMM configuration in a memory slot. Notice the notch in the lower right hand corner that prevents the memory from being installed incorrectly.

You'll find that these are relatively easy to install and come in configurations from 256K to 64MB, the most popular being 1MB, 4MB, 8MB, and 16MB. It's also important to note how many pins fit onto your motherboard. SIMMs come in 72-pin and 30-pin versions, with the 72-pin now being the most common.

Because memory comes in different sizes, you need to check with the motherboard manual or manufacturer to make sure of the type of RAM you will need. Some systems let you mix different size SIMMs or make you install them in specific groups—for example, two at a time.

Other memory that you may find, usually on older 386 or 486 computers, is in *dual in-line packages (DIPs)*, as shown in Figure 5-6. These aren't as common. They're also harder to install, and take up more chips.

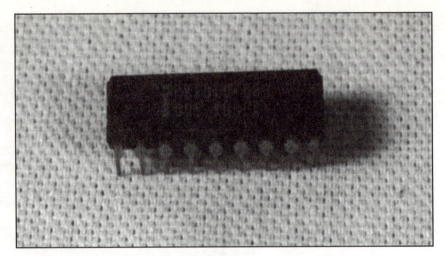

Figure 5-6: Memory in a DIP configuration.

Most 386, 486, and Pentium motherboards already come with a place (a *socket*) for holding memory. If you install memory directly onto your motherboard, you'll get the fastest performance. Always use these sockets first, before resorting to expansion cards.

Some boards can use proprietary expansion cards to hold additional memory. You'll have to check with the manufacturer of your motherboard, but some require that you add memory in pairs or only in certain configurations. You'll need to know this in advance to make your purchase.

Another option for adding RAM is SIMM conversion cards that let you install multiple SIMMs onto a special board, then install the board into a standard SIMM slot. This way, you can use your 30-pin memory in a 72-pin slot. Some companies will sell you a blank conversion board, but most will want to sell it to you with memory already installed. Again, you should check with your motherboard manufacturer for more information on these.

One last option: You can try to sell your existing RAM to mail order houses and see what price you can get (it won't be high, but it's better than nothing) and buy new RAM at a higher price.

> ## *Cost: Looking to the Future*
> When making RAM upgrades, you may want to consider your future needs. In the future, it won't be unusual for systems to have 32MB or even 64MB of RAM. If you can, you should try to leave room in your upgrades to do even more upgrades later. For example, if you're moving up to 16MB of RAM, you might purchase two 8MB SIMMs instead of four 4MB SIMMs. This way, if you want to get to 32MB, you can easily add two more 8MB SIMMs.

When shopping for memory, keep these issues in mind:

○ How much memory do you need?

○ How is it packaged (SIMM, DIP)?

○ How fast is the memory (70 ns, 60 ns, etc.)?

○ What type of memory?

○ Can you use an expansion board?

○ Can you use a SIMM conversion card?

There are lots of sources for buying memory. Most computer specialty stores sell memory. When shopping this way, be sure to check that the memory will work with your motherboard and system: Call the memory manufacturer if necessary. Another, potentially lower-priced source is mail-order firms. Also, if you can't use your old memory in your upgrade, some firms, depending on the type of memory you have, will buy your old memory from you. While you can't expect much money for old memory, regardless of what you originally paid for it, it can be a small downpayment toward new RAM.

Again, ask hard questions before you give up your credit card number. For installation instructions, please refer to Chapter 16, "Replacing or Adding RAM." For more on shopping for computer parts, please refer to Chapter 12, "Bargain Basement."

Moving On

In this chapter, we discussed that all-important memory. As you have seen, memory affects your PC's performance, can be configured in different ways, and comes in different configurations that affect the type of upgrades you can perform. From here, we'll move into an in-depth discussion of video cards in the next chapter to show you how a video card affects the performance of your PC, what factors to consider in a video card, and how to purchase one that meets your needs.

Video Cards

Whether it's text, graphics, or mind-blowing games, everything appears on your computer's monitor. To display images effectively, your system needs a graphics or video card, which compiles the information from the computer and converts it to a form that can be displayed on the monitor. In all PCs, the video card is a board that plugs into the system's expansion bus on the motherboard, as shown in Figure 6-1.

As you might expect, there are different video cards on the market, and they play a significant role in determining how fast your computer will display images on your monitor. While a video card's speed isn't too important when you're just displaying text, its performance is crucial when you're working with graphics, especially animation and video.

Figure 6-1: A video card.

If your system has a relatively fast CPU (a 486 or higher), but it takes a long time to draw images on the screen, new windows are slow to open, animation and video sequences are jerky, and it seems to take forever to scroll through a long document or image, you may need a new and better video card.

You might also consider a video card upgrade if you want to view better *resolution* on your display, which gives you more detail, or if you want to see more onscreen colors.

Definition, Please

Resolution refers to the number of dots, or *pixels*, on a computer screen. The more dots that appear, the higher the resolution and the better an image looks.

For example, 640x480 (the minimum for working in Windows) means that there are 640 pixels across the top of the screen and 480 down the sides, which translates into 640 columns of pixels running up and down on the screen and 480 rows of pixels running left and right. Higher resolutions include 800x600 and the ultrahigh numbers, 1024x768 and above. You can see an example of this in Figure 6-2.

A pixel is the smallest unit or dot of color that a computer monitor displays. Looking at a picture in a newspaper in magnification, you see dots in black or other colors. Pixels are electronic dots that make up the pictures on your computer screen.

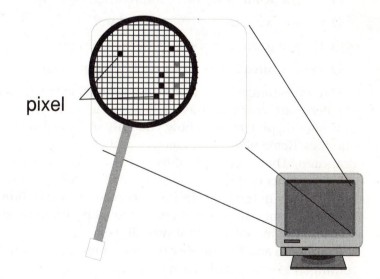

pixel

Figure 6-2: Resolution refers to the number of lines on your screen. Pixels are the electronic dots that form onscreen images.

Keep in mind that while a video card is an important factor in your system's ability to rapidly display graphics, that capability also is closely tied to the speed of your CPU. If you're experiencing some of the conditions below and you have a slow processor (a 386 or lower), you'll probably be better off upgrading your CPU first. Otherwise, a lot of "yes" answers indicate that a new video card would be an excellent upgrade.

○ Does it take too long for images or windows to be drawn on the screen?

○ Do videos or animation in multimedia titles tend to be jerky or jumpy?

○ Does it take a long time to scroll from one part of a document to another?

○ Do individual windows take a long time to open on the screen?

○ Do colors sometimes appear distorted?

○ Do you want to see more information on a Windows screen?

○ Do you want to display more colors?

○ Do you want to work at higher resolutions?

○ Do you already have a 486 or higher processor?

Like everything else related to computers, video graphics adapters have changed drastically over the years. In the old days, computer displays could show you only plain text with simple graphics. Remember those green or amber monitors of about 10 years ago? They were state of the art at the time. Also, the first color monitors that were made for the PC displayed low-resolution graphics in four simple and garish colors. Color brought in a new era of entertainment and educational programs even though it wasn't fun to look at. But it was all we had.

Resolution and the number of colors a monitor could display continued to evolve with each new video standard. And with each new standard, computer images became more attractive to view, and text became easier to read. Today, *VGA* and *super VGA* are the clear standards, but as you'll see, there are many variations.

Definition, Please

VGA stands for video graphics array. It has been, for some time, the basic industry standard for computer graphics display. For our purposes here, super VGA has gained wide acceptance and describes higher resolutions beyond that of the standard VGA. Other adapters are the monochrome display adapter (MDA), the color graphics adapter (CGA), and the enhanced graphics adapter (EGA). Each of these is a video standard that defines a certain resolution and the number of colors that can be displayed on a monitor.

For a brief look at the evolution of video standards with their resolutions and ability to display more colors, please refer to Table 6-1.

	Resolution	Number of Colors
MDA	720x350	2
CGA	320x200	4
EGA	640x350	16
VGA	640x480	16
	320x200	256
Super VGA	640x480	256
	800x600	16
	800x600	256+
	1024x768	16
	1024x768	256+

Table 6-1: Graphics adapters over the years.

Note: The higher resolutions aren't limited to only 256 colors and can, depending on the video card, display thousands of colors. The more memory your video card has, the more colors and the higher the resolution you can display.

Upgrading Video

In most ways, upgrading a video card is relatively easy. All you have to do is shop around for a better card that meets your needs and install it by replacing your existing card. Keep in mind that when you install a new video card, you'll need a monitor that can display the images it sends. You'll need a VGA monitor to display VGA graphics, a super VGA monitor to display super VGA resolutions and colors, and so on. For more on monitors, please refer to Chapter 8, "Monitor This."

Another type of upgrade involves adding extra memory to your video card. We won't dwell on this type of specialized upgrade here, but you may want to check with the manufacturer of your video card to see what type of memory it uses and if it's possible to add to it. I'll discuss memory issues a little later in this chapter. For the most part, you can purchase video cards with different amounts of memory on them. For some guidelines, you can refer to the memory recommendations for video cards listed in Chapter 3, "What Upgrades Will You Need."

The Video Card

At its most basic level, your system's video affects the way you can display video. Aside from speed and performance issues, this involves the resolution of your display (which is also tied to the capabilities of your monitor) and the number of colors you can display.

Resolution, as I mentioned earlier, refers to the number of pixels that are displayed on your monitor and is expressed in the number of horizontal and vertical lines on the screen.

As you can see in Figures 6-3, 6-4, and 6-5, resolution makes a big difference in how your display looks. Figure 6-3 displays a Windows screen at a resolution of 640x480. Notice that the displayed window takes up most of the screen.

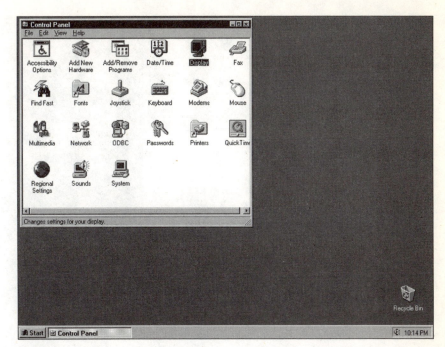

Figure 6-3: Windows at 640x480.

Figure 6-4 depicts a Windows screen at a resolution of 800x600. As you can see, the same window takes up less space (I didn't resize it), which gives you room to view other applications. Notice also that the fonts look cleaner.

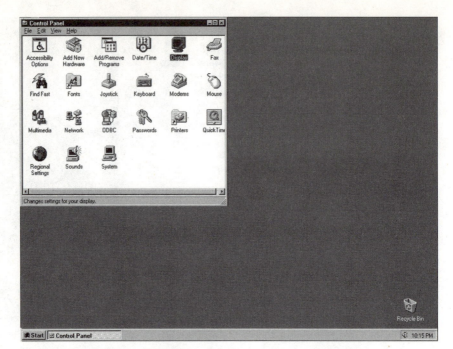

Figure 6-4: Windows at 800x600.

Finally, Figure 6-5 depicts the same window at 1024x768. On a large screen, it's easy to read the smaller and cleaner text, and you definitely have more room to work with. For example, if you're doing a page layout, a higher resolution screen lets you see the entire page, not just part of it.

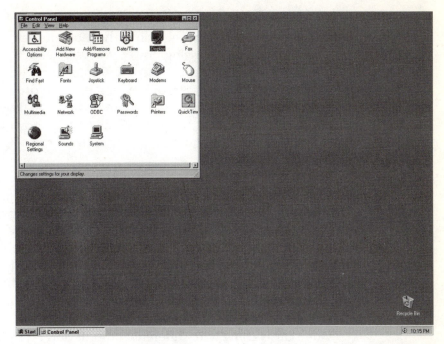

Figure 6-5: Windows at 1024x768.

In general, the more pixels on your screen, the cleaner and more attractive your display will look. But as with all things, there are drawbacks. The more pixels you display, the more processing power your computer needs, which means more CPU processor time and a more powerful video card.

Earlier, I mentioned VGA and super VGA. VGA actually refers only to the 640x480 resolution with 16 colors. Anything above that—800x600 and beyond—usually is considered super VGA. Today, you'll definitely want to buy a video card and monitor that can handle at least super VGA. The resolution you set usually will depend on the size of your monitor—the larger the monitor, the higher the resolution that you probably will want to run.

You must consider, besides resolution, the number of colors that you can display on your screen. You might have a video card that can show only 16 colors at a time (such as EGA), or one that can show 256, 16,000, or up to 16 million. Just as with resolution, the more colors that you show at a time, the more attractive the display and the more processing power you will need.

In most cases and for most users, 256 colors look just fine. At resolutions of 640x480 or 800x600, you'll have no problems running most multimedia titles, games, and educational programs. If you're going to be doing image or video editing, however, you'll want more colors and you'll definitely want to run at one of the higher resolutions.

The first consideration is how much memory a video card has in which to store images before sending them to your monitor. This directly affects the resolution. For example, running a screen at 640x480 and showing 256 colors requires some 350K of memory. If this is the case, a low-end, low-cost video board with 1MB of memory will work just fine. If this is all you're going to run, paying extra for more memory doesn't make sense. The higher the resolution you want to display, the more memory your video card will need.

Video cards come with different amounts and types of memory. The least expensive, DRAM, is the most readily available. You'll also find that some cards come with memory called EDO RAM, which offers better performance than DRAM. At the high end, there's video VRAM, which is the most expensive and offers the best performance.

Cost

Unless you need the improved performance for running high-end applications, you'll probably do just fine with a video card that's equipped with DRAM. This way, you'll save some money when compared to buying a card that's equipped with EDO RAM or VRAM.

Although 640x480 at 256 colors may be fine for a lot of uses, most people like to run in higher resolutions when they can. If you buy a 64-bit board with 2MB of memory, you'll have a good solid configuration for running the higher resolutions and getting more onscreen colors (we'll explain that "64-bit" part in a minute).

Without going into an in-depth discussion of buses here (please refer to Chapter 4, "The CPU & the Mother of All Boards," for more information), you need to know that the type of video card you can use will depend on what type of expansion bus you have on your motherboard. Today, all new video cards come in popular PCI versions. In the past, video cards were mainly available for ISA, local bus, or VESA. For all practical purposes, they are no longer available. The ISA bus dates back to the 286 ATs and runs at a slower speed than the later local bus and VESA, which are, in turn, slower than the PCI bus. If your motherboard supports PCI, you'll definitely want a video card that supports it.

A few years back, local buses could accept only proprietary video cards, which worked only with specific motherboards. If you've upgraded your system's motherboard, you may not be able to use your old VESA or local-bus video cards. Also, if you are keeping your old motherboard and want to upgrade its video card to gain better performance, you may have trouble finding a video card that will fit in its existing slots, whether it's a VESA or local bus. Again, for more information on buses, please refer to Chapter 4.

You may want to consider buying an *accelerated video card*. Just remember that an accelerated board has faster performance than an unaccelerated one. Accelerated boards come with additional capabilities that help process the video information and speed up the computer's performance.

Definition, Please

An accelerated video card offers faster video performance. With an unaccelerated video card, all of the video information is processed by your computer's CPU. An accelerated video card, on the other hand, has the means to process image information and send it to the card's memory, where it's temporarily stored and then sent to the monitor. The better the card, the faster the performance.

Another factor that affects a video card's performance is its internal data pathway, which you'll see listed as "64-bit" or "128-bit." These numbers tell you how much data a video card can transfer internally between its accelerator chip and video memory. As you may remember from my discussion on data paths, the more bits, or the wider the path, the more information that can be transferred and the faster the computer will perform.

While a 128-bit internal bus sounds like a lot more than 64-bit, the actual difference in the final performance isn't that great. You'll pay top dollar for a 128-bit card but gain only a little speed. So unless you need the 128-bit performance for some higher-end application, save the money and buy a 64-bit. Keep in mind that "64-bit" and "128-bit" don't refer to a card's compatibility with a motherboard's expansion bus—they are strictly internal video card factors.

Cost

Unless you have high-end video requirements, you probably can get by with a 64-bit or even a 32-bit video card. There's usually no need to pay a bundle for only a marginal increase in performance.

Another video factor is the *refresh rate*. Look for boards with re-fresh rates that are at least 70 megahertz (MHz). Anything slower will probably make the screen flicker.

Definition, Please

The *refresh rate* indicates how often a video card redraws the picture on your screen. The slower the refresh rate, the more chance that you'll see flicker. If you think of old black-and-white movies, like newsreel footage from World War II, in which you can see brief lapses between frames, you already know about flicker. Keep in mind that if you choose to purchase a video board with a higher refresh rate, your monitor must be rated to display it.

Some of the latest trends in video cards involve such things as *3D accelerators*, *MPEG video*, and *TV tuners*. Depending on what you want to do, you may want to consider boards with these add-on capabilities.

Definition, Please

3D accelerator cards are special boards that can process data quickly in order to display 3D-style games, such as Quake or flight simulators.

An MPEG video card comes with special functions that allow it to play MPEG-style video faster and at higher resolutions. MPEG video refers to a certain type of video designed to run on a computer that optimizes how it's stored and played for the best results.

TV tuner cards handle computer visuals and also can turn your monitor into a TV, as long as it's hooked up to an antenna. Many tuner cards also act as video capture boards, so you can play video from your camcorder or VCR.

> ### *Cost*
> Be sure to buy only the video card that you need. For the most part, the more complicated and expensive cards are necessary only for high-end applications that have special needs, such as image or video editing.

Bottom Line

If you own a 486 or Pentium-based PC that offers good performance but has slow or jerky video, upgrading the video card makes sense. Just be careful when treading these waters. Video speed and clarity also depend on your processor, so it may make more sense to upgrade your CPU first, particularly if you have a slow 486 or lower. For a summary, refer to Table 6-2 for factors in the video card-buying decisions.

Factor	Impact on Performance
Memory	High
Accelerated/Unaccelerated	High
Internal data path	Marginal
Expansion bus type	High
3D graphics	Personal preference
MPEG	Personal preference
TV tuner	Personal preference

Table 6-2: Factors in the video card-buying decisions.

Moving On

In this chapter, we discussed video cards, how they work, how they affect your system's performance, and what to look for when buying them. In the next chapter, we'll look at another important component in your system: the hard drive.

Hard Drives

Like a desk or file drawer, your hard drive stores all of the applications and data that you use on your computer. And like a desk or file drawer, it can never be too large.

A hard drive is different from random access memory (RAM) in that it retains data even when the computer is shut off. When you work with your software or files, the hard drive loads these into memory, where the computer can use and process them.

Today, as applications get bigger, hard drives continue to grow. For now, the standard size is a gigabyte (1G), which is 1,000 megabits (MB) of storage space. While 1,000 megabits may sound like an endless expanse, like the great prairie of the American Old West, it doesn't take a lot of effort to fill it.

Some CD-ROM games offer installations that run the program faster by loading as much data as possible onto the hard drive, and some of these are beginning to creep into the 90MB range. Also, operating systems such as Windows 95 and many business applications—word processors and spreadsheets, for example—require huge chunks of disk space. As you can see, a 100MB hard drive that once seemed like an immeasurable amount of storage space is no longer enough. (There was a time when a mere 10MB seemed huge.) If you need to do image editing, run video, or desktop publishing, you'll find that the sky is the limit when it comes to your hard drive and storage space.

Storage Space: A Final Frontier

Deciding how to expand your system's storage space will depend on what type of hard drive already resides in your system. You can add another hard drive to supplement what you have, or you may have to buy an entire new controller and hard drive.

Like all things associated with computers, hard drives have evolved over the years, and several standards have come and gone. Today, integrated drive electronics (IDE) and enhanced IDE (EIDE) rule the hard drive market. EIDE is similar to IDE, but can handle larger drives (up to 8GB), can transfer data at a higher rate, and support tape and CD-ROM drives.

If you own a 286 or 386 machine, you already have a hard drive, but chances are (particularly with the 286) that these are based on older technologies, such as the once-standard RLL (Run-Length Limited procedure) and MFM (Modified Frequency Modulation procedure). These older drives, compared with the behemoths we have today, are small—usually 20, 30, or maybe as much as 60MB. Nowadays, you can buy huge IDE-style drives, which can hold more than a gigabyte (1G) of data, for just a couple hundred dollars. If you have an old 60MB RLL or MFM drive and need more space, it's just not worth holding onto.

The problem with upgrading an older drive is that you'll have a hard time finding an MFM or RLL drive of any significant size. Also, if you do find an older style drive that will work with your system (maybe a 60MB drive), you'll pay top dollar for it, probably even more than if you bought a 1.2G IDE drive and a new controller. Besides, the old drives are a lot slower than newer models and will slow your computing.

Another standard drive that is still popular is the kind that conforms to the *small computer system interface (SCSI)*. A newer version, the SCSI-2, is immensely popular on the Macintosh, where it has become a plug-and-play standard that lets you easily expand and add new hard drives and peripherals. If you are using SCSI with your PC, it does have advantages, but IDE is the clear favorite.

Definition, Please

SCSI is a popular standard for connecting peripherals, such as hard drives and CD-ROMs, to a computer. While SCSI is used on the PC, it's most popular on the Macintosh.

You may want to consider upgrading to a SCSI drive, since it is actually faster than an IDE drive. In fact, SCSI is the drive of choice for those who use computers for high-end graphics and video work. If you have monstrous storage requirements, you can purchase SCSI drives in sizes up to 8G (IDE drives currently top out at 4G). Also, when you look at the per-megabyte cost of a SCSI drive, it's really fairly close to that of an IDE drive. Although IDE and EIDE are used on most systems being made today, if you already own SCSI drives, it makes sense to stay with SCSI.

For a summary of hard drive standards and their upgradability, please refer to Table 7-1.

Hard Drive Type	Upgrade Path
MFM (ST-506)	Replace the system with an IDE drive
RLL (ST-506)	Replace the system with an IDE drive
IDE	Add a new IDE drive
SCSI	Add a new SCSI drive

Table 7-1: How to upgrade different hard drives.

Cost

If you have a fairly decent-sized hard drive—say, 540MB—and storage is an issue, you might be able to get by with software-based disk compression, which will give you more hard drive space without the expense of buying a new drive. If you use a utility such as DriveSpace that comes with Windows, you can effectively gain more hard drive space without spending a dime—the ultimate shoestring objective.

Definition, Please

Software *disk-compression utilities* are programs that cram more data on your hard drive as you work. The end result is that you can store more of some kinds of data. Popular disk-compression schemes include DoubleDisk and DriveSpace 2 and 3, which come with different versions of Windows.

If you're considering disk compression, be warned that it's not a free ride. First, because the system has to rearrange data on your hard drive and store it in a different way, the data are one step removed from your operating system. Should something go wrong—a relatively remote chance, but it can happen—you can lose data that you'll have a hard time retrieving.

Another factor is that the actual disk space you gain depends on the kind of files you are storing on your hard drive. In general, if you store data files, you can expect to see compression of about 2:1 or more (up to 16:1 for some CAD and image files). But program or application files typically compress far less, usually less than 1.5:1, if that.

In all, I know lots of people who successfully use disk compression, but I don't personally use it, nor do I usually recommend it.

The Need for Speed

So far, I've talked only about storage and haven't considered the speed of hard drives. The speed at which your computer operates is an issue that depends on what kind of work you are doing. In general, programs that load and work mostly in RAM won't run much faster when you have a fast hard drive. But databases and other applications that constantly access the hard drive can greatly benefit from a speedy drive.

Of course, the speed of your system's hard drive affects how fast your system will load programs. The faster your hard drive and your CPU, the faster your programs will load.

Your hard drive's speed (along with your CPU and memory) also plays a role in how well Windows runs. Windows uses something called a *swap file*, which acts like an overflow buffer for applications and information. When you run Windows programs, they usually load into RAM or memory. The more programs you use and the larger they are, the more RAM they take up. When Windows runs out of RAM, it starts using your hard drive as if it were memory. This is called *virtual memory*.

Definition, Please

A *swap file* is a part of your hard drive that's set aside to accept overflow of programs and data from RAM or memory. When Windows uses your hard drive in this way, it's called *virtual memory*.

When Windows uses your hard drive as overflow memory, the performance of your system radically changes. A hard drive is a lot slower than memory, and using your hard drive as memory slows down your system. As mentioned in the chapter on memory, you can add more memory to increase the performance of your system, but when you exceed the system's memory, it's nice to have a fast hard drive to back it up.

The speed of your hard drive depends on three major factors: *data transfer rates*, *average access time*, and *average seek time*. When you're shopping for a drive, you can use these figures to get an idea of how fast it will perform.

Definition, Please

The *data transfer rate* tells you how fast data can move from the hard drive to the CPU. It's one of the most important indicators of hard drive performance and is measured in megabytes per second (Mbps). IDE drives can transfer data at around 11 to 16 Mbps, and SCSI-2 drives are supposed to reach somewhere around 40 Mbps.

Average access time is the amount of time it takes for the heads (the devices that read and write information to the drive) to move to the different tracks on a disk. In general, look for drives that have an average access time of around 10–12 milliseconds (ms).

Average seek time tells you how long it takes for the read/ write head to move between two adjacent tracks. This figure is not as important as the data transfer rate or the access time.

For a summary of the speed parameters, please refer to Table 7-2.

Look For	
Data transfer rate	11–16 Mbps
Average access time	10–12 ms

Table 7-2: Hard drive speed specifications.

Another factor that affects your hard drive's speed is the way data are stored on the drive. Files are stored on the hard drive in units called *clusters*.

Definition, Please

A *cluster* is a unit of measure of information that is stored on a hard drive. When a system stores a file, it doesn't find one place on the drive for the entire file; the operating system breaks up the file into clusters and stores each cluster, sometimes in different areas of the drive. You can think of clusters as subsets of a file.

In practice, clusters can become separated and spread over disparate parts of the drive. When that happens, the hard drive has to read them from different parts of the drive, which slows it down. The optimum situation is for clusters to lie right next to each other. This way, the hard drive can simply read the clusters one after another and barely even have to move, thus increasing the speed at which it reads information.

To achieve this state on your hard drive, you can use software that's called a *defragger or defragmenter.*

Definition, Please

A *defragger* or *defragmenter* is a special software program that rearranges a hard drive's clusters so a drive can operate as efficiently as possible. If you have a drive that has data spread all over the disk (a condition that occurs naturally over time), you will see some performance gains by using defragmentation software. While the gains may not be quite what manufacturers claim, they are noticeable.

You might consider using a defragger periodically, and especially if your computer seems a bit sluggish. Depending on how far the clusters are distributed across the drive, you can see some performance improvement. In my experience, however, I've never seen anything better than a 10 percent increase in speed. Thus, using a defragger is more of a system maintenance item than an upgrade.

Hard Drive Nuts & Bolts

An IDE drive doesn't actually need a drive controller or separate board as an MFM does, but to connect a hard drive to your motherboard, you usually rely on what's called a paddle board, or paddle card, depending on the construction of your motherboard. You'll find that some motherboards come with this capability built in. As mentioned in Chapter 4, "The CPU & the Mother of All Boards," whenever you buy motherboards with built-in input/output (I/O) ports or other capabilities, there's a chance that they may not fit correctly into your case.

Tip

When buying a hard drive, get one as large as you can comfortably afford. All new hard drives seem spacious at first, but it won't be too long before you're bumping into space limitations and deleting files to fit in new ones.

Buying a New Hard Drive

First, decide how much hard drive space you need. For guidance, you can refer to the charts in Chapter 1, "Why Upgrade?" and Chapter 2, "What Do You Want to Do With Your System?" that help you consider want you want to do with your computer. The second major consideration is whether a drive will fit inside your computer case. Most drives sold today come in a 3.5-inch size, but you should take a careful look at your case and more specifically at the drive bay, which is a cage that holds hard drives in your computer. For more on this, refer to Chapter 20, "Installing an IDE Hard Drive & Floppy."

Hard drives are sold in kits or are sold "bare." Unless you're already comfortable with installing drives, buy the kit, as it will be more complete and include related hardware and instructions. Before buying, be sure to check what type of documentation comes with the drive and verify that everything you need is in the kit. This way, you can tell ahead of time how difficult the installation will be.

In general, make sure that the kit comes with the *mounting components*, *adapters*, and *cables*. There's nothing more frustrating than buying a kit and then having to make several trips back to the computer store to buy related parts.

Definition, Please

The mounting components are the physical adapter rails, nuts, bolts, and other hardware that let you mount the drive in your PC, some of which are shown in Figure 7-1. The adapters and cables, as their names imply, let you connect a hard drive to power and to the controller card.

Figure 7-1: You can purchase hard drives in kits that come with mounting components.

Also, be sure to check our buying instructions in Chapter 12, "Bargain Basement." Before you put out your money, check to see whether the kit includes:

○ Cables

○ Adapters

○ Instructions

○ Mounting components

When buying your hard drive, you can compare the following:

○ Size

○ Data transfer rate

○ Access time

○ Average seek time

○ Cost

○ Cost/MB

Note: To determine cost per megabyte, simply divide the price of the hard drive by its size in megabyte. The lower the number, the better the deal.

Don't Forget the Floppy

While we're talking about system storage, it's worth taking a minute to talk about floppy drives. Of course, a floppy drive, as shown in Figure 7-2, is that device on the front of your computer that accepts the little disks that store programs and data. Floppy drives, like hard drives, have evolved over the years, mainly getting smaller while holding more and more data.

Figure 7-2: Floppy drives read and write data to floppy disks.

Today, the standard floppy size is the 3.5-inch disk, which can hold 1.44MB of data. If you already have a disk drive that supports this, great. If you have an older 5.25-inch or 3.5-inch drive that accepts disks that hold only 720K of data, you may want to upgrade, particularly if you're still using a 5.25-inch drive.

While it's not absolutely necessary to upgrade your floppy drive, you'll find that all software distributed today comes on 3.5-inch disks formatted as 1.44MB. If you don't have the right drive, you won't be able to read the program disks. For a look at various size disks and their storage capacity, please refer to Table 7-3.

Disk	Disk Size	Capacity
360K double side, double density	5.25 inch	360K
1.2MB high density	5.25 inch	1.2MB
3.5-inch	3.5 inch	720K
3.5-inch high density	3.5 inch	1.44MB

Table 7-3: Capacities of various size disks.

Installing a new floppy drive is pretty straightforward, as you'll see in Chapter 20, "Installing an IDE Hard Drive & Floppy." The one thing that you'll have to consider is the controller card. Most PCs have a card that acts as the floppy controller, which sometimes serves other functions as well: It can be a serial or parallel port or even a joystick interface. Some older motherboards come with these controller features built in, but that is rare today. If you have such a motherboard, you'll probably be replacing it during your upgrade.

More Storage & Backups

When a computer is a part of your life, you'll find that you store a lot of important information on it. It's not a stretch to imagine that you'll ultimately rely on your computer to store complete financial and tax information, crucial business records, client data, various contracts and proposals, resumes and other personal documents—even your kid's school report on dinosaurs.

But computers aren't perfect, of course, and any act of man or God can cause computer glitches that make your system lose data. Other factors, such as computer viruses, can maliciously or inadvertently erase data. And if you're tired or not thinking, it's easy to accidentally erase key files.

This past year, for whatever reason, was not a great year for my computers. I had two major hard drive crashes and my modem went bad. If I hadn't had back-ups for many of the chapters in this book, and for lots of the other important data, I would have lost all of it. Fortunately, I'm pretty good about keeping double back-ups. I even go so far as to keep copies of all my data in my briefcase, which goes wherever I go. I always knew there was a reason why I carefully backed up all my data, but it wasn't until I had a serious hard drive crash that it made perfect sense and saved the day.

If you have a hard drive crash, there are companies that can retrieve lost data from the damaged drive. But this service is extremely expensive (last time I checked it was in the thousands of dollars). At these prices, only rich corporations can probably afford it. Your data may be important enough that you resort to paying for such a service, but a little expense and thought before-hand will make it a lot easier—and cheaper—to get through a disaster. Because virtually everything that you do with your computer resides on your drives, you need to back up your data. I can't over-emphasize the importance of this.

Definition, Please

Backing up your data means to make a copy of the data on your hard drive, or storing a copy of your entire hard drive, on another hard drive, a removable drive, a series of floppies, or on tape.

Back in the old days, when a 20MB hard drive was considered state of the art, it was feasible to back up your hard drive onto a series of floppies. You could get most of that 20MB drive onto some eight or nine 1.2MB floppy disks (with disk compression).

These days, however, 1GB hard drives are the norm. If you tried to use floppies to back up these monstrous drives, you'd end up with a stack of some 400 disks, depending on the data. Not only would you have to store that stack of floppies somewhere, but during the back-up process, you would have to swap these disks, one by one, into the drive—a tedious process that could take hours. The bottom line is that floppies are no longer a reasonable way to back up large amounts of data and today's hard drives.

Fortunately, as you would expect, there are alternatives for backing up. We'll explore several that can be excellent upgrades to your current system.

One solution is to install a second hard drive in your computer. At the end of each day, you simply copy all of your data files to it. Then if you have a crash on your main drive, you'll have a backup of data already on your system.

The advantage to this relatively cheap solution is that you also get more hard drive space, which you can use to store more applications. The down side is that you can't take the data with you. Should someone steal your computer, or there's a fire or flood, or you accidentally drop your computer out the window and down three stories (anything's possible), both your main and backup data would be gone. That's why, in addition to storing data twice on my computer's hard drive, I also store data on another medium, usually a Zip drive, which I'll talk about later.

Caution

There is one precaution that you need to take with the hard drive backup method. Be sure that if you back up data onto a second drive that you are, indeed, using a different physical drive. If you simply partition a large hard drive into two smaller ones, these are physically still the same drive. If a crash occurs, both of your drives would be knocked out, and all your data would be irretrievable. To make the hard drive backup scheme work, you must have two physically different drives installed in your PC.

Personally, I only back up my data, but I know many people who back up their entire drives, so if something happens they can restore the programs as well as the files. I find that it's not worth my time to back up my applications. First of all, applications like Microsoft Office are huge, and since they come on CD-ROM anyway, installation is not a major task. Of course, if you installed a huge application from a stack of 35 floppy disks, you might think otherwise. But a CD-ROM installation is fairly painless, and I usually don't have that many macros or templates to lose (I back these up, anyway).

If you take my approach and don't back up your applications and operating system, you also stand to lose your settings in Windows, including wallpapers, arrangements of groups, icons, and other aspects. If you have Windows set up in a particular way and it would take you days to reconfigure a fresh installation, by all means, back up that entire hard drive. I'm just not all that attached to my screen savers and desktop.

Get It On Tape

An excellent backup choice is a tape backup drive. You can find these at fairly low prices (under $100 for a 450MB) and they can store a lot of data, up to 8GB. Most experts consider tape drives to be quite reliable for storing data. The down side is that these devices are very slow at reading and writing data, and backing up a large amount of data can take hours.

Definition, Please

Tape Backup refers to a technology that saves digital computer data onto special cassette tapes.

While a tape drive is very slow, most of them come with software that let you schedule automatic backups at any time you set. This way, you can have your system perform the backup on its own, after your normal working hours. While you sleep, your computer can back itself up for you (and you can sleep peacefully, knowing that your data is safe).

If you do want to perform unattended backups, you'll need to make sure that the tape cassette has enough space to store all of the data (a tape backup drive can't swap tapes for you). Recording data on a tape drive is much like using a VCR to tape your favorite show on television while you're away. If the VCR tape runs out just before the detective in the movie dramatically fingers the killer, you're going to have to wait for reruns, or call your friends to fill you in.

I talked earlier about backing up data on two mediums. For the same reason, I recommend that if you use a tape drive, you should rotate two tapes for each of your daily backups. It is possible—see my earlier comments regarding Murphy's Law and computers— that some malevolent force could destroy your main hard drive, and only then would you discover that the backup tape you've been using for weeks is faulty. If you switch tapes each time you back up, you'll have your data on two tapes, and lessen your chance of losing anything important.

When it comes to losing data, I can speak from personal experience. I once had a hard drive crash *and* one failed backup. As I brought out my second backup, I was literally holding my breath—some three weeks of work, plus nine months of financial data, were riding on this. Fortunately, the second backup worked just fine and I was immediately up and running. I have friends who laugh at me for my "paranoid" backups, but in this one case it definitely saved me. I can't emphasize enough the importance of backing up your files.

If you need to back up a hard drive that's over 1GB, a tape backup is an excellent choice.

Recordable CD-ROM

Another medium that is gaining in popularity is recordable CD-ROM. You may recall from my earlier discussion of CD-ROM that that you can't record to this medium. I wasn't fibbing—you can't record with a conventional CD-ROM drive, like those mentioned in Chapter 9, "CD-ROM." But there are devices now on the market that let you make a single recording to a CD-ROM disk.

Definition, Please
Recordable CD-ROM refers to a technology that uses a special drive to save data onto a CD disk.

The problem with recording on a CD is that it's permanent. You can record about half a GB onto a CD-ROM, but it's one-time only. In other words, you can't go back later and re-record over the CD-ROM with other data, or the next day's backup. For this reason, CD-ROM is really only useful for archiving data that is fairly fixed, like all of last year's financial records. One thing that the CD-ROM has going for it is that a CD can store data for a long period of time without going bad, unlike floppy disks and magnetic tape, which fade over time. For this reason, CD-ROM is an excellent archive and storage medium, but it's not practical for day-to-day backups.

Recordable CD-ROM is also quite pricey. Just a year and a half ago, the drives cost over $5,000. Today, some are under $600. At this writing, blank CD-ROMs are around $8 each.

Removable Drives

Another technology that is gaining in popularity is removable hard and floppy drives. Until recently, these drives were extremely pricey. While it's still a bit expensive now, removable drives offer many advantages.

Definition, Please

A removable hard or floppy drive is one that lets you store large amounts of data—usually from 100MB to 1GB—and can be removed easily from the computer.

The obvious advantage is that a removable hard drive can hold lots of data, some as much as 1GB. As with a floppy, you can take this data with you wherever you go—in fact, most of these removable drives are much like large floppies. If you need more space to store data, all you have to do is buy another disk, the same way that you would buy more floppy disks. Therefore, your ultimate storage backup space on a removable drive is virtually unlimited.

A popular removable hard drive is the Syquest EZ125, which uses a 135 MB 3.5-inch cartridge. An immensely popular removable floppy drive is the Iomega Zip Drive, which uses 100MB 3.5-inch cartridges. Both of these products are available for under $200, and the cartridges are around $20.

I've been mostly pleased with the Zip Drive, which comes in a SCSI version that attaches to a SCSI port, and a parallel version that connects with your system's printer, LPT1, or parallel port.

The beauty of the parallel port model is that you can easily use the Zip Drive on different machines by simply attaching it to a system's parallel port. You don't have to open the case and install the drive.

In fact, I frequently use my parallel Zip Drive to move data from one system to another by plugging the drive into the parallel port of one machine, copying data, connecting the drive to another machine, and copying the data again. I've also had good luck using the Zip Drive as a second backup to my second hard drive.

If you have visions of using a Zip Drive as a hard drive from which to run programs, you'll find that the parallel version is far too slow. However, the SCSI version runs quite fast and will give you acceptable performance, if you have the hardware to run it. Also, when you have to send a lot of data to someone else, a Zip cartridge is a fairly inexpensive, and standard media that you can send through the mail, since more and more people own them. I have used Zip cartridges to send large presentations to others.

The advantage of the removable hard drives—the Iomega Jaz and Syquest EX135, EZFlyer, and SyJet—is that they are just about as fast as regular hard drives and can quickly copy data, or even be used to run applications on different machines.

If you need to make backups for projects or under 100MB of data, the removable floppy and hard drives are excellent choices. They also work well if you have to load and unload large files from your hard drive. If speed is an issue, definitely go with one of the removable hard drives.

Re-writable Optical Disk Drives

At the entry level, Magneto optical (MO) drives are compact 3.5-inch drives, for under $500, that store about 128MB. At the high end, the 5.25-inch drives, which sell for thousands of dollars, can store several gigabytes.

Optical drives are known for being rather slow, but they are also recognized as the most reliable medium for storing data for long periods. Most re-writable optical discs are rated to maintain data for some ten years. On the other hand, most magnetic media, such as floppies and tapes, are rated to last only five years. Optical drives are less sensitive to shock, too, so they can take more abuse than a removable hard drive or other media.

Popular MO models include the Olympus Sys.230 and the Fujitsu DynaMO 230, both of which can store 230MB drives, and the Panasonic PD/CD drives, which come in both parallel and SCSI versions and store up to 650MB. By the way, unlike the removable floppies and hard drives, which only work with one company's system, the 230 optical drives are more standardized and can work with drives from different manufacturers. Also, the PD/CD, while not standardized, will work as both a quad-speed CD-ROM player and a re-writable drive. If you're thinking about buying a new CD-ROM, this may weigh into your decision.

Moving On

I've discussed the various factors and issues involved with hard drives, what the parameters and specs mean, and what to look for when buying one. In Chapter 8, "Monitor This," we'll discuss the all-important monitor, something you look at and use each and every time you compute.

Monitor This

What you see, as they say, is usually what you get. And what you see on your computer depends greatly on your monitor. Your computer's video card takes data from your computer and converts them into a signal that your monitor can display, but it's the monitor—your computer's screen—that is the link between you and your computer. It's what you stare at and interact with, day after day after day.

At its most basic level, a monitor is a lot like your television set. Both rely on the same technology: a cathode ray tube (CRT), which is a tube of glass with phosphorous materials on the inside of a screen, and a gun, controlled by a magnetic field, that rapidly "fires" electrons onto the screen. The screen phosphors, arranged in groups of three for three primary colors (red, green, and blue), light up when they're hit by the electrons, lighting up *pixels*, and forming the onscreen images.

But a computer monitor is different in that it displays at a much higher resolution than your television set. You may remember, in the early days of computing, doing word processing on a television set. If so, you'll recall that those large, blocky letters just couldn't compare to the clean letters displayed on a computer's monitor.

As a side note, a new generation of color *liquid crystal display* (*LCD*) monitors is just coming on the market as I write this.

Definition, Please

A *liquid crystal display* (LCD) uses technology that is strikingly different than that used in a traditional cathode ray tube. LCD displays rely on tiny wafers that polarize light to create images. Since they don't rely on a gun that "shoots" electrons, LCD displays are very thin.

These monitors are large versions of those flat (and very thin) color displays that you find on color notebook computers. They are now available in larger sizes, to be used as stand-alone monitors. The difference is in the physical size, particularly the depth, of an LCD display when compared with that of a conventional monitor.

Because the LCD screens are flat, they don't take up as much room as a regular CRT-style monitor. In fact, you can mount these monitors on the wall, hanging them like a picture, which is going to drastically change the way we use our systems and set up our computer-based offices. Despite its advantages, a color LCD panel is a new technology and costs quite a bit more than a CRT monitor. If you want to buy one, you can apply many of the same considerations that you would use when buying a conventional monitor but expect to pay a lot more.

Upgrading a Monitor

Do you need to upgrade your monitor? If you currently own a monochrome monitor, you'll certainly want to move up to color to run the latest applications. If you own a color graphics adapter (CGA) or enhanced graphics adapter (EGA) monitor, you'll want to upgrade to super VGA (video graphics array). Otherwise you won't be able to run the latest multimedia programs. Besides, super VGA will give you clearer and more attractive images and text, which also can reduce eyestrain.

Video arrays and adapters were discussed in Chapter 6, "Video Cards."

Even if you're already running a VGA monitor, its age and capabilities can affect how you run Windows applications. For example, a low-resolution screen with a small display will let you view only one application at a time effectively, as shown in Figure 8-1.

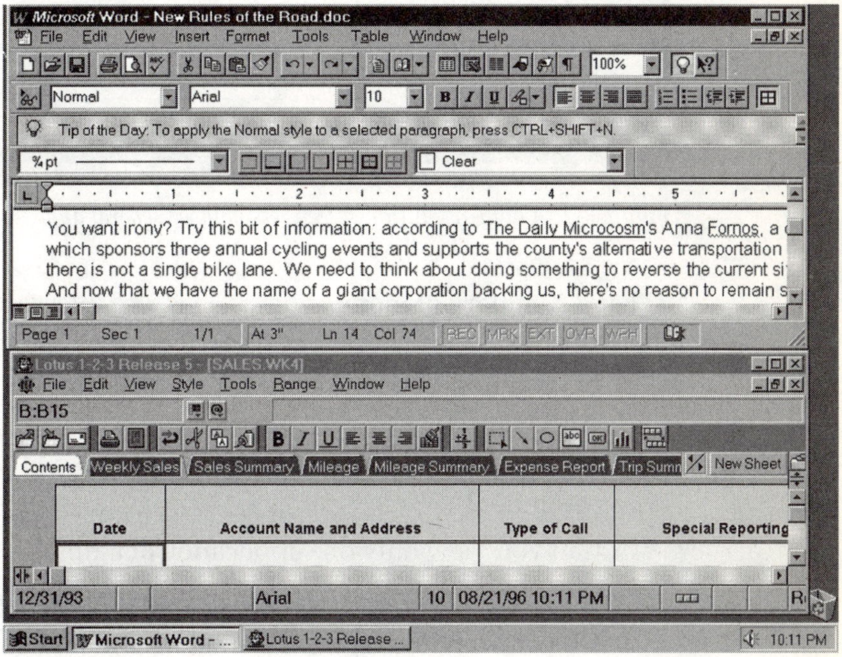

Figure 8-1: A low-resolution screen practically lets you work with only a single application at a time.

With a high-resolution screen and a large display, you can have several applications open at a time and see them all at once, as shown in Figure 8-2.

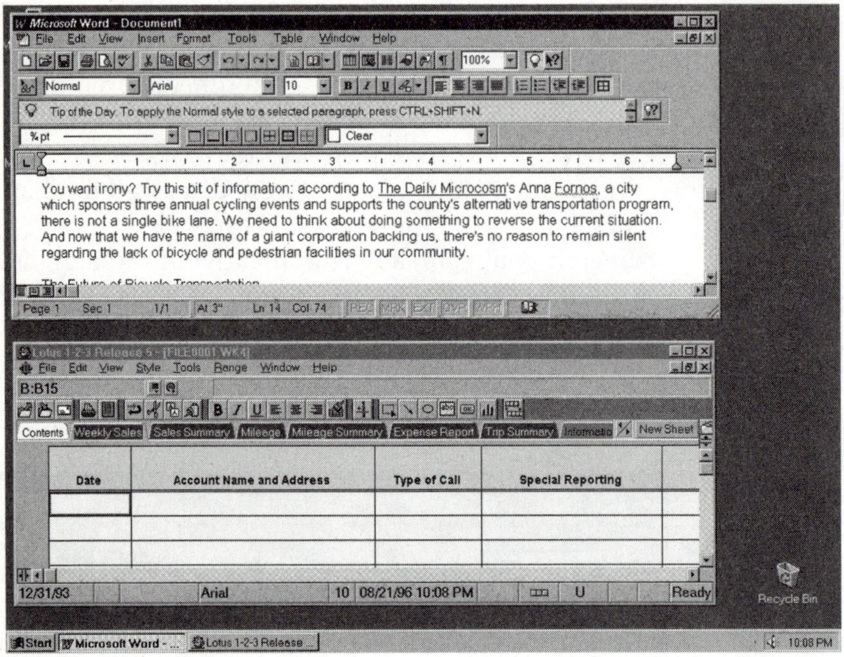

Figure 8-2: A high-resolution screen lets you see several applications at a time.

For a summary of monitor upgrade issues, please refer to the following list:

○ Do you find that your eyes often feel strained after working with your PC?

○ Do you sometimes get headaches when working on your computer?

○ Can you view only one application at a time?

○ Do you want to view more than one application at a time?

○ Do you want to display more colors and higher resolutions?

○ Do you need a larger display to do intricate desktop publishing or CAD work?

○ Does your current display look fuzzy?

Unfortunately, there is currently no way to add or replace a component to upgrade your monitor: You have to buy a new monitor to replace an old one. Also, keep in mind that what you can display on your monitor goes hand in hand with the capabilities of your system's video card. For this, please refer to Chapter 6.

By the way, I didn't discuss monitors in Chapter 3, "What Upgrades Will You Need?" because many of the upgrades—particularly those with enhanced video cards—assume that you already have a color monitor of VGA quality or better. When you consider how much you look at a monitor in the course of your daily work or play on your computer, you can see that a decent monitor is a good investment, particularly if you currently have a CGA or low-resolution monitor.

I can speak from personal experience on this. In the late '80s, I made do with a CGA monitor that kept tagging along with all of my various system upgrades. When I finally moved up to a VGA monitor, I found that my eyes felt so much more relaxed when I was working. I still kick myself for taking so long to make that upgrade.

Adding a new monitor is one of the easiest upgrades you can perform. All you have to do is buy a new monitor, connect it to your video card, and plug it into power, and you're ready to go. Of course, if you're upgrading from older standards such as CGA or EGA, the upgrade also will involve a new video card installation. On the other hand, when you're actually shopping around for that new monitor, there are lots of things to consider.

Bigger Is Better

The first thing you have to think about when buying a new monitor is its physical size. Today, most monitors are between 14 inches and 21 inches, measured diagonally like a television screen. Larger monitors are available, but they are mainly for special purposes—for example, for use in multimedia presentations. These superlarge monitors also come with astronomical price tags, in the thousands of dollars.

While a 14-inch monitor can certainly do the computing job, a larger screen offers several advantages. First, because of the larger size, you'll get a bigger image. With a larger screen, you can run your graphics applications, particularly those in Windows, at higher resolutions for more clarity.

On the other hand, the lower the screen resolution, the more "blocky" the text will appear. While a smaller screen can display the high-resolution images, it tends to shrink them down in size. A larger display keeps high-resolution text at a more readable size. For graphics, desktop publishing, drawing, or CAD work, you'll definitely want a larger monitor, at least 17 inches.

For more general use, you can buy a monitor based on the type of work that you will do and, more important, the resolutions you will want to run. In general, you'll want at least a 15-inch monitor to run in resolutions of 800x600. A 14-inch monitor will be okay to run 640x480. For the ultrahigh resolutions, such as 1024x768, you'll definitely want at least a 17-inch monitor. On a 14-inch monitor, the high resolution will be so small that you'll probably have trouble reading it. For a summary of resolution versus monitor size, refer to Table 8-2.

Resolution	Monitor Size
640x480	14 inch or bigger
800x600	15 inch or 17 inch
1024x768 or higher	17 inch or bigger

Table 8-2: General guidelines for resolutions and monitor sizes.

Definitely avoid any monitor that can't meet a resolution of 640x480. When you buy a new monitor, be sure to check what resolutions it can display. While most monitors can display all of the popular resolutions, some can't; these might be the ones you'll see at a far lower price.

On the downside, larger monitors are more expensive, so check your budget and see how much you can spend. If you'll be buying a 14-inch monitor, keep in mind that you usually can buy a 15-inch, or maybe even a 17-inch, monitor for just a little more money. Buying the size you actually want may be well worth this extra expense. By the way, a 17-inch monitor might not sound like all that much of an improvement over a 14-inch one, but when you look at the math, the 17-inch monitor has some 50 percent more screen area.

The largest monitors, such as the 21-inch jobs, will give you vast amounts of screen space. If you're doing desktop publishing and want to view two full pages on your screen, for example, these monitors are definitely the ones to consider for the job. On the other hand, you'll pay a lot of money for such a monitor, and it will take up a lot of space on your desk.

If you're considering a large monitor, 21 inches or larger—or even a 17-inch one—you should measure your work space to be sure that there's adequate room and that the desk can hold the 70 pounds or so that the device weighs. Be sure to check both the depth and height of the monitor you're considering, and don't forget to add the height of the tilt-and-swivel stand, which you'll need so you can adjust the screen to your preferred viewing angle.

I've actually known people who have bought 21-inch monitors for their homes and couldn't get the carton through their doorways. Before you lug a new monitor home or pay hefty mail order shipping charges, be sure to check the dimensions. You don't want it to be like the time Dad brought home a Christmas tree that was too big for the door and too tall for the living room.

One last tip: When buying a monitor, be sure to actually measure the screen size. Because there are few standards in the computer industry, many manufacturers have taken liberties with their screen sizes. If you measure the screen, you'll know exactly what you're getting.

The Rest of the Story

A common screen specification is its *dot pitch*. This term refers to the size of the pixel or dot that a monitor displays. The smaller the dot pitch, the better; look for a monitor with a maximum of a 0.28 dot pitch. For serious work, you might consider a monitor with a dot pitch of 0.25 or lower. You can save some money by going with a larger dot pitch—say, a 0.31 dot pitch—but this is a personal call. For some it's unacceptable, while others won't see any problems. In general, the smaller your monitor's screen, the larger the dot pitch you can get away with.

As I mentioned before, you also have to consider what resolution your monitor can display. Some older monitors can display only lower resolutions, but most new monitors will handle the higher levels.

Another factor related to the monitor is the physical flatness of the front of the screen. Generally, the flatter the monitor, the better—and the more expensive—it is. Less expensive monitors have curved screens, which can distort onscreen images. The amount of distortion you'll accept is a personal call—as always, you'll want to take a look at the screen before you buy to see that the monitor meets your needs and preferences. I definitely prefer a flat screen and recommend that you purchase the flattest screen you can.

A parameter called *scanning frequency* tells you how fast a monitor will draw an image, from the top left corner of the screen to the bottom right corner. Look for a refresh rate or *vertical scan rate* of at least 70 Hz. At the high end, this parameter can go up to 100 Hz. Another parameter, called the *horizontal scan rate,* looks at this same measurement across the screen: Look for a monitor that has a horizontal rate between 30 and 70 KHz.

When shopping for a monitor, you might run into the terms *interlaced* versus *noninterlaced.* For the most part, you should go with a noninterlaced monitor. Again, this is a personal call, and there are cost trade-offs.

Definition, Please

Interlaced and *noninterlaced* describe the way a monitor displays data on the screen. An interlaced monitor draws each screen image in a way that results in a slight flicker, while the noninterlaced monitor reduces the flicker.

For a summary of monitor specifications to look for, refer to Table 8-3.

Monitor specifications to look for	
Dot pitch	0.28 or lower
Flatness	Personal preference
Supported resolutions	640x480, 800x600, 1024x768
Interlaced versus non-interlaced	

Table 8-3: Monitor cost and feature issues.

Cost

You can save money on a monitor by considering your needs for dot pitch, flatness, and interlaced versus noninterlaced monitors. The best thing you can do is check out the monitor ahead of time with the video card to see if the result meets your personal needs. Remember that the monitor is what you will be staring at when working on your system. It makes sense to buy one that you know you can live with and use for a long time.

The Intangibles

Some monitors are energy efficient and offer different modes of operation that cut down on the amount of power they consume when you're not working on your computer. Some monitors sense when you stop working on your computer and go into a low-power mode to save energy. To reactivate the screen, you just move the mouse or press a key on the keyboard.

Also, because many people are concerned about electromagnetic emissions, some monitors have met a standard called MPR-II, which limits the amount of electromagnetic emission the monitor sends out. If you are concerned about this, be sure to look for a monitor that meets this standard. Be warned, though—you will probably pay more for it.

Buying a Monitor

One last concern is the placement of your new monitor's controls. On some, the various adjustment dials can be found in interesting places, including the back, where they're hard to get at. I like a monitor with clearly marked controls mounted in the front, where they're immediately accessible. Also, it doesn't hurt to get a feel for the responsiveness of the controls for brightness, contrast, vertical and horizontal position, size, and other adjustments before you buy. For a summary of these controls, refer to Table 8-4.

Control	Description
Brightness	Adjusts how bright the image is, just as on your television set.
Contrast	Adjusts the contrast between the darkest and lightest parts of the screen.
Vertical position	Adjusts the vertical position of the display so you can move the image vertically, up or down, and center it.
Horizontal position	Adjusts the horizontal position of the display so you can move the image horizontally, right or left, and center it.
Vertical size	Adjusts the size of the image, making it shorter or taller.
Horizontal size	Adjusts the size of the image, making it wider or narrower.

Table 8-4: Monitor adjustments.

Like other computer components, monitors come in a variety of price ranges and features. The best monitors generally come from such companies as Eizo (Nanao), NEC, and Sony. You probably won't go wrong with one of these reputable manufacturers.

This isn't to say that there aren't excellent monitors from other companies. The best test is to check them out and see if you like the way they display images. If you purchase through mail order, be sure that you can return the monitor if you don't like the way it looks. Better yet, check out the monitor at a local computer store to compare its price and features against others. With the general guidelines given here, you should be able to find a decent monitor that will work for you, yet not have to pay top dollar for it.

For a summary of all of the monitor issues and what you need to look for, please refer to Table 8-5.

Issue	Look For
Resolution	
640x480	14 inch or bigger
800x600	15 inch or bigger
1024x768	17 inch or bigger
	Interlaced Vs Noninterlaced
Dot pitch	0.28 or smaller
Vertical scan rate	70 Hz
Horizontal scan rate	30 through 70 KHz
Controls	Brightness
	Contrast
	Vertical position
	Horizontal position
	Vertical size
	Horizontal size
Physical size and your work space	
Physical weight and your computer desk	

Table 8-5: Summary of monitor issues.

Moving On

In this chapter, we've reviewed dot pitches, emission standards, size, resolution, and lots of other factors that will help you purchase the right monitor. In Chapter 9, "CD-ROMs," we'll enter the realm of multimedia when we begin our discussion of CD-ROMs and, following that, sound cards.

CD-ROMs

If your computer isn't equipped with a *CD-Read Only Memory (CD-ROM)* drive, you won't be able to run many of the latest programs on the market. Today, most games and educational programs are packaged solely on those little silver-colored disks, which look just like the audio CDs that you buy at the music store. You'll find that, in addition to entertainment programs, many business applications and even operating systems such as Windows 95 now come on CD-ROM. While the games and educational titles usually read data direct from the CD-ROM as you run the programs, other titles simply use a CD, instead of disks, to store and conveniently install the programs.

Definition, Please

In function, a CD-ROM drive on your computer is quite similar to the one in your stereo system. Both rely on the same technology—a moving laser head that reads the grooves in a CD's surface. The difference is that a computer's CD-ROM holds data for programs, while the audio CD holds data to play music. Also, like an audio CD drive, a computer CD-ROM drive usually can't write or save data to a CD-ROM.

There are specialized computer CD-ROM drives that can "write" or record data, but they are for users with special applications—usually developers, presenters, and those who want to store large amounts of information. They are not something the average PC user will probably need, at least for now.

With its impressive storage capacity of some 650 megabytes (MB), a CD-ROM can hold a lot more data than a floppy. In fact, one CD-ROM is equivalent to more than 400 3.5-inch disks, each of which holds 1.44MB of data. A publisher can save money by distributing programs on CD. Yes, it comes down to cost savings. Instead of spending approximately 25 cents for each floppy disk (some larger programs can require 20 or more), a publisher has to reproduce only a single CD-ROM for less than 50 cents.

On CD-ROM, you'll find titles that take advantage of the medium's extraordinary storage capabilities. These include multimedia encyclopedias that illustrate their text with live-action videos, sound effects (you can hear part of Martin Luther King's "I have a dream" speech or the songs of a humpback whale), and animation.

Games and educational programs use CD-ROM to store their considerable graphics, video, and audio effects. These programs require greater storage space as they become more sophisticated. For instance, Sierra's Phantasmagoria requires an astounding seven CD-ROMs. Installing these programs direct to your hard drive isn't practical. Some recent titles can take up to 100MB of hard drive space for the fastest operation, and it's not unusual to have a CD-ROM program install more than 30MB of data.

These days, many organizations use CD-ROMs to distribute reams of timely information. It's not unusual to find monthly CD-ROMs with the latest information on bugs in an operating system, legal mumbo jumbo and case studies, and even software demos that come with magazines. You'll also find collections of clip art, pictures, videos, and even sound effects distributed on CD-ROM, all of which you can use in your own presentations, multimedia productions, and publications.

From our perspective as users, installing a program from a CD-ROM is convenient. Imagine a program that comes on 30 floppy disks (like some of the business suites that come with a word processor, spreadsheet, and database in one package) and requires you to insert all those disks, one by one, in your floppy drive—a royal pain. With a CD-ROM installation, all you have to do is insert the disk and walk away. The program does all of the work for you.

There's no doubt that to run today's latest programs, particularly those involving multimedia, you'll want a CD-ROM drive. As an additional bonus, you can play your audio CDs on your computer—high-tech whistling while you work.

What to Look For

When you buy a CD-ROM drive, the most talked-about factor will be the data transfer rate, expressed as 2X, 3X, 4X, 6X, and 8X drives. As you'll see, this is an important factor, but it's not necessarily the entire story. (You'll find more information about data transfer rates and access times in Chapter 7, "Hard Drives.")

Years ago, when the first CD-ROM drives came onto the market, they could transfer data at a rate of 150 kilobytes per second (Kps). This means that every second, the heads on the CD-ROM drive could read 150K of information. These original pioneering drives became known as "single-speed" CD-ROM drives.

As usual in the computer industry, faster drives were soon on the horizon. The next revolution came in the double-speed or 2X drive, which could transfer data at 300 Kps. From here, it's easy to see how the ratings work: 3X is three times 150Kps, the speed of the original single drive, or 450Kps, and so on.

CD-ROMs need to be specifically made to run on a faster drive; otherwise, they won't take full advantage of the drive's capability. For the most part, though, a 2X drive is faster than a single speed, a 3X faster than a double, and so on. These days, you shouldn't buy anything slower than a 4X and should try to buy the best that's within your budget (up to 8X, with a data transfer rate of 1200 Kps).

While the 2X and subsequent multiple drives are indeed faster, other factors, such as seek and access time, also play a role. Usually you don't find these parameters clearly spelled out. Transfer rate tells you how much data a drive can read in a second; access time tells you how long it will take a drive to find the information. A common CD-ROM access time is around 200 milliseconds (msec.), and that will give you decent performance. For a summary of these criteria, please refer to Table 9-1.

Data transfer rate	600 Kps (4X) or faster
Access time	200 msec. or less

Table 9-1: CD-ROM seek times and data transfer rates.

Cost

If you will not be doing any multimedia, you can probably get by with a slower CD-ROM drive. However, be warned: The slightly slower drives are only slightly less expensive (if you can find them), so it really makes sense to purchase the fastest drive you can afford.

Another consideration is what's called *multisession* capability, although with newer drives this is almost a given. For the most part, you will want to purchase a drive with multisession capability just in case you later need it, particularly to support Kodak PhotoCD.

Definition, Please

Multisession is a technology that can burn new data onto a CD-ROM at different times, instead of all at once. This technology was developed to support the Kodak Photo CD, with which you can develop film and have the photos placed electronically on CD-ROM, so you can immediately use them on your computer.

Because a CD-ROM can hold some 100 electronic photos, the developers of this technology recognized that even the most avid shutterbugs won't always need to develop 100 photos at a time. They developed the multisession technology so that users can have more developed pictures added to a CD-ROM whenever they wish. This way, you can receive your first batch of pictures on a CD-ROM, and then let the developer add more photos at a later date.

Making the Connection

Another factor in your CD-ROM purchasing decision is whether to buy an IDE or a SCSI CD-ROM drive. For an explanation of these and other drives, see Chapter 7.

In the old days, all CD-ROM drives were connected to a PC via SCSI or through proprietary ports. In fact, most of the proprietary ports were actually variations on SCSI. If you have SCSI hard drives, you already have a way to connect a SCSI CD-ROM drive. Also, if you have an older sound card, chances are that the card provides a port to connect a SCSI CD-ROM drive. To find out if your sound card has such a port, you'll have to check its documentation.

Caution: Windows supports standard SCSI but does not necessarily support proprietary solutions or even proprietary SCSI connections, which can create compatibility problems. If you use a SCSI, you'll be able to add other peripheral devices, such as scanners and hard drives, without inserting additional expansion cards.

Today, the most popular way to connect a CD-ROM drive to your PC is through something called the ATAPI (AT attachment packet interface) standard. Using an ATAPI drive, you can connect your CD-ROM drive directly to your EIDE (you'll recall from Chapter 7's discussion of hard drives that this is an enhanced IDE drive connection) or IDE controller. Also, as with SCSI, some newer sound cards provide a connection that specifically supports an ATAPI CD-ROM drive. Again, you'll have to check the documentation that comes with your sound card.

Keep in mind that once you purchase either a SCSI or ATAPI CD-ROM drive, it will work only with that standard.

Buying the CD-ROM

You can buy a CD-ROM drive by itself or as part of a *multimedia upgrade kit*. You'll find such kits available from a variety of hardware manufacturers, such as Creative Labs, Diamond Multimedia, and Turtle Beach.

> ### Definition, Please
> Multimedia upgrade kits are packages that contain everything you need to upgrade your computer to handle multimedia. In this regard, you'll find that these kits include a CD-ROM drive, sound board, all connections, and some applications.

Multimedia kits are usually decent deals, and since the sound card and CD-ROM come together, you can be fairly confident that they will work together.

Cost

It makes lots of sense to purchase a multimedia kit if you are planning to upgrade your computer to run the latest multimedia. However, if you aren't planning to add a sound board or if you already have a decent sound board, a multimedia upgrade kit may not be the best buy. If you already own a sound board, check out my suggestions in Chapter 10, "Sound Cards," to see if you might want to upgrade it.

Innie or Outey

CD-ROM drives come in both internal and external versions. It's usually more convenient to own an internal version, as shown in Figure 9-1, since it doesn't require extra desk space and costs less. On the other hand, if you're planning to use a CD-ROM drive with several computers, then the more expensive external version does make sense.

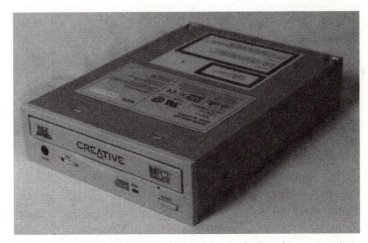

Figure 9-1: An internal CD-ROM drive is designed to mount into your PC, and is the most popular style.

Another variation in CD-ROM drives is that some require you to first load a CD disk into a holder, called a caddy, before inserting the disk into the drive. Most of the older drives require caddies. It's more convenient to have a CD-ROM drive that doesn't need a caddy. This way, you can load a CD disk the same way you load an audio disk into a stereo player. With caddies, you'll have to find one before you can use it, and if your computer desk looks anything like mine, this is a definite disadvantage.

For a summary of CD-ROM buying considerations, refer to Table 9-2.

Speed	4X	6X	8X
SCSI versus EIDE			
Access time	(200ms or lower)		
Internal versus external			
Buying a multimedia upgrade kit			

Table 9-2: CD-ROM drive buying considerations.

Moving On

In this chapter, we talked about CD-ROM drives: what you use them for, their available speeds and configurations, what to look for when you buy them, and how to purchase them. Now that you know how you can use a CD-ROM drive to play a multimedia program, it's time to learn how to listen to one. We'll talk about that in the next chapter, where I cover sound cards. Read on for the latest on sound boards, the various types and which will make your multimedia sound the best.

Sound Cards

I can vividly recall, from the early days of computing, the programs that were supposed to teach kids to read—except that the kids had to read onscreen instructions to figure out how to play the game. Of course, this was long before we had the convenience of sound on our PCs. In fact, that early computing period is almost akin to the era of silent movies, although I doubt any user looks back fondly on any silent computer game as a "classic."

These days, sound is an integral part of multimedia programs that provide voice narrations and instructions, music, and the magic of sound effects. With these capabilities, kids can learn about reading and math with whiz-bang music playing in the background, and their elders can play flight simulator games and hear the roar of a jet engine and a crash landing when their virtual plane buys the proverbial farm.

If you want to listen to sound on your PC, it has to be equipped with a *sound card*, such as the one shown in Figure 10-1. This is a special expansion card that takes data from the CPU and translates them into signals that can be played through speakers, a stereo, or headphones. These cards also connect to microphones so you can record your own sound effects, voice-over narrations, and music and even play audio CDs by working with your CD-ROM drive.

Figure 10-1: A sound card.

If you already own a sound board, it may do just fine with today's multimedia. However, older cards lack some of the latest features that will enhance your computing experience. In this chapter, I'll discuss what sound capabilities you will need and what's available.

Which One Sounds Best?

Sound cards come in a variety of configurations and types for different uses. There are also PC-based sound systems that connect to your parallel port—useful mostly for those who are performing multimedia presentations on portable notebooks. As you would expect, sound cards cover a wide range of capabilities and support different types of sound standards.

Games People Play

To provide sound effects in games and educational programs, you'll want a board that is both SoundBlaster and AdLib compatible (although many can use Wave and MIDI files as well; I'll explain these later). You don't have to actually understand exactly what these terms mean, but if you want to play games, these two are definitely the standard. If you buy a board that has these designations, you can listen to sound in a variety of programs and open up a whole new world. While there are lots of sound boards on the market today, by far, the SoundBlaster card, from Creative Labs, is the standard.

Keep in mind that you don't have to actually purchase a real SoundBlaster board (this is the brand name of a board that's manufactured by Creative Labs). Many boards on the market from companies other than Creative Labs are compatible and can be bought at a lower price. Some of the less-expensive boards, however, have compatibility problems with certain games. I recommend buying a Creative Labs board if you can afford it—this way, you should have no problems.

Cost

You'll definitely pay more for a name sound card from a company such as Creative Labs, but if you'll be playing a lot of games, the extra cost is well worth it. With a board from another manufacturer, you can have audio problems if the boards aren't 100 percent compatible—the sound just won't play and these problems can be difficult to correct. On the other hand, if you'll be using your sound card primarily with Windows multimedia, a lower-cost compatible board will probably work just fine.

Catch a Wave

The best-known sound file format is the .wav ("wave") file that Windows uses to play system alerts and special audio effects. If you're already using Windows with a PC sound system, you know the "ta-da" sound that plays every time you start a Windows session; Windows is just playing a .wav file. For our purposes, a .wav file is simply a recording—similar to an audio tape—that is stored in a digital format and can be played back at any time, using tools in Windows.

Definition, Please

A .wav, or "wave," file is a recording that may be played back through any program that supports the file format. Working with programs such as Windows' Multimedia Player, you can essentially record and playback sounds, and even perform some basic sound editing.

Any multimedia software—whether it's a presentation, a multimedia authoring tool, or even some creativity tools for children—will play wave files. Most of these programs include collections of wave files for sound effects and music, and Windows comes with some of its own. Another fun aspect of wave files is that you can mix or play with these files with audio-editing software, which lets you play sounds backward, add echoes, and apply other special effects. When you record a wave file, you can actually see how your computer represents sounds as a wave form, as shown in Figure 10-2.

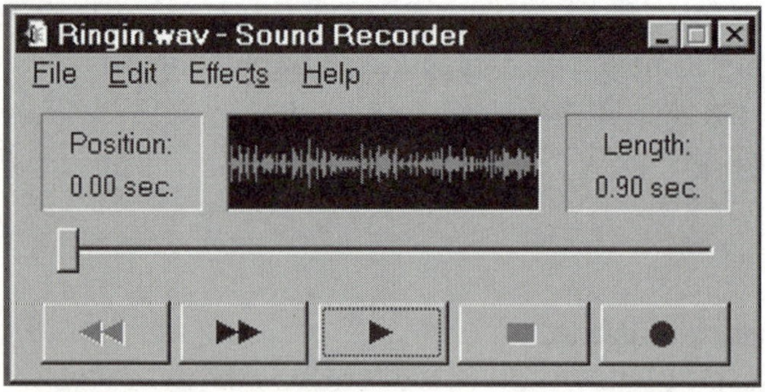

Figure 10-2: Viewing a wave sound file.

You can choose to save wave files in different ways. The better the quality, the more space the recording will take up. The two factors that affect the quality of the recording are the *sampling rate* and the *number of bits* used to store the data.

Definition, Please

Sampling rate refers to how often your sound card samples, or records, the sound, and is measured in hertz (Hz). The more times the sound card samples the sound, the higher the quality of the recording.

The second measurement that affects the quality of a recording is the number of bits that a PC uses to store a sound. The more bits used, the better the quality of the recording and the resulting playback. Most sound boards record in either 8 bits or 16 bits. This is why you'll see the term "16 bit" associated with many sound cards. Audio CDs, the type you buy in music stores, are recorded in 16 bits.

In general, sounds recorded with only 8 bits will play back like a tinny AM radio. But at 16 bits, you'll be working with the same level at which audio CDs are recorded. The only downside, of course, is the extra disk and storage space required for better recordings. By the way, an audio CD, like its computer counterpart, stores some 650 megabytes (MB) of data—approximately equivalent to one hour of sound recorded at 16 bits. So you can see where your audio CD gets its time limit.

Any Windows sound board and many older DOS boards that are SoundBlaster compatible will be able to play wave sound files. If you already own a sound card, it probably will play wave files.

MIDI (Musical Instrument Digital Interface)

MIDI sound files, unlike wave files, provide instructions to the computer so it can play musical and instrumental sounds. Think of a MIDI file as one that tells a computer how to re-create music—in a rough sense, like a roll on a player piano.

Definition, Please

Unlike a .wav file, a MIDI file contains instructions for playing music. Any program that supports this file format can read the file and re-create a song that's complete with instrumentation. Because MIDI files contain instructions and not actual recordings like a .wav, they make it easy to make immediate changes to a song, and take up far less space.

The MIDI standard, besides defining a file format, also provides a means to communicate with *MIDI instruments*.

Definition, Please

A MIDI instrument is any musical instrument—usually an electronic keyboard—that supports the MIDI standard.

If your sound card has a MIDI port, you can attach MIDI keyboards or other instruments to your PC and have the computer record songs as you play them on the instrument or even have it write out the score with musical notations. It also will play back the music on your system's speakers. What's really cool about working with MIDI is that you can use it to define and play instruments: It can, for example, re-create the sound of a trumpet or a xylophone.

If you want MIDI sound, you need a sound card that specifically supports it. There are two basic levels to look for. The less expensive, lower-end sound cards re-create instrument sounds through a process called *FM synthesis*. This kind of sound card tries to re-create or mimic the sound of an instrument, but the results are always less than satisfactory. If you've ever played with one of those cheap electronic keyboards that feature instrument sounds for flutes, saxophones, and violins but they all sounded the same (like a synthesizer), you already know the results.

The higher-end, more expensive sound cards use a process called a *wavetable*. Instead of trying to re-create the sound of an instrument by tweaking frequencies, the sound card actually holds samples or recordings of the real instrument and plays them, on command, at the correct pitch. The result is that a clarinet sounds like a clarinet, and a harpsichord sounds like a harpsichord. If you want to have wavetable capability, you must purchase a board that offers it, and you will pay extra for it.

Until now, MIDI capabilities were the domain of serious musicians and composers, both professionals and hobbyists. Sound cards with wavetable features were expensive—$500 plus—and weren't compatible with .wav files or with SoundBlaster for games. Today, some boards combine all three capabilities for less than $300, and some games take advantage of a wavetable to offer first-rate music that sounds like the London Symphony, not some kid on a toy piano.

Audio CD

A third type of sound is an audio CD (the kind you buy at the music store), played on a PC that's equipped with a CD-ROM drive. In fact, some entertainment programs actually play audio from a CD-ROM game just as if it were an audio CD. Most sound boards that support this capability come with software that lets your CD-ROM drive read and play tracks, just like any other CD player.

Hearing Voices

You've probably heard a lot recently about voice recognition on the PC. With voice-recognition capabilities, you can use a microphone to control a computer: For example, you could dictate a letter, tell your computer to search a database for all of your customers who live in Oregon, and then have the computer print out letters and envelopes. Or you could even conduct research by telling a computer to look for all occurrences of, say, "Eisenhower" and "World War II" in an electronic encyclopedia or online reference.

Ideally, a computer with voice recognition would allow hands-free operation; you wouldn't have to lift a finger or touch a keyboard or mouse. You would simply speak into a microphone, and the computer would understand what you are saying and carry out your orders. Another popular use for voice recognition is for dictation: You just talk into a microphone and the computer enters the corresponding text.

Many sound boards come with limited voice-recognition software. But for now, these capabilities are probably not a major factor in your sound card decision. If you're serious about voice recognition, you're better off, for now, purchasing a specific software solution that works with certain hardware (sometimes proprietary), such as those offered in products in Dragon System's DragonDictate for Windows and Kurzweil's Voice for Windows.

Sound Shopping Advice

You can buy a sound card by itself, and you'll find that a variety of stores, even the software stores, carry them. You'll usually find sound cards in their own section, where you can compare the features on the boxes. If you understand your sound needs and look for capabilities that support them, you can probably find a decent price.

Buying a sound card means weighing what you want to do with your system and what you can afford. For general use in games, educational programs, and Windows, you can get by with a board that is SoundBlaster and AdLib compatible. Most of these boards already have 16-bit capabilities (you probably can't find an 8-bit board these days). They'll play sounds and music in most games, wave sounds in Windows, and audio CDs when used with your CD-ROM drive. Also, most of these have basic MIDI capabilities built in.

By the way, most sound cards have connectors that let you attach powered speakers or headphones direct, or you can connect them to a stereo system with the right cables. As part of your sound card purchase, you might want to consider buying some speakers. But if you have headphones or a small stereo that already accepts external inputs, you probably can save the money.

As you shop, you'll find that many sound boards already come with MIDI and even some voice-recognition capabilities. While you might not have any plans to compose a musical score for your kid's elementary school play, basic MIDI capabilities do come in handy in supporting a lot of games. If you can find a board with this capability built in, at a competitive price, it's worth a little extra money.

On the other hand, wavetable capability is definitely nice to have, but it's not essential. You'll find this capability only in the high-end boards. If you need it, of course, you probably won't mind paying extra for it. But for many users, it's probably an expensive novelty. For a summary of sound card options, refer to Table 10-1.

Option	Description
SoundBlaster and AdLib compatibility	Games, entertainment, and "edutainment"
MIDI interface and support	Music—some games and serious music
FM synthesis	Music—some games and serious music
Wavetable	Higher-end music
Voice recognition	Can recognize your speech to command the computer or convert your speech into text.

Table 10-1: Sound card options.

Cost

For the most part, SoundBlaster, AdLib, and wave compatibility are a "must have" with sound boards. This is not necessarily a bare minimum—these capabilities are everything a lot of users will need. If you want MIDI and, particularly, wavetable capabilities, you will pay extra.

One other item worth considering in your purchase is the software that comes bundled with new sound boards. Most packages usually include programs for mixing audio files, playing audio CD-ROMs, basic musical notation and instrumentation software, and some simple voice-recognition features. Usually, the more expensive the board, the more of these features you can expect. If you're serious about music and sound on your computer, these may weigh into your decision.

Also, as I discussed in Chapter 9, "CD-ROMs," you might be better off buying a sound card as part of a multimedia upgrade kit. These kits come with a CD-ROM drive, a sound card, and lots of multimedia software. As a general rule, they can be a less-expensive way to purchase multimedia capabilities, but you have to watch out: Sometimes you'll pay more. One advantage, for certain, if you buy a CD-ROM with a sound card, you probably won't have compatibility problems. In many cases, the sound card comes with a port so you can connect your CD-ROM drive. For more on CD-ROMs, please check out Chapter 9. Also, be sure to shop around.

Moving On

I have been talking about sound cards—what they are, the different types, and how to purchase them. Using this information and the CD-ROM information in the previous chapter, you're armed and ready to go looking for your complete multimedia system with CD-ROM drive and sound card. Whether you purchase the components separately or in a kit, you'll be set for a new computer experience. In the next chapter, I'll talk about how to buy a modem so you can use your computer to accelerate onto the information highway.

Modems

If you want to surf the Net, send and receive faxes from your PC, communicate with other computers, obtain information through your telephone line, or even use your computer to answer the phone and record messages, you'll find that you can do all of these things by buying and connecting a *modem* to your computer.

Definition, Please

At its simplest, a modem is a device that lets your PC talk with another computer over a telephone line. A modem (short for **mo**dulator/**dem**odulator) converts signals from your PC into a form that can be sent across a telephone line. At the other end of the phone line, a modem converts the signal back to its original form so that a computer can read and use the information. As you can see in Figure 11-1, modems act as translators between two computers so they can connect over telephone lines.

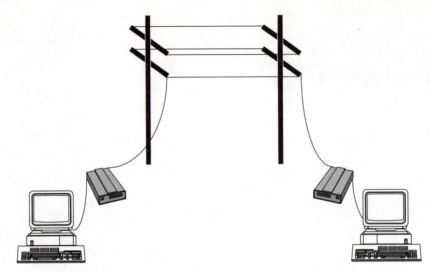

Figure 11-1: Modems let computers communicate with each other.

A World of Information

With a modem, your PC can work through telephone lines to connect with other computers to obtain information. When you go *online*, you can connect to other computers to get copies of (or *download*) program files, find information to help your kids with their homework, check stock prices and other current happenings, reserve airline tickets, investigate a company's site or join its *forum* (an online area set up by a company to distribute information about its products), and participate in groups that exist to explore a particular interest—pets, movies, computer games, or whatever.

> ### *Definition, Please*
> *Going online* is a generic computer term that refers to using your computer and a modem to connect with other computers across a telephone line, usually to obtain information or communicate with other computer users. You can go online and connect to the Internet or Web or any commercial service, such as America

Online, CompuServe, or Prodigy. These days, all of the commercial services have jumped onto the Internet bandwagon. You can access the Internet through America Online, CompuServe, and Prodigy as well, but it's usually more expensive. All of these are essentially computers that you connect with in order to obtain information. Figure 11-2 shows some of the online research tools available on America Online.

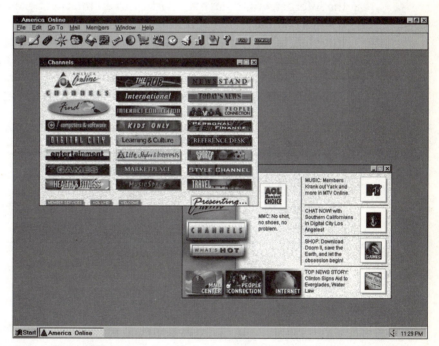

Figure 11-2: Online services such as America Online offer research tools and lots of information.

Today, the most popular online destination, and the one that has received the most attention, is the Internet, one particular portion of which is called the World Wide Web. The Internet is a world-wide network of computers that can readily communicate with one another. Most of what you hear about today when anyone talks about the Internet, or "information superhighway," is the World Wide Web. You also can obtain services through commercial online providers such as America Online, CompuServe, and Prodigy. These companies offer subscription services that allow you to connect to their computers to obtain and exchange information.

To connect with these services, you must have a modem and the right software. Companies such as Prodigy, CompuServe, and America Online have their own software, which you install on your PC and which works with your modem to get you connected. For the Internet, you'll have to work with an Internet Service Provider (ISP), a company that specializes in providing connections to the Internet. Table 11-1 lists some popular communications packages that let you connect with popular commercial services and the Internet. Also, keep in mind that both Windows 3.1 and Windows 95 come with their own basic communications packages.

Software	Publisher
ProComm Plus	DataStorm
Smartcom	Hayes
WinComm Pro	Delrina
FocalPoint	Global Village

Table 11-1: Popular communications packages.

Just the Fax

If you equip your PC with a special modem, called a fax/modem, you can send and receive faxes right from your computer, a capability that can replace your stand-alone fax machine.

The advantages of using your computer as a fax machine are that you can fax documents direct from your computer, where you're probably creating them, instead of printing pages out and then feeding them into a separate fax machine (you'll save paper as well).

The quality of your sent fax will be better, since the document doesn't have to be scanned and translated into computer code by the fax machine before it's sent. When a fax is sent direct from your PC, it's already in the computer code in which you created it, so it looks cleaner when read at the receiving end.

Fax software displays a list of all received faxes, as shown in Figure 11-3. When you receive faxes on your computer, you can choose the ones that you want to print out (again, saving on paper) and delete those that don't interest you, particularly junk faxes.

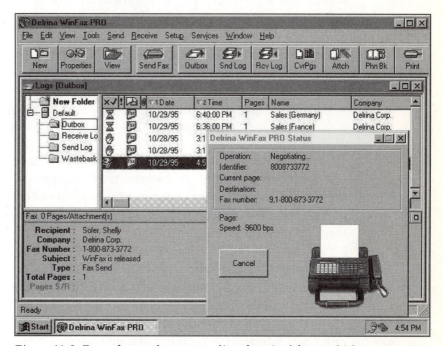

Figure 11-3: Fax software shows you a list of received faxes, which you can view, print, or delete at your leisure.

Finally, when you use your own printer, you can print to plain dry paper. You don't have to deal with expensive, greasy paper—the kind used in inexpensive fax machines—that curls and smudges in your hands.

All fax programs install a *driver* for your print application. With it, you can send a fax from any Windows application on your computer simply using the print menu. For example, if you're working in a word processor—let's say, Microsoft Word—you can just "print" the document to your fax/modem. The program asks you for the name and number of the person you want to send it to, and off it goes. With fax software, you also can send one fax to several locations or even schedule them to be sent at a later time (when phone rates are lower).

Definition, Please

A driver is a set of instructions that tells software how to work with an external device, such as a printer or a fax/modem.

On the downside, if you use your computer to receive faxes, you'll have to leave it on and connected to the phone. In fact, you might have to leave your computer on 24 hours a day, as it's not uncommon for businesses to send faxes late at night. If you don't leave your computer on, you can be jolted out of a restful slumber by a phone call that plays only that irritating high-pitched fax tone (believe me, I've been there). If you hand out a fax number, others will assume that your fax machine is on night and day and that you have a dedicated line.

When fax calls come in, they usually take control of your computer and interrupt what you are doing. So if you're working—in your word processor, for instance—you have to wait for the entire transmission to finish before you can continue. Some Windows 95 fax packages now promise something called *background processing,* which allows them to receive faxes without interrupting work you are doing in another application. From what I've seen, background processing isn't entirely invisible, but it is a big help.

Another issue, if you don't have a scanner attached to your computer, you'll have no way to fax a document that's already on paper. With a stand-alone fax machine, you can simply send the document.

Today, virtually all modems on the market are fax/modems, which means that you can use them to send and receive faxes, as well as connect to other computers to transfer data. Most of the modems come with fax software so you can immediately try out these capabilities. Table 11-2 lists popular fax programs to use with your fax/modem. Keep in mind that Windows 95 comes with its own faxing capability, called Microsoft Fax.

Product	Publisher
FaxTalk Plus	Thought Communications
HotFax	Smith-Micro
SmartCom	Hayes
WinFax Pro	Delrina

Table 11-2: Popular fax programs.

Hearing Voices

If you buy and install a special kind of modem, called a *voice modem*, you can use your computer as a sophisticated answering machine. When you're not at your desk, your computer can answer your phone, play your greeting ("I'm not here right now . . . "), and record the caller's message. When you get back to your desk, your computer will tell you that you have a message waiting and play it for you.

The voice modem's capabilities go well beyond those of a simple answering machine. Your PC can work much like the sophisticated (and aggravating) voice mail systems that you often encounter when you call a business. Your PC can answer your phone, route calls to individual mailboxes ("press '1' for sales, '2' for customer service," etc.), and record messages in these separate boxes. When you get back to your computer, you can open your mailbox, and the software lists all recorded voice messages so you can choose to play, save, or just delete them. As shown in Figure 11-4, you can see a voice modem effectively turns your PC into one powerful answering system.

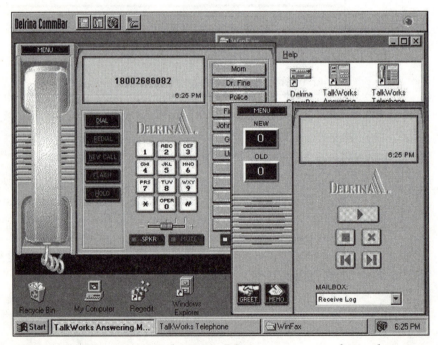

Figure 11-4: Using a voice modem, your PC can answer your phone, play your greeting, and record and organize your messages.

Voice systems are good if you're running a business, since you can create a system that sends callers to separate mailboxes to leave messages. The other advantage is that these systems make it sound as if you are a big company with an expensive phone system.

Any voice modem on the market today will have fax capabilities built right in and come with fax and voice message software. Theoretically, this means that your PC can answer the phone, determine if the call is a fax or voice call, and then either receive the fax or record the voice message. However, I've never gotten this to work perfectly. Software products with these capabilities are listed in Table 11-3. Normally, you'll get telephone support in all-purpose communications suites, along with faxing and communications.

Software	Publisher
Delrina CommSuite	Delrina
FocalPoint	Global Village

Table 11-3: Popular voice modem programs.

Remote Computing

Remote computing, or *remote access,* allows you to use your system and a modem to actually control a PC that is in another location, even thousands of miles away.

Using remote-computing software, you run other computers from your own, just as if you're sitting in front of them. You can use applications on the other computer's hard drive, type in commands from your keyboard, use your mouse, copy files back and forth, open and save data files within applications, and even print at both locations. The entire process is kind of eerie. When you look at the monitor in front of you, what you're seeing is the other computer, as shown in Figure 11-5.

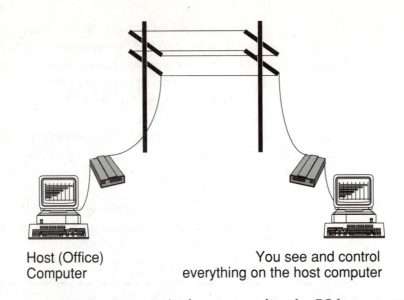

Host (Office)
Computer

You see and control
everything on the host computer

Figure 11-5: Remote computing lets you control another PC from your own computer. Everything you see on your monitor actually is being processed by the other computer.

Remote computing offers lots of possibilities. If you have office work to finish, you can go home and eat dinner with the family, then use your computer to connect to the office system and complete the unfinished business. You can even print documents so they're waiting when you arrive the next morning.

Executives on the road can log on to office computers to catch up on e-mail or use applications that can't be loaded conveniently onto notebook computers. Remote-computing programs also are great for demonstrating software over the phone and for trouble-shooting software problems in the field.

Any two computers with modems can connect with each other. The key is the software: The same package must be running on both systems. Popular remote-computing software includes such programs as Norton pcANYWHERE, Avalan's Remotely Possible, and Microcom's Carbon Copy. For remote computing, you'll want a fast modem, because the faster the modem, the more responsive the other computer that you're controlling will be. In any event, remote computing is the next best thing to being there.

Modem Considerations

When you buy a new modem, your first consideration, besides the type (fax or fax/voice), is the modem's speed. The fastest modems you can buy today are rated at a speed of 33,600 *bits per second* (*bps*). If you look around, you can probably find lower-cost modems at 14,400 bps. Modem speeds usually are referred to in kilobits per second (Kps), as in 33.6 Kps.

Definition, Please
Bits per second (bps) is a measurement of the number of information bits that a modem can send and receive in a second. The more bits it can send, the faster you can exchange information.

As you might expect, the faster the modem, the better the performance and the higher the price. And while you can save some money by purchasing a slower modem (for example, 14.4) and live with slower performance, you probably won't come out ahead (see "Cost"). For the most part, you'll want to buy a faster modem just so your computer's performance is zippy. It doesn't take too long to become frustrated with slow performance, and because the price difference isn't that great, it's worth buying at least a 28.8 Kps modem.

Cost

You might feel that you can live with a slower modem, but you have to consider your time online. As the adage goes, time is money.

Commercial online services charge you by the hour. If much of your activity will involve obtaining or downloading files, a faster, more expensive modem will pay for itself in a short time. When downloading huge files, such as program files, you can easily spend an hour or more just waiting for them to be transmitted to your PC. At $2.95 an hour, the going rate for time on CompuServe and America Online, you can make up the cost difference between the modems in a relatively short time, depending on the number and types of downloads that you perform.

If you're going to use the Web, a 28.8 Kps modem will give you far better performance and reduce your frustration level. I know several people who have tried to use a 14.4 Kps modem on the Web and have been completely frustrated with waiting. For online purposes, I highly recommend that you buy at least a 28.8 Kps modem.

Playing the Numbers

When you go shopping, you'll also find other numbers and gobbledygook associated with modems. Without going into minute detail, here's what they indicate: You may see designations such as V.22, V.32, and V.32 bis on the package. Like most designations of this kind, the "V" indicates that a modem meets a standard so it can perform at a certain level. Each designation is a standard that refers to the speed at which a modem will operate, as summarized in Table 11-4.

Standard	Modem Speed
V.22	2.4 Kps
V.29	9.6 Kps
V.32	9.6 Kps
V.32 bis	14.4 Kps

Table 11-4: V standards.

Another standard that's often displayed on modem packaging is that of the Consultative Committee of International Telephone and Telegraph (CCITT), an international organization that develops standards and protocols. In the past, some manufacturers could play games with these designations and try to make a modem appear to be faster than it is. Today, if you purchase a 28.8 Kps modem—particularly a major brand—it will perform as indicated.

Fax Considerations

When you buy fax capabilities with your modem, check that it is compatible with Group II, the current standard. This way, you should have no problem using this modem to connect with any fax machine.

Another issue, which relates solely to software, includes designations such as Class 1, Class 2, and Communications Application Specification (CAS) support. These standards define how your fax software communicates with the modem itself. Most of the major fax software packages support all three. If your modem comes with fax software, you can be reasonably assured that the software will work with it.

Voice Considerations

Unfortunately, there aren't clear standards for voice modems. Until the industry establishes standards, the only thing you can do is to make sure that the software you want to use works with the voice modem you wish to buy. If you have no software in mind, you probably can use the software that comes with the modem.

Internal vs. External

Modems come in two major types—external and internal. An external modem, as shown in Figure 11-6, is a housing that holds the modem's electronics outside of your computer and attaches to your PC's serial port.

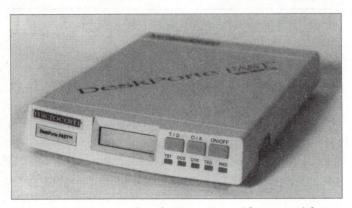

Figure 11-6: An external modem connects with your serial port.

The advantage of an external modem is that you can move it from place to place and easily attach it to other types of computers, such as Macintoshes. External modems also feature a front panel of LED indicators that show you the status of your connection. Without a doubt, external modems are easier to install because they connect with an existing serial port. Internal modems sometimes cause system conflicts that make them harder to get up and running.

Internal modems don't require a serial port or any desk space and install into a slot inside your computer. You'll find that internal and external modems by the same manufacturer are basically identical, except for their physical appearance. An external modem has a housing and power supply and uses a cable (usually included). Internal modems, like that shown in Figure 11-7, are expansion cards.

Internal modems are more difficult to install than external ones because you're installing a modem as well as a new port, and it's not unusual to run into configuration problems. In fact, in the old days, computer users had to learn a whole new language of terms when installing a modem for the first time. These days, Windows Plug N Play (an approach that automates the setup) makes the installation a lot easier.

Figure 11-7: An internal modem is an expansion card that installs inside your computer.

If you have to go on the road with a notebook computer, you may want to buy a small portable modem instead of one designed for your desk.

As with most components, compatibility is an issue when you select a modem. Here it makes sense to purchase a name-brand modem, because all software publishers make sure that their modem software works with the most popular modems on the market.

If you buy an unknown brand, it will be compatible with most software, but it may have slight inconsistencies that tie up some software programs. For this reason, even though it will cost a bit more, I recommend that you purchase a name-brand modem from a manufacturer such as Cardinal, U.S. Robotics, or Zoom. The following is a list of popular modem brands that are compatible with most commercial software.

- ○ Cardinal
- ○ Creative Labs
- ○ Hayes
- ○ Practical Peripherals
- ○ U.S. Robotics

Sometimes, at higher speeds, you have to consider your computer's universal asynchronous receiver/transmitter (UART), particularly when you're upgrading an older PC. Check to see if your computer's UART is a 16550A. If not, you probably will have to replace the UART so that your system can handle higher modem speeds. If you are upgrading an older computer, such as a 286 or 386, you should count on having to replace the UART. To check to see what type of UART your PC has, you can check your system's documentation, use a system diagnostic software utility, or, on some machines, you can check your system's CMOS configuration screen (the menu that you can access at boot-up that shows information about your PC).

In all, there are many factors in your modem-buying decision, as well as the potential for gaining lots of capability. Review the following list of buying issues before you go shopping.

- ○ Speed; as fast as you can afford
- ○ Group II fax compatibility; definitely look for this
- ○ Voice capabilities; optional, and there are few standards
- ○ Name brand; less chance for incompatibilities

Moving On

I have talked about some of the things you can do with a modem and what to consider when purchasing one. Using this information, you will be well on your way to cruising the Web and the information superhighway. In Chapter 12, "Bargain Basement," I'll talk about general considerations and strategies to consider when purchasing computer components for your upgrades and ways to get the most for your money.

Bargain Basement

The key to upgrading and repairing your PC on a shoestring is to buy inexpensive parts and perform the upgrades yourself. Most of this book talks about the components that you can buy and how to install them. In this chapter, I'll discuss where to buy parts and provide guidelines on getting the best deals, plus some warnings about potential pitfalls.

Despite their popularity, PCs—and particularly their components—are still specialty items. Although you can buy computers in department stores, you'll have to turn to a specialized source to get the parts you need for a repair or upgrade. These sources include dedicated computer stores, general warehouse stores such as Price Club/Costco, computer superstores, computer swap meets, and mail-order firms.

Generally, the warehouses and superstores have fairly competitive prices, while the small computer stores vary in the deals they offer. Some are quite a bit more expensive but provide excellent service. However, there are times when such stores advertise great prices, especially if they tend to carry a specialty item.

Mail order often offers great prices as well, but you have to wait to receive your parts (although many companies will ship them to you by overnight express if you pay for it). If something doesn't work, it takes more effort to return it for an exchange or refund.

Without a doubt, swap meets offer the best deals. However, you have to be very careful when you buy computer equipment at such an event.

As when purchasing anything, shop around and compare prices to get the best value for your hard-earned dollars, and make sure that you thoroughly understand each vendor's return policy.

Let's look at each of these sources, what you can generally find at each type, and at which you're likely to find the best deals. These are general guidelines, and there are always exceptions.

Specialty Computer Stores

These stores are classic mom and pop outfits, specializing in computers, that spring up in local shopping centers and along Main Street in your hometown. Most of the time they offer repair services along with new computer systems, parts, and software.

Generally, these small stores have the highest prices, mainly because they can't (and don't) buy parts in enough quantity to get their stock at a lower cost. They often won't have the part you need in stock and will have to order it, which can take a day or two.

The best time to opt for a small computer store is when you need expert advice or one-on-one attention, and you're willing to pay for the service. Watch out though—some smaller computer stores don't want you to install your own components and will only test them for you before you buy. Then you're on your own. If something goes wrong with the part, they won't want to accept returns or exchanges. For this reason, be sure you understand the return policy, and get it in writing. When I've shopped at small stores, I've generally paid top dollar; however, they do sometimes offer special deals that can match the mail-order houses.

In all, a small specialty store will not be your first choice for getting the best deal, but they surely are convenient and helpful. For a summary of advantages and disadvantages, refer to Table 12-1.

Advantages	Disadvantages
Good service	High prices (usually)
Convenient location	Don't stock most items
Expert advice	Have to order parts

Table 12-1: Pros and cons of specialty computer stores.

Warehouse Stores

Warehouse stores have changed how we buy products (and store them). Most of these stores sell food and other goods in bulk quantities (such as 3-gallon jugs of maple syrup or 3-pound blocks of cheddar cheese). You'll also find computers and a limited selection of accessories. Stores of this kind include Price Club/Costco, Sam's Club, and Pace.

Although these stores often carry a decent supply of printers, scanners, floppy disks, modems, and software, the only type of upgrade components you'll probably find are hard drives, RAM chips, and the occasional CPU upgrade chips. Their prices usually are competitive, but you have to know exactly what you want to buy.

If you have any questions, you'll have a hard time finding anyone who knows anything about computers, let alone the components. The person selling car wax or serving frozen pizza in the next aisle probably is not a reliable source for computer information. And the warehouse store's return policy often requires you to go back to the manufacturer if you want to return the item after you open the package. For this reason, you want to be very sure of your purchase.

You won't find rock-bottom prices at a warehouse store, but they're competitive. These stores are also good sources for hard drives and RAM chips, as long as you know what you need to buy. If you go to one of these places, just try to walk out without extra books and CDs that you never intended to buy (they are just such great deals). For a summary of advantages and disadvantages, please refer to Table 12-2.

Advantages	Disadvantages
Competitive prices	Little selection and few parts
	No expert advice
	Limited return policies

Table 12-2: Pros and cons of warehouse stores.

Computer Superstores

For any computer enthusiast, a computer superstore is a high-tech candy shop, stuffed with the latest and greatest cutting-edge PCs, hardware, and software. It's easy to lose yourself in dreams as you admire the output on a new printer and browse through endless aisles of books and software. In these stores, you'll also find a good selection of computer components at decent prices. Well-known computer superstores include CompUSA and Computer City.

The best thing about a computer superstore is that it offers a great combination of knowledgeable salespeople and selection from an established dealer. Since most of these stores have repair departments, their people have a lot of technical expertise, and you'll find that most of the sales staff know what they're talking about. I've had good experience buying components from these stores, although they don't have the absolute lowest prices.

A subset of the computer superstores are office superstores, such as Staples and Office Depot. In these establishments, you'll find everything you need for an office, including furniture, pens, and copy machines, along with computers and software. You can find some components at these stores, but the selection isn't as great as at a dedicated computer superstore. I also would classify in this subset the electronics superstores, such as Circuit City and Silo, which also dabble in computers. These stores are more like the warehouse stores (particularly the consumer electronics shops), but the office clubs have more knowledgeable sales staffs.

For a summary of advantages and disadvantages concerning computer superstores, please refer to Table 12-3.

Advantages	Disadvantages
Great selection	Not available in some areas
Decent prices	
Expert advice	
Established store	
Lots of stock	

Table 12-3: Pros and cons of computer superstores.

Mail Order

Like clothing, food, and just about anything else you can name, computer parts are available by mail order. All you have to do is peruse the ads in any computer magazine, and you'll find lots of mail-order companies that will sell you components or entire systems. Often you can find companies that specialize in a single item—RAM, for example—at excellent prices. I've done my share of buying by mail order and have never had a problem. In fact, they have been downright pleasant experiences.

While all computer magazines have mail-order ads, the king is *Computer Shopper* magazine. This weighty tome is easy to find at any newsstand—it's twice as large and twice as thick as the others. Open an issue, and you'll find evaluations, articles with a mail order/direct purchase slant, and lots of ads. In fact, if you can't find it in *Computer Shopper,* it probably doesn't exist. If you want to make life hard for your mail carrier, you can order a subscription to this behemoth (it dominates my mailbox the same way that it dominates the newsstand).

Buying anything by mail order has pluses and minuses. Prices vary, but you usually can find great deals. It's a definite advantage that you don't have to pay sales tax on your purchase, unless the mail-order firm has a retail outlet in your state. This can mean significant savings, even if the local computer store can match the price. On the other hand, you do have to pay shipping charges, which vary according to the size of the package and how fast you want the product in your hands. If you don't have your purchase sent by overnight mail, it may be a week or more before you get it.

While shopping by mail may seem to be a stretch for many of you, most vendors who advertise in the major publications are reputable. You can't tell just by reading an ad which firm is reputable and which is not, but there are ways to find out. You can go back a few issues to see that the firm is placing ads consistently, and check out the addresses. You can call the firm's home city government to ask about it and contact the local Better Business Bureau. It's also wise to avoid companies with only a post office box address. As long as you use a credit card, which is the preferred form of payment, you'll probably do just fine. (I'll talk about credit card issues later in this chapter.)

Most firms have set return policies, and some offer technical advice hotlines. If the installation isn't going exactly the way you want it to, expert advice is a phone call away—a plus. Many mail-order houses have Web sites, where you can get up-to-date prices for quick comparison shopping. Most companies have 800 numbers, so calling and comparing prices won't cost you a dime.

For a summary of advantages and disadvantages of mail order, please refer to Table 12-4.

Advantages	Disadvantages
Competitive prices	Have to wait for product delivery
Expert advice	Have to pay for shipping and handling
Save on sales tax	Can't see the product ahead of time
Huge selection	
Easy to comparison shop	

Table 12-4: Pros and cons of mail order.

Computer Swap Meets

While computer swap meets aren't available in every part of the country, their popularity is spreading. They're like the swap meets held in parking lots and at drive-in theaters but offer only computers and computer software, accessories, and parts for sale. You'll find tables set up by vendors who will sell you anything related to a computer at prices that can't be beat by any of the other sources I've discussed previously. You might even be able to wheel and deal to get a vendor to cut a price in order to match or beat swap meet competitors. Sometimes a dealer will pay the sales tax for you.

On the other hand, while you'll find the best prices at swap meets, you really have to know what you're buying, and it's hard to pick out the reputable dealers. When shopping this way, more than any other, the rule is *caveat emptor*—"let the buyer beware." At the largest swap meets, you may be charged for parking and admission and could be out $10 before you walk in the door.

Most of the booths are staffed by dealers and vendors who also sell from storefront or factory locations. I've had success with attending a swap meet and first picking up the fliers for deals that interested me. Between swap meets, I check out the store or factory to make sure that it is a legitimate business (although this isn't always practical, as some sellers come from a long distance), then make my purchase at the next swap meet so I can get the special show price. Many of the sellers offer their best prices as swap meet specials. Occasionally, I've found a vendor who will give me the swap meet price at the store.

Another thing you'll find is that the vendors at swap meets want to deal in either cash or checks—very few will accept credit cards. This makes it extra important to know whether you're dealing with a reputable business.

When buying at a swap meet, be sure that you understand the seller's return policy, and get it in writing if possible. Unfortunately, you'll find that some sellers hand-write their invoices, and dealings at swap meets generally are not very formal or businesslike. You also want to make sure that you actually see the component before it goes into the bag, to ensure that you are getting the right part (sellers can make mistakes). For a summary of swap meet advantages and disadvantages, please refer to Table 12-5.

Advantages	Disadvantages
Lowest prices anywhere	Hard to determine firm's reputability
Expert advice	Returns might be difficult
Ready stock	Few accept credit cards

Table 12-5: Pros and cons of computer swap meets.

Where to Buy

Where you buy your components is up to you. If you don't feel too confident about wheeling and dealing and making spot decisions, computer superstores and mail order probably are the best options. You'll save money over other sources and shop in a comfortable place with information available from knowledgeable salespersons or written copy.

On the other hand, if you're looking for the absolute lowest prices, you're not going to beat the swap meet. However, you have to know exactly what you're buying and dig a little to make sure that you understand return policies. Swap meets involve more legwork, but the savings are worth it. If you're one of those people who thrive in a wheeling-dealing environment, head for the swap meet and enjoy.

General Buying Tips

When buying computer components, be sure that you clearly understand the seller's policies and get them in writing whenever possible, whether you're dealing with a store, a mail-order firm, or a vendor at a swap meet. If you're purchasing by mail order, you'll usually find the seller's policies clearly stated in the ad.

First, check and understand the return policy. Can you return the part in its original condition and get your money back? Is there a restocking fee? In that case, the firm will give your money back but deduct a percentage, sometimes as high as 15 percent. Some firms will accept only a defective product for a cash refund. Because you usually can't bring your computer to the store to see if a part will fit and work, you need to have a clear understanding of this policy, just in case the installation doesn't go smoothly.

Most vendors should give you 30 days to return parts, and give you your money back whether you have problems or just decide that you don't want the part, as long as you return it in salable condition. Make sure that the vendor provides tech support should you encounter any problems.

Be sure that you understand whether you are buying just a part or an installation kit. This is particularly important when you're purchasing a hard drive. Unless you have lots of spare parts lying around plus experience installing a particular part, you'll want to buy the kit so everything you need—rails, adapters, cables, and connectors—is included.

When you are purchasing by mail order, the vendor shouldn't bill you until the product is shipped. You can call your credit card company to see if you've been charged. If it sounds as if you've been charged but no product has been shipped, you can call the vendor and ask for a shipping bill number. If the vendor can't come up with one, call your credit card company and ask for a charge-back (that is, to have the charge removed from your bill).

Be sure to double-check the manufacturer, model, and part number to make sure you're getting the correct part. If you can, get these facts in writing by fax or mail. Sometimes unscrupulous vendors will sell reconditioned parts as new, so beware. If a price sounds too good to be true, it probably is.

When purchasing, it's best to use your credit card so that you have a way to stop payment should a seller refuse to accept a return or exchange for a defective product. Problems aren't too common but do happen. A firm might charge your credit card but go out of business before delivering the product to you. Or more likely, you may not receive what you thought you ordered. Because a credit card gives you an easy way to stop payment, you should never pay by check or money order.

If you're not sure of a company's reputation or stability, check with the Better Business Bureau in the company's area to see if there have been any complaints lodged against the firm. It's probably a long shot, but it is one more thing you can do to protect your interests.

If you have a disagreement with a company, you can contact your credit card company for a charge-back. To do this, report your grievance to your credit card company within 60 days of the billing statement. While it investigates the problem, the credit company holds the payment at no interest. If the vendor is at fault, you won't be charged. Be sure to always keep good records— dated notes of any related phone calls and every scrap of correspondence. You might want to check with your credit card company to double-check its policies, your options, and what proof you would need, before you make a major purchase.

Consider and compare warranties. You can rely on extended coverage if you have the right kind of credit card. This extra coverage usually is automatic when you use your card, but there are always exclusions and exceptions. Again, you need to keep detailed records including the shipping bill, credit card receipt, and written warranty. If your warranty terminates and you run into problems, inform your credit card company within 45 days of the malfunction. They'll send you a form to fill out and probably direct you to a service provider. Again, double-check with your credit card company.

Finally, there's nothing like a recommendation from a satisfied customer to help you find a good dealer. Check with your friends, relatives, and acquaintances who might recommend an excellent source for parts. If you work in an office with a network, you might talk with the network administrator, who has a lot of experience buying and putting parts together.

Most of the time you should have decent luck with shopping for parts. In this chapter, I've tried to give you a good idea of what you should be looking for; if you keep my comments in mind, you should do quite well. Price isn't everything, but with some investigation and comparisons, you can save some serious money. For a summary of your purchasing options, please refer to Table 12-6, and look to Table 12-7 for a summary of buying considerations.

	Selection	Service	Price	Notes
Local computer store	Good	Excellent	High	Usually emphasizes service
General ware-house store	Fair	Poor	Fair	No expertise
Computer superstore	Excellent	Excellent	Low	Knowledgeable staff
Office superstore	Good	Excellent	Low	
Mail order	Excellent	Excellent	Low	Have to wait for deliveries; no sales tax on out-of-state purchases
Swap meet	Excellent	Fair	Lowest	Need to know what you are buying

Table 12-6: Purchasing summary chart.

Fair price
Quality and value
Return policy (try to get it in writing)
Warranty
Available tech support
Installation kits
Reputable company

Table 12-7: Buying considerations.

Moving On

In this chapter, we looked at sources for components for your upgrades—including various kinds of stores, mail order, and swap meets—and considered where you can find the lowest prices. I've also offered suggestions on ways to protect yourself as you make the deal. Now, with upgrade components in hand, you're ready to proceed to the next chapter, in which I'll discuss how to set up your work area to actually perform the upgrades.

The Tools & Work Area

There's nothing like having the right tool when you have a job to do. You wouldn't use a mixer to squeeze oranges or a sledgehammer to dig a hole in the ground. In the same sense, the correct computer tools will help you perform your upgrades more efficiently. In this chapter, I'll talk about the most essential tools plus a few extras.

When I worked on cars as a teenager, I often struggled with my tool set, which was limited to a pair of pliers, three screwdrivers, and a crescent wrench. Unfortunately, my lack of both tools and mechanical prowess were reflected in the way my car ran. I recall being especially stymied once by a nut that I just couldn't reach to turn. When my car and I broke down (literally) and I took the car to the shop, I watched in amazement as the mechanic used a special wrench with all the right curves and lengths to turn that nut easily. He had the right tool, while I was trying to get by with whatever I could find in the trunk of my mother's car. Fortunately, computers aren't as complicated as cars. (*Upgrading & Repairing Your Automobile on a Shoestring* is a book I won't try to write!)

You probably can get every tool you need for making computer upgrades for less than $30. And like Dorothy in the land of Oz, you may have some of them already in your own backyard or at least in your garage.

If you do need to buy a tool set, it'll come in handy whenever you need to work on your computer and be well worth the investment. I've used the same tools (a small $30 set that I bought more than six years ago) for almost everything that I've done, and I've never been without the right tool (if anything's missing, it's always a connector or cable). My kit includes some tools that I've never even used.

Having the right tools reduces the frustration of working on your computer and makes it safer for both you and your machine. For example, you could use a knife to turn a screw, but the knife could slip and injure you or damage the screw or nearby components. I can't emphasize enough the need for the right tools.

Tools for All Your Needs

I'm going to discuss the basic, minimum tool set and then talk about the ones that are nice to have.

As a minimum, you'll want to have at least the tools described in the following sections.

A Basic Set of Screwdrivers

You'll need both Phillips and standard screwdrivers in a variety of sizes, as shown in Figure 13-1, all of which you can find at any hardware store. The tip of the standard screwdriver has a flat edge; the tip of the Phillips forms an **X**. You probably have some in your toolbox already. I've also had good luck with a switching screwdriver, which has several interchangeable tips that fit on a single handle. Just avoid any cheap tool that costs $2.99 at the grocery market. It will be worthless in the long run.

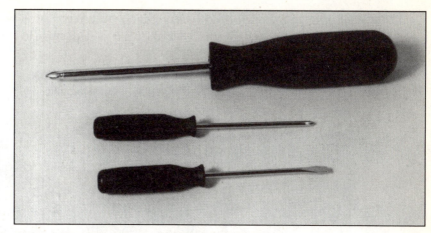

Figure 13-1: Standard and Phillips screwdrivers.

Caution

Although a magnetized screwdriver may be convenient for picking up small screws that you drop, you don't want to use magnetic devices around your computer equipment. Because computers store data magnetically, any magnetized tool or magnet that's brought near the internal components of a PC, or the diskettes, might erase information.

Needle-nose Pliers

You probably have one of these if you have a home toolbox. In fact, I use the same needle-nose pliers on my computer that I use to remove hooks from fish when I go fishing. This may sound crazy, but I use my pliers for two things that I like to do and save money. No, my computer doesn't smell fishy, either.

You'll find that needle-nose pliers are handy when you need to pinch and remove standoffs (more about standoffs in Chapter 16,

"Replacing the Motherboard"), and you never know when else you'll need them. Figure 13-2 shows a pair of needle-nosed pliers.

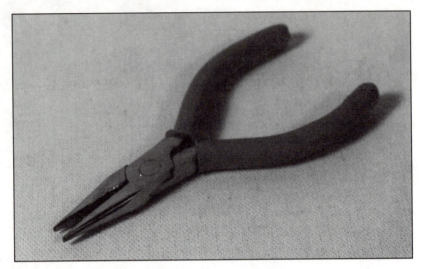

Figure 13-2: Needle-nosed pliers.

Tweezers

Yes, this is the very same tool that you use to remove splinters from the soles of your feet. Tweezers are invaluable for picking up small objects and are particularly good for setting jumpers on a board. You can buy plastic versions for use on computers, to minimize the possibility of shorting a circuit as you use them.

Keep in mind that tweezers come in all shapes and sizes to suit different purposes (dentists, gemologists, etc.). While I've only used general purpose tweezers to help me with my upgrades, you may find that there are some specialized types that work well for you.

Three-prong Extractor

This tool may not be familiar to you. It looks something like the claw in those machines you see at the local arcade or pizza parlor: you know, that glass box of enticing stuffed animals. You put in a quarter and manipulate the claw to see if you can pluck a prize. The difference is that a true three-prong extractor has real gripping power—unlike the one at the pizza parlor—and is invaluable for picking up screws and small items that fall into your computer case. When I didn't have an extractor, I had to lift my entire computer and turn it upside down to retrieve a tiny object that I lost in the case. Figure 13-3 shows a three-prong extractor.

Figure 13-3: A three-prong extractor used for picking up tiny objects.

Caution
Do not use a magnetized device in place of the extractor as this may cause you to lose data.

Flashlight

Another tool that comes in handy is a flashlight. At times, you may have trouble seeing the bottom depths of your case, or your head may cast a shadow that obscures what you're looking at.

Of course, flashlights come in different types and styles. Some people like to use those flashlights that mount on your head so you can easily direct the light where you need it and keep your hands free. I've had good luck with one of those snake-style flash-lights that you can bend in different ways. The kind of flashlight you need will depend on your work area and available lighting. A flashlight can definitely shed a little light on the subject.

Fine-point Permanent Marker

This comes in handy when you want to label something in your computer. No one else will be looking inside your case, so a little graffiti there is no problem and can save you hours when you're trying to put things back together.

DOS Boot Disk

While a DOS boot disk isn't a piece of hardware, it's a primary tool in any computer worker's troubleshooting arsenal.

Definition, Please

A *DOS boot disk* is a floppy disk that contains the necessary information to boot, or start, a computer. You can create one of these disks by formatting a floppy and telling the computer to add system files.

If you're using Windows 3.1, it doesn't hurt to have key files, such as Fdisk.exe and Format.exe, on this boot floppy, for use as diagnostic tools. You can find these files in your DOS direc-tory and copy them to your floppy. Of course, if you own Norton Utilities or a similar program that helps make your system run at its peak and comes with tools to "rescue" your data in a catas-trophe, by all means use it.

Foam Padding

Nonconducting foam padding is a good surface to use as a resting place for expansion boards while you are working on your com-puter. A foam surface also can help prevent damage to a board or other internal component should it fall or get dropped.

Small Adhesive Labels

Labels are good for marking cables so that you can find what you need when it's time to put everything back together. Also, it doesn't hurt to label your internal components with info such as the date you purchased or replaced them and other information.

Antistatic Wrist Strap

An antistatic wrist strap will ground you so you won't build up static electricity. It consists of a strap that goes around your wrist and is connected to a cable. At the other end of the cable is a clamp that attaches to a ground, usually your computer's case. All right, I don't know anybody who uses one of these all the time, and, the repairmen in the shops I've been in never seem to use them at all. But you should consider using one to minimize your chances of frying your boards with static electricity, although it will literally tie you down (a great excuse not to answer the doorbell).

Work Space

Finally, you'll need a good work area. Obviously you need to be close to electrical power so that after you make an installation you immediately can plug in and power up to see the results. You'll want a large surface on which to spread out your tools and components. I've worked on kitchen tables and coffee tables. I don't recommend the coffee table (too low), but the kitchen table works just fine, at least until dinnertime.

The best setup is a big workbench, the kind that some lucky people have in their garages. Make sure you have adequate lighting—it's easy to lose small parts, and you might have to refer to those poorly written instructions that come with components.

If you run a multiple-outlet power strip from the nearest outlet, it'll minimize the number of electrical cords dangling from your work area, so you won't trip over them or get them tangled up.

You want to be sure that your workspace has good lighting. There's nothing like squinting at tiny parts and trying to read little numbers when a little more light easily solves the problem. Also, you do want an area that is free from things that can fall onto and into your open system, and it doesn't hurt to clean the area so it's free from dust that can more easily collect in your system as you're working on it.

Additional Tools You Might Need

A few other tools might come in handy. Of course, because I say they're optional, chances are good that you'll absolutely have to have one of them on Sunday night when all the stores are closed and you need to be back up and running on Monday morning at eight for your most important client (computer users are especially subject to Murphy's law). With that caveat in mind, these are tools that you might need, depending on your system. Sometimes they're included in the aforementioned inexpensive tool kits.

Nut or Hex Drivers

These tools look much like screwdrivers but are designed to turn nuts, as shown in Figure 13-4. You can get away with using a Phillips screwdriver to turn most hex nuts (the hex nut has a slot that accepts a Phillips screwdriver), so while the nut driver is nice to have, it's probably not absolutely necessary.

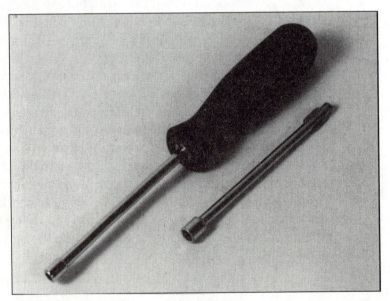

Figure 13-4: Nut drivers.

Torx Screwdriver

Another type of screwdriver is called a Torx screwdriver, as shown in Figure 13-5. Only a handful of manufacturers—one of them Compaq—use these oddball screws, so your need for the screwdriver depends on your system.

Figure 13-5: Torx screwdriver.

Chip Puller

These are special tools that are designed to grip a chip, especially a CPU, and pull it up with an even amount of pressure. Chips have tiny metal legs or pins that plug into a socket, and it's quite easy to bend them out of shape—or, even worse, to break them off. A chip puller, as shown in Figure 13-6, can help minimize the chances of such damage.

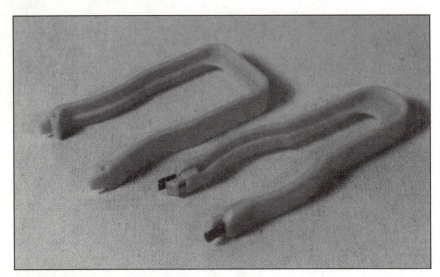

Figure 13-6: A chip puller.

When I didn't have a chip puller handy, I had good luck using a screwdriver to gently pry under each end of the chip. Note the word *gently*. I also found that many chips, particularly some of Intel's OverDrive chips, come with pullers of their own (prying devices that look like forks). I haven't used a chip puller very often, but when you have to remove a chip, it's the safest way to go.

Containers

Whether you use paper cups, Tupperware, or those little plastic boxes that hold lures when you go fishing, you will want to have a few containers around to store small parts. In particular, containers come in quite handy when you're removing screws from your computer. And instead of simply setting them down where they can fall off the workbench, roll around, or get lost, you can keep them organized in compartments or containers so you don't lose them and can easily find them when you need to.

You may even want containers with lids so items don't fall out should you knock them over. A quick trip through the kitchen should yield all the containers that you could ever need. This could also be an excellent time to finish up that half-eaten yogurt so you gain an excellent upgrade tool.

Moving On

In this chapter, I've talked about the basic and optional tools you need to perform your own upgrades. Once you have these tools, you're ready to learn how to open up your computer and swap expansion cards, as I'll explain in Chapter 14 "Opening Up Your Computer & adding Expansion Cards." The basic skills that you learn in the next chapter will carry you through the upgrades in the rest of this book.

SECTION III

Nuts & Bolts

Opening Up Your PC & Adding Expansion Cards

Just as you can't work on your car with the hood closed, to work on your computer, you have to open your case so you can get at the components inside. And before we go about swapping CPUs or motherboards, you can get your feet wet by adding an expansion card, which I will explain later in this chapter.

You'll find that while these tasks initially sound daunting, they're actually quite easy to perform. Also, they're the very first step you'll make before performing upgrades on your own.

Opening Up Your Computer

You'll find that most cases are designed so you can remove some screws and slide the top cover off, but other covers fit in different ways.

Caution–Data

Back up all of the important data on your computer before you begin any kind of work on its innards. I can't overemphasize how important this is. Although you probably won't lose data when you make an upgrade, it isn't impossible, and it's only sensible to back up data and have it in a safe place in case something goes awry.

Also, before you open your PC and begin any installation, take a minute to record the information on your hard drive—the type, cylinders, etc. You'll find this information in your computer's setup, which you usually can see by booting up your PC and then holding down a key to view a menu screen (computers vary; check your manual). Write this information down and keep it somewhere. If you have the hard drive documentation, it will include this information. For more on this, please refer to Chapter 20, "Installing an IDE Hard Drive & Floppy."

Caution–Safety

Before you open your PC, turn it off. I always unplug my PC, too, although some experts will tell you to leave it plugged in (just as long as it's turned off). When working on your system, don't probe screwdrivers in areas that you're not working on, particularly the power supply.

To Open Your Case

1. First disconnect all of the cables and connectors attached to your computer—power, printer cables, keyboard, mouse, video connections, and so on. Then you're ready to remove the screws, which you'll usually find along the back side of the computer case, as shown in Figure 14-1.

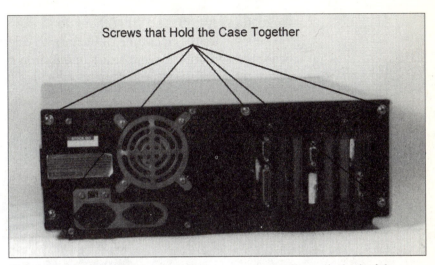

Figure 14-1: The screws that hold the case on are usually on the back of the computer.

Caution
When removing screws from the back of the case, be sure to remove only those that appear to hold the case. If you go over-board and remove all the screws, you may hear internal compo-nents—the power supply, for example—drop loose and fall down inside your computer. Be conservative. Remove the obvious screws first and then see if the case cover budges.

2. When you have removed the screws, gently push the cover to see if it moves. If it does, slide the cover off the case. If it doesn't, you probably missed a screw. Check for any errant screws and then try to budge the cover again. On a desk-top machine, as shown in Figure 14-2, the cover usually slides backward, away from the front of the computer. On a tower case, the cover can slide either forward or back-ward, as shown in Figure 14-3. Of course, your case may not fall into any of these categories. Some cases swivel,

while others lift off, and still others don't even use screws, you simply depress a couple of buttons to open the case. Please refer to your system's documentation for more on how to open the case.

Figure 14-2: A typical desktop case cover opens by sliding back from the front of the computer.

Figure 14-3: A typical tower case cover opens by sliding either forward or backward off the case.

3. With your PC's cover off, you're ready to begin working. Go to the appropriate chapter of this book to read about whatever you want to install.

Installing Expansion Boards

When you install a new video card, sound board, serial port, or anything other than a motherboard, you'll be working with expansion cards. In this section, I'll talk about how to install these cards. The techniques that you learn here apply any time you install a card or board.

A good precaution before removing any expansion board is to carefully label any connectors or cables attached to the board. This way, you can make sure that they go to the right connectors on the new board. If you can, identify the function that each cable connects to and in what direction it attaches. This way, you can be sure that you will reconnect components correctly when you add new boards. If applicable, you also might record such items as *dip switch* and *jumper* settings.

Definition, Please

Some boards have switches, called *dip switches* and *jumpers*, that let you apply settings and configure the boards. For example, in the old days, you would set switches on a video board to get different video modes. If a board has jumpers, refer to that board's documentation for information on correct settings.

Assuming that you are replacing a card already in your system, you'll have to remove the existing card. Here's how you do so:

1. Remove the retaining screw that attaches the expansion card to the case, as in Figure 14-4.

Figure 14-4: Removing the retaining screw.

2. Remove any system connectors and cables attached to your expansion boards. I highly recommend that you label any connectors before removing them and, if possible, write down to what the connectors are attached. Different boards perform much the same functions, but often look radically different. You will often find that connectors and various dip switches and jumpers will be in different places, and the boards can be different sizes.

3. After removing the retaining screws and any connectors and cables, hold the expansion card by its edges, as shown in Figure 14-5, and rock the board a little as you gently pull it out of its slot.

Figure 14-5: Hold the expansion card by its edges and gently rock it, parallel with the slot, as you pull to remove it.

Caution
Always hold a board by its edges. The static electricity in your body can fry a component on the board. Also, never touch the connectors on the bottom of the board. It is essential that they make good contact in the future.

If there is no existing board, just remove the retaining screw and cover as shown in Figure 14-6.

Figure 14-6: If you don't already have a board in place, prepare a slot by removing its retaining screw and the cover.

You're ready to install your new board.

Installing a New Expansion Board

1. Make sure that there are no connectors or cables in the way of the slot. Also, measure any cables that will have to connect to your new board and verify that they will reach easily. If the cables don't reach, you should rearrange the boards so they will.

2. Hold the expansion board by its edges and gently push it into its slot. You may have to rock the board a bit to make it connect properly, as in Figure 14-7.

Figure 14-7: Gently rock the board in place to gradually seat it in its slot.

3. After the board is firmly seated, replace the retaining screws.

Just a Few More Tips Before You Begin Working

1. Don't rush. When you're working on your computer, allow enough time and don't work under any pressing deadlines. When you're under pressure, you're more likely to make mistakes.

2. Keep all documentation. Be sure to keep every shred of documentation that comes with any new component. It will come in handy later, when you need it most.

3. Take careful notes and draw diagrams. Note the way things come apart and where and in which direction connectors go, so you can put everything back together again.

4. Be gentle. Computer parts should go together without being forced. You don't need to be an Arnold Schwarzenegger to work on a computer.

Moving On

I've talked about how you open your computer and install expansion cards. Once you have mastered these techniques, you can go to the next chapters, where I will show you how to perform the actual upgrades. You now have the knowledge, the tools, and the basic skills, and you should be pumped up. Take a deep breath and turn the page. The moment of truth is about to arrive.

Upgrading Your CPU

If there's any task that resembles computer brain surgery, this is it. But that resemblance has to do with the part being operated on, not the operation itself. As I mentioned in Chapter 4, "The CPU & the Mother of all Boards," you can upgrade some motherboards for 486SX and 486DX chips by adding an Intel overdrive chip. If after reading Chapter 4 and examining your system you've decided to upgrade your processor this way, you'll find everything you need to know about the process in this chapter.

If you're not sure whether this is the correct upgrade path for you, read Chapter 2, "What Do You Want to Do With Your System?" That will help you decide whether a CPU upgrade will meet your computing needs. In any event, it's a fast and simple upgrade that can boost your computer's horsepower significantly.

As mentioned in Chapter 4, you need to check with your dealer or manufacturer to be sure your motherboard can accept an overdrive chip. I can't emphasize the importance of this enough. You might, for instance, see something on your motherboard that looks like an upgrade socket, which is really for a math coprocessor. I've also seen boards that have a socket that looks as if it should accept the overdrive—in fact, the overdrive chip does physically fit in it—but it doesn't work. Finally, you need to check for the type of overdrive chip that your motherboard can accept, as there are several different kinds. After you have verified which chip your motherboard can accept and have bought it, the upgrade should be downhill (in the positive sense) from there.

This chapter covers replacing the CPU on your motherboard; Chapter 16 explains replacing the motherboard itself. Upgrading the CPU usually means simply substituting one chip for another (an overdrive chip replaces the current CPU chip). Or, depending on your motherboard, you may be adding a new chip in a spare socket and keeping your current CPU.

As just mentioned, some motherboards, like the one shown in Figure 15-1, come with only one socket. In this case, you will have to remove the current CPU and replace it with the overdrive CPU.

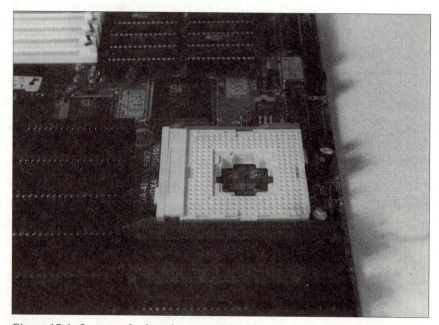

Figure 15-1: Some motherboards come with only a single socket for the CPU or overdrive chip.

Fortunately, many motherboards that will accept an overdrive chip come with a Zero Insertion Force (ZIF) socket. This type of socket has a mechanism that actually clamps down on the pins of the chip to hold it and releases to let it go. This makes it easy to remove one chip and install another. You can recognize a ZIF socket by the lever that's attached to it. On the other hand, some motherboards don't offer a ZIF socket. For these you'll have to use a chip puller (one usually comes with the overdrive chip) and install the replacement chip by gently pushing it in.

The other type of motherboard features an additional socket that holds the overdrive chip in addition to the CPU already on the board. In this case, you'll simply add a chip to the board, and the chip takes over the CPU's function.

Tip

The Intel OverDrive technology makes for a fast and easy upgrade. If you don't run into any snags along the way, this very straightforward upgrade should take less than 30 minutes. From a time-and-cost perspective, it's a winner. Most of your work lies in verifying that your motherboard will accept this upgrade and in buying the right part.

Caution-Data

Back up all of the important data on your computer before beginning any upgrade or repair and take a minute to record information about your hard drive and other system information listed in your BIOS, as outlined in the last chapter.

Overdrive Chip Installation

First shut off your PC and unplug it. Following the directions and cautionary notes in Chapter 13, "The Tools & Work Area," and Chapter 14, "Opening Up Your Computer & Adding Expansion Cards," open your PC's case. With the cover off and the motherboard located, you're ready to begin.

Replacing Your ZIF-Socketed CPU

1. Lift the lever on the ZIF socket to release the CPU chip, as shown in Figure 15-2. Gently remove the chip.

Figure 15-2: Lift the lever on the ZIF socket to release the CPU.

2. Insert the overdrive chip into the socket. You may need to move it around a bit, but the chip should fall into place the instant the legs are completely aligned. Once the chip drops down into the socket, it's correctly placed. Take a quick look to make sure that all pins are in contact.

3. With the chip in place, close down the handle of the ZIF socket.

Replacing Your Non-ZIF-Socketed CPU

1. Intel should provide you a specialized tool—it looks like a small fork—that helps you remove your current CPU. Use it to pry up the chip carefully, one side at a time, until it releases.

2. With the socket free, you now can install the overdrive chip. Carefully align it with the socket and gently push it in.

Installing the Chip in a Socket Near Your CPU

1. Place the overdrive chip on the open socket and line up its pins.

2. Carefully push the chip down into the socket. It helps to apply pressure evenly across the chip.

Now, Test the System

Before you close up your computer, it's a good idea to test your system. Double-check your chip installation, plug your computer in, and see if it boots up normally.

> ### Caution–Safety
> *Don't forget that when you test your computer with the cover off, you have a live machine.* Under no circumstance should you probe your PC or touch any internal component when your system is running. *Always* shut off power and unplug your computer before doing any work on your PC or before removing or adjusting any component. Not only can you get a dangerous shock, but you also can fry your components.

If everything looks normal but the machine is running faster, you have successfully replaced the chip. Congratulations! At this point, you can replace the cover on your machine and reconnect the cables, and you're done. On the other hand, if your computer isn't booting correctly, read the next section.

Troubleshooting

If your computer doesn't work correctly after you replace your CPU with an overdrive chip, something in the installation has caused a problem. After all, the computer worked fine before you made the upgrade.

Double-check the chip installation. Make sure the chip is installed properly and seated securely in its socket. Also verify that you didn't disconnect any other cables or components while replacing the chip. After inspecting the connections, expansion boards, and chip, try booting again.

Sometimes when working on your PC, your BIOS can become erased. To check for this, reboot your computer and bring up the system configuration screen (the way you bring this up varies from system to system—check your PC's documentation). In this case, you'll need to re-enter the BIOS information that you wrote down before you began the upgrade.

If you're absolutely sure that your connections look right and the computer still won't boot, see if the chip's manual has any other suggestions. As a last resort, you can reinstall your old CPU chip and see if the computer runs. If it does, there's probably something wrong with the new chip. However, if your old chip doesn't run anything, you've inadvertently changed something in your system. Check those connections again, then try booting again. If it still doesn't work, please refer to the troubleshooting instructions in Chapter 22, "You've Got Trouble, My Friend."

Moving On

In this chapter I've gone over the steps necessary to replace the CPU on a motherboard. If this is not an option for you or if this is not the CPU upgrade path that you want to take, I'll show you how to replace a system's motherboard in Chapter 16.

Replacing the Motherboard

Now we're talking major surgery. This chapter on replacing your motherboard comes rather early in this hands-on, how-to section, but this is, quite frankly, the most involved task covered in this book. Performing the upgrade itself is fairly straightforward, but it takes time and careful, steady work. If things go perfectly, you should be able to complete it in less than three hours. However, things don't always go as they should, and you can get stuck trying to reinstall the cables. I'll do my best to help you avoid problems.

At this point, you're probably sitting there with your new motherboard in hand, ready to put it in. I hope that Chapter 4, "The Central Processing Unit & the Mother of All Boards," helped you decide what type of motherboard you need and that you're now excited about the new possibilities of your upgraded machine. If you're still wondering what type of motherboard upgrade you want to make, take a look at Chapter 2, "What Do You Want to Do With Your System?," which discusses your options.

RAM for Your Motherboard

If you have random access memory (RAM) to install on your motherboard, it's best to do this before you actually install the board in the computer, as you'll have a much easier time getting at the sockets. For more on installing RAM, please refer to Chapter 17, "Replacing or Adding RAM."

Opening Your PC

> ### Tip
> Before you open your computer's case and begin, please take the time to read this entire chapter for an idea of all the tasks involved and the overall scope of this project. Just in case, allocate a lot of time. Don't try to squeeze this upgrade in between appointments, or you'll inevitably find yourself with your system completely dismantled and your biggest client breathing down your neck.

> ### Caution-Data
> Back up all of the important data on your computer before beginning any upgrade or repair, and take a minute to record information about your hard drive and system settings in your PC's BIOS. To access the BIOS, please check your system's documentation.

Shut off your PC and unplug it. Following the directions and cautionary notes in Chapter 13, "The Tools & Work Area," open your PC's case. With the cover off, you're ready to begin.

Removing the Motherboard (Bye, Mom!)

At this point you'll need to remove components so you can get at the motherboard. Before you begin removing expansion cards, be sure to disconnect all cables that connect to the power supply, the expansion cards, and the motherboard. Here, it's a good idea to write down exactly where each connector goes and preferably label each.

You're now ready to remove each expansion card. To do this, unscrew and remove the screw that secures the board to the case's slot, as shown in Figure 16-1 and as explained in Chapter 14, and gently lift the board out, using a rocking motion if necessary as shown in Figure 16-2.

Caution–Removing Expansion Cards

Always hold expansion cards by their edges and try not to touch the metal connectors that fit into the PC's slots. Your body can build up enough static electricity to fry an entire card or one of its components, rendering it useless.

Tip

Some internal connectors and cables may be stretched to their maximum lengths in order to reach their boards. After you install your new motherboard, you'll probably have more success getting the cables to reach their boards if you replace each board in its original place first. On the other hand, you might need to switch the order of some boards to make it easier to route the cables. If you need to, do so. If you label your boards and slots (on the case) as you install them, it will be easier to reinstall them next time.

After pulling out the expansion cards, disconnect all cables and connectors, including the power cables, between the motherboard and other components. As with the expansion cards, it helps to label the cable connectors so it's easy to figure out where they go when you reassemble your system. With a new motherboard installed, things can look different, although most components will go back in their original place in the case.

> ## Tip
> When removing connectors that have flat ribbon cables (these look like a bunch of wires taped together in a flexible flat cable a couple of inches wide), look for the stripe on one side of the cable and note how it connects with the motherboard. You can use this as a reference when you connect it to a new motherboard. The stripe, as shown on the ribbon cables in Figure 16-1, represents the wire that connects to a connector's first pin.

Figure 16-1: The stripe on one side of the ribbon cable is a distinguishable mark that you can use as a reference.

You'll find that most power connectors are of the Molex variety, as shown in Figure 16-2. While these can be stiff, you can work them off by carefully rocking the connector back and forth and pulling gently to get them apart. However, you probably won't have to remove your power supply to take out the motherboard—at least, I've never had to do so.

Figure 16-2: A Molex power connector.

Caution

When removing cables, pay particular attention to how the power cables—the ones that come from the power supply—are connected. You need to check their orientation as well as placement. If you reconnect these incorrectly, you can fry your new motherboard. Take notes or make a sketch.

The hard drives and floppy drives usually are mounted with screws in a metal cradle or cage, as shown in Figure 16-3.

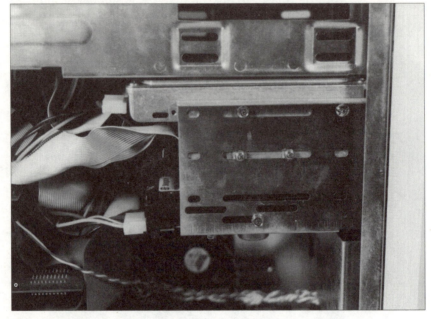

Figure 16-3: The drives are mounted in a metal cage.

To remove the drives, carefully loosen the screws that hold them to the cage. Most systems use four screws. Once you loosen these, you'll find that the drives can move a little. At this point, if you can, remove the connectors and cables, noting where and to which drive they attach. Then remove the screws and pull the drive out of the front of the cage. Be gentle with drives, particularly the hard disk one.

Please refer to Chapter 20, "Installing an IDE Hard Drive & Floppy," for more information.

Tip–Removing Components & Fasteners
An old auto repair trick that works for me is to place components in a circle as you pull them out. Then, when you put them back in, you reverse their order. If you also label each component, this approach is virtually foolproof.

After removing the cables and components, you should be at the motherboard itself, as shown in Figure 16-4.

Figure 16-4: After removing expansion boards, connectors, and system components, you should be right over the motherboard.

Most motherboards are attached to the case with screws and little plastic fasteners called *standoffs*. You can identify standoffs by their plastic heads, as shown in Figure 16-5.

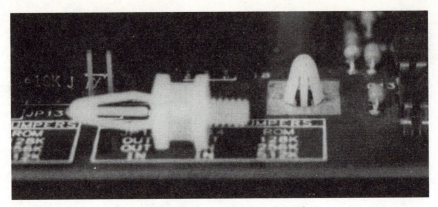

Figure 16-5: Plastic standoffs hold the motherboard in place.

To remove your motherboard, simply remove the screws one by one. After that, you should be able to slide the motherboard away from the power supply to free the board. If the board doesn't move, check to see if you missed any screws.

Once you remove the motherboard, you'll want to remove the standoffs and use them to hold your new motherboard. Use your needle-nosed pliers to gently pinch and remove the standoffs.

Stay with me—we're halfway there.

Putting It All Back Together (Hi, Mom!)

To put all the components that are now sitting on your workbench back together in your case (in the right place), begin by lining up your new motherboard at the bottom of the PC case.

As you look through the holes in your motherboard, you should see corresponding holes underneath in the PC case. Don't worry if you can't match all of the holes. It's not unusual to have to skip some holes; boards don't always line up 100 percent. You'll have to make a decision as to whether there are matchups for enough screws to adequately hold the board in the case or if you'll have to return the motherboard to the store and find another that will fit. While I can't provide any firm guidelines here, in general, count the holes you can use and see if you think there are enough to safely and securely hold the board in the case.

There is one other option, but it is not for the fainthearted. You can drill your own holes in the board. Of course, you also could ruin the board, void the warranty, and have no way to exchange the board for another one, even it proved to be defective. I haven't and probably never will do this and recommend you pass on this option.

After verifying that the holes line up, hold the board in place and make sure that the slots on the motherboard also line up with those of the case. Again, there's not much you can do if they don't, and you'll have to make a judgment call as to whether this motherboard is worth keeping or should be exchanged.

When the holes and slots line up reasonably well, you're in business. If you haven't added your new RAM chips, do it now before you place the motherboard into the case. (Installing RAM is covered in Chapter 17.)

Now, hook the standoffs in their respective slots and slide your motherboard toward the power supply, reversing the process that you used to remove the old one. Standoffs sometimes get caught, so you have to persevere until they fall into place. With the board seated, replace the screws.

After the motherboard is in place and before putting back the rest of the components and the expansion boards, it's a good idea to test the motherboard to make sure it works. Discovering a problem motherboard at this point will save you a lot of trouble-shooting later.

Caution–Safety

Before turning your computer on to test the new motherboard, be sure to recheck the power connection to the motherboard. It could be dangerous to turn the power on if the motherboard is not connected.

Caution–Safety

Don't forget that you have a live machine. Under no circumstance should you probe your PC or touch any components while your system is running. *Always* shut off power and unplug your computer before doing any work on your PC or before removing or adjusting any component. Not only can you get a dangerous shock, but you also can fry your components.

To test the motherboard, reconnect power to the board (refer to your diagrams), install the graphics card, and connect the keyboard and monitor. When you turn on the power, the computer should display a picture and text that shows the amount of memory in your system and other configurations. (By the way, it's okay at this point if your computer gives you error messages; that's natural, since you haven't configured the system yet.) If you get the picture and text, you can assume that everything thus far is fine. Switch off and disconnect power and continue reassembling your computer.

The next step is to reinstall the components and their connectors. Here's where the notes and labels that you wrote during disassembly will come in handy. (You did write them, didn't you?) Now you just reverse the process. Don't forget to reconnect those wires that drive such things as the lights on the front of the case. With components and most connectors in place, you now can reinstall the expansion boards.

At the end, be sure to check to see if you have any extra parts left over—not usually a good sign, depending on what the parts are. Double-check your installations and cabling, and make sure everything looks secure and connected.

Now, before you slide the cover back on, you'll want to see once again if the PC is working. Reconnect the video monitor, mouse, and keyboard and fire up your machine.

> ## Caution–Safety
> Recheck the power connection to the motherboard. It could be dangerous to turn the power on if the motherboard is not connected properly.

> ## Caution–Safety
> *Don't forget that once again you have a live machine.*

If you get a picture again, so far, so good. Now, to make everything run, you'll have to configure the system via your PC's setup or configuration screen—the BIOS, also known as the *complementary metal-oxide semiconductor* (CMOS). (The name comes from the semiconductor technology used in microcomputers.) Once you enter the parameters for your hard drives and other information, you'll be ready to roll. For more on system configurations, please refer to Chapter 20.

As you boot up your computer, listen and look for the usual order of sounds and events (your computer will sound slightly different with the cover off). If nothing happens or the system hangs up, shut everything off and try again. If it continues to hang up, unplug the system and recheck all of your installations and cable connections. If things still are not working, please refer to the following troubleshooting guide.

Troubleshooting

If your system doesn't power up: You may have forgotten to reattach the power cable to your system.

If your system stops during boot-up: Examine the messages displayed as the computer boots to see if the system identifies any problems. Try booting with your floppy boot disk and then getting into your system to examine it for problems. If you can't access the hard drive, the culprit may be your setup, which you'll probably have to reset. In this case, reconfigure your PC settings and double-check the connections to your hard drive.

If this doesn't work, another strategy is to remove all of the expansion boards and then reinstall them one by one, testing the system at each stage. If a board is the problem, you'll be able to identify it.

If none of these options works, use the diagnostic instructions described in Chapter 22, "You've Got Trouble, My Friend," to see if the problem is with your motherboard.

This Is It

If your system seems to be running normally—except presumably a lot faster because of your new upgrade—you're set. You can turn off your machine, pull out all of the power cables and peripheral connectors, reinstall the cover, reconnect everything, and you're ready to roll. Congratulations on a job well done.

Moving On

Following the instructions in this chapter, you've actually installed a new motherboard. (Please pause to pat yourself on the back and brag to everyone within earshot.) Now that the motherboard is in place, I'll discuss in the next chapter how to install RAM. For a memory-jarring experience, please turn the page.

Replacing or Adding RAM

It would be great if I could improve my own memory capacity as easily as I can improve that of my computer. Medical science is a long way from letting us simply add new brain cells, but adding memory to a PC is not a difficult process. In fact, most of the work involves deciding how your system's memory is configured currently, then determining what type of RAM you can add.

In this chapter, I'll show you how to add *SIMM (single inline memory modules)* memory to your PC. If you've just upgraded your motherboard or you have a newer motherboard—a 486 or a Pentium—your motherboard will no doubt accept SIMM-type memory.

Definition, Please

SIMM stands for single inline memory modules. This is simply a standard configuration for memory that you can buy and install in your motherboard.

SIMMs come in both 30-pin and 72-pin configurations, and today's most popular style by far is the 72-pin. For more background on memory, please refer to Chapter 5, "Thanks for the Memory."

Tip

As mentioned previously in the book, when you add memory, it's important that you match the memory that's already on your motherboard. (For more on this, please refer to Chapter 5.) Matching memory, in most cases, involves maintaining memory of the same speed and type. There are times, however, when you might encounter a system that only accepts memory from a single manufacturer. Fortunately, these are usually the exception rather than the rule. When you're unsure, it's always best to contact the manufacturer of your motherboard.

In some cases, when the existing memory configuration limits how you can effectively add memory, it makes sense to simply sell your existing memory to a vendor and start over. Many memory vendors will buy old chips, but don't expect to get a lot of money for them.

How much RAM you want to add will depend on what you want to do with your PC. In Chapter 5. I discussed how adding memory can help your PC run larger, more memory-intensive applications and keep your system from spilling overflow onto your hard drive, since that slows your computing to a crawl. One thing's for certain—you can be confident that you are making one of the best upgrades possible to improve the performance of your system. For an outline of memory requirements versus particular uses for your system, you can refer back to Chapter 3, "What Upgrades Will You Need?"

Adding a SIMM to Your Motherboard

Adding a SIMM is actually a fairly straightforward process. Some motherboards hold memory modules at an angle, while others hold them straight up. Regardless of the orientation of the socket, you install the SIMM in the same manner.

> ### Tip/Caution
> Always store the SIMM in an antistatic bag until you're ready to use it. Memory is one of the components most easily damaged with static electricity. Also, always try to hold the SIMM by the edges and not touch the connectors. If you aren't using a wrist strap, be sure to ground yourself before handling any SIMMs. To do this, simply touch the metal case of your PC before picking up the SIMM.

> ### Tip/Caution
> Back up all of the important data on your computer before installing new memory and take a minute to record information about your hard drive and system settings. Keep this information in a place where you can always refer to it later, if needed.

Shut off your PC and unplug it. Following the directions and cautionary notes in Chapter 14, "Opening Up Your PC & Adding Expansion Cards," open your PC's case. With the cover off, you're ready to begin.

Caution

Be sure to shut off your PC and unplug it.

Take a look at the motherboard in Figure 17-1 and the location of your memory sockets. Although the placement of these sockets varies from board to board, you'll be looking for the same type of sockets. For a close-up view of the memory sockets, refer to Figure 17-2.

Figure 17-1: Memory sockets on the motherboard.

Figure 17-2: A closer view of the memory sockets.

To Remove Existing SIMMs

1. First, you must release the latches that hold the SIMMs in their sockets. You'll find latches at the sides of the memory sockets, as shown in Figure 17-3. Gently press them toward the side to release a SIMM.

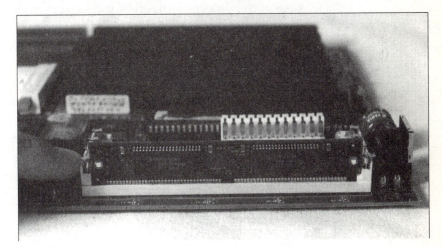

Figure 17-3: Latches hold SIMMs in their sockets.

2. After unlatching the sockets while holding the SIMM, pull the SIMM forward to disengage it from the socket, as shown in Figure 17-4.

Figure 17-4: After releasing the latches, gently pull the SIMM forward to disengage it from its socket.

3. Repeat the process with all of the sockets from which you want to remove old SIMMs.

Inserting New SIMMs

1. Gently position the SIMM so the contacts rest in the socket.

> **Tip**
> If your board already has memory chips installed, notice how they are set in. This will help you correctly orient your new SIMMs.

You should hold the SIMM at a slight angle. Look for a notch on the SIMM that will help you align it correctly with the socket. This notch, shown in Figure 17-5, prevents you from installing the SIMM in the wrong direction.

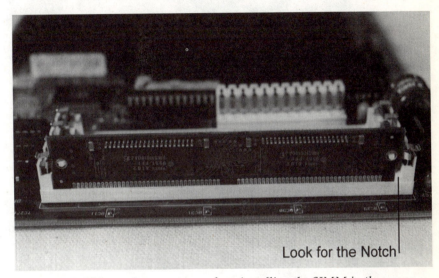

Look for the Notch

Figure 17-5: This notch prevents you from installing the SIMM in the wrong direction.

2. Gently push the SIMM into the socket until it engages with the latches. You won't have to force it—the chip should engage easily, as shown in Figure 17-6.

Figure 17-6: Gently push the memory module into the socket until it engages with the latches.

3. Before you replace the case cover, connect the monitor to your PC, connect your keyboard and mouse, and reconnect power to the system. You'll want to perform a quick test to ensure that everything is okay and that your system accepted the new memory.

> **Caution**
> *Don't forget that you have a live machine.* Under no circumstance should you probe your PC or touch any components while your system is running. *Always* shut off power before doing any work on your PC or removing or adjusting any component. Not only can you get a dangerous shock, you also can damage or ruin system components.

4. Turn on your PC. You should see the usual initial screen that tells you that your computer is starting up and testing its memory. If this screen shows that there's more random access memory (RAM) in your system, so far, so good. This number won't necessarily reflect the exact amount of RAM in your system, but if the number is within 384 kilobytes (K) of the RAM that you have installed, it's okay.

   At this point, the computer may kick you out into the complementary metal-oxide semiconductor (CMOS) setup screen, because it has realized that it has more RAM than it was configured to have. At this point, the CMOS should list the correct amount of RAM. All you have to do is save the CMOS to configure your system properly.

5. If everything appears to be normal, you can shut off your system, disconnect the power, reconnect all of the cables and connectors, and reinstall the case cover. After that, you're ready to go.

SIMM Troubleshooting

If your system doesn't boot properly, shut off your PC and unplug the power. Recheck your RAM installation. The SIMMs should be well seated in their sockets. Also, make sure that while you were working in your computer, you didn't inadvertently loosen other connectors or cables. For this, check around for dangling or loose connectors and verify that all are seated properly.

If you have a problem, to check whether your new RAM is the cause, you can remove your new RAM and reinstall the old RAM (if you completely replaced your existing RAM). If you installed additional RAM, you can check to see if the old RAM works without the new RAM.

If your old RAM works correctly, the problem is likely to be your new RAM installation. The RAM chips may not be the proper ones for your system, your system may not be configured correctly to recognize them, or the RAM chips may be faulty. Try reinstalling the new RAM chips. If they don't work, review your system's documentation to check what type of RAM you can add. Also, you can contact your motherboard's manufacturer to double-check.

Don't forget, if you're installing additional RAM, you must account for the existing RAM that you already have. Sometimes, if you're mixing SIMMs of different speeds, they will not configure correctly unless you go into your system's CMOS setup to change something called *wait states*. For this change, you'll have to check with the manufacturer's instructions. Also, double-check how you can add new RAM. In many cases, motherboards require that you install in pairs.

If you check all of these things and still have a problem, you may have a bad SIMM. In this case, you'll want to return the SIMM to the manufacturer and exchange it for another set.

Moving On

In this chapter, we've discussed how you easily can add RAM to greatly enhance your system. You should see the difference it makes in your system's performance immediately. In the next chapter, I'll talk about how to add a new video card to your system to speed up your PC's ability to display images.

Replacing the Video Card

What you see is what you get, and with a new video card, what you get will be more speed when your system displays graphics. In this chapter, I'll explain how you can replace and upgrade your video card—then in Chapter 19 we'll also learn how to install and configure a modem, so you can get up and running on the information superhighway.

Upgrading to a new video card simply means removing the existing video card, installing a new one, and setting it up. The most time-consuming work is deciding what you want to do with your computer and ensuring that you buy the right video card to get there. I hope that Chapter 6, "Video Cards," gave you a feel for what type of video card you need. If you're still wondering what type of upgrade you might want to make, take a look at Chapter 2, "What Do You Want to Do With Your System?" and Chapter 3, "What Upgrades Will You Need?" Those chapters discuss your options.

Replacing a Video Card

As mentioned earlier, your video card is usually an expansion board that you can replace in your system.

Before installing a video card, check to see if your motherboard has built-in VGA (video graphics array) video, which it usually doesn't. If yours does, you may have to check your documentation or call the motherboard's manufacturer to learn how to disable the VGA before installing your new video board. Some boards disable their VGA capabilities automatically when they sense another video board, while others have to be changed manually.

Caution

Back up all of the important data on your computer before beginning and take a minute to record information about your hard drive and system settings.

Also, before you install your new video card, be sure to remove your old one, using the following instructions.

If You Have to Remove an Existing Video Board

1. Before you do anything, turn on your computer, go into Windows and change the resolution and setting to 640x480 standard VGA. This way, when you install your new board, you can bring up a basic Windows screen that's supported by all video cards to change the resolution and setting:

In Windows 3.1

Locate your video card's utility that changes the resolution and video. You may find this under the control panel in the Main group, or there may be a group that holds software tools for your video card.

In Windows 95

Click on Start Settings | Control Panel | Display and then click the Settings tab. Use this, as shown in Figure 18-1, to change the video mode to 640x480, 16-color VGA.

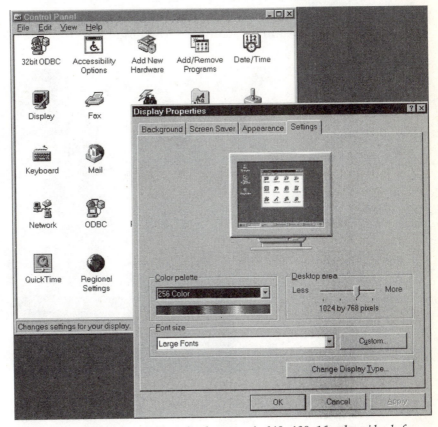

Figure 18-1: Set your system to display generic 640x480, 16-color video before you switch video cards. This is where you set it in Windows 95.

2. Shut off your PC and disconnect it from power.

Caution
Be sure that your PC is shut off. Also, if you aren't using a wrist strap, be sure to ground yourself before handling any components. To do this, simply touch the metal case of your PC.

3. Following the directions and cautionary notes in Chapter 13, "The Tools & Work Area," open your PC's case. With the cover off, you're ready to begin. Unscrew the board's retaining screw as shown in Figure 18-2.

Figure 18-2: Remove the retaining screw.

4. Grip the board and gently pull it up, using a back-and-forth rocking motion, as shown in Figure 18-3.

Figure 18-3: Grip the board and use a gentle rocking motion to pull it out of its socket.

Caution–Removing Expansion Cards

Always hold expansion cards by their edges and try not to touch the metal connectors that fit into the PC's slots. Your body can build up enough static electricity to fry an entire card or one of its components, rendering it useless.

To Install Your New Video Board

1. Find a slot that's appropriate for your board (PCI to PCI, 16-bit ISA to 16-bit ISA, etc.). For an examination of the type of boards and their matching slots, please refer to Figure 18-4.

Figure 18-4: Matching different boards with their slots.

2. After finding an appropriate slot, unscrew the retaining screw and remove the slot cover, as shown in Figure 18-5. You can replace this cover on any other open slot, if you have one.

Figure 18-5: Unscrew the retaining screw and remove the slot's cover to prepare it for your new video board.

3. Slide the new video board into the slot and use a rocking, pushing motion to seat the board into the socket, as shown in Figure 18-6. Make sure that the board is well seated in the socket.

Figure 18-6: Gently push down, using a rocking motion if necessary, to install the board into its socket.

Caution

Be sure that the video board is not touching any other expansion board. In fact, it makes sense to keep some room between them when you can. This way, air can circulate between them and the boards stay cooler.

4. Replace the retaining screw to secure the video board in place.

5. Before you replace the system's cover, connect the monitor to the PC card and reconnect power to the system so you can test it.

Caution

Don't forget that you have a live machine. Under no circumstance should you probe your PC or touch any internal component when your system is running. *Always* shut off power before doing any work on your PC or before removing or adjusting any component. Not only can you get a dangerous shock, you also can fry your components.

6. Turn on your PC and ensure that your system appears to be working correctly. If it's not, please refer to the video card troubleshooting tips at the end of this section.

7. At this point, you need to install the drivers for your new video card. For this, look for one or more disks that came with your new video board. Place the first disk into your system's drive. If you're running Windows 95 or Windows File Manager, use Microsoft Explorer or My Computer. If you're running Windows 3.1, use the Run command and run the installation file. In most cases, the file probably will be named Setup, but check with your video card documentation. The basics are as follows:

If You Are Running Windows 95 & Have Installed a Plug & Play Video Card

Reboot your computer. Windows 95 should boot up and immediately recognize that a new video card is installed in your system. At this point, the program will ask for a disk that contains your video card drivers, and you usually can follow the instructions on the screen, which will tell you to insert your driver disk. Windows 95 will perform most of the configuration for you.

If You are Running Windows 3.1

Click on Windows Setup in the Main Group. When the dialog box opens up, select Settings. When the window displays a list, select Other Display (Requires Disk From OEM). Now you can insert your video card driver floppy, and Windows will read and load your drivers. You should see some new resolutions and color depths from which to choose.

If You Are Running Windows 95 & Have Installed a Non-Plug-&-Play Card

To Use Windows 95 Explorer

1. Right-click your mouse on the Start button on the left side of the task bar.

2. Select Explore, as shown in Figure 18-7, to open the Windows 95 Explorer.

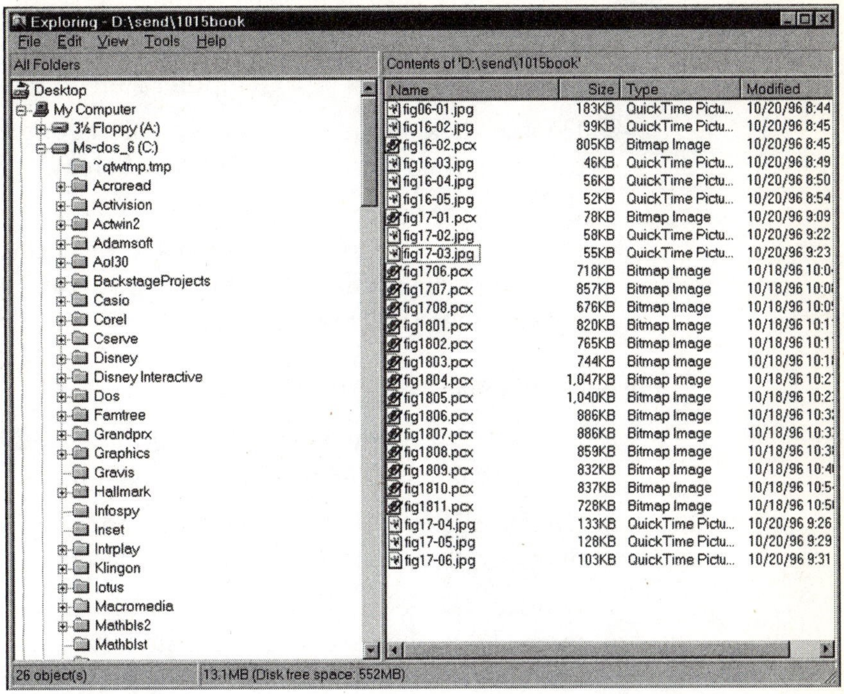

Figure 18-7: Use Windows Explorer to set up your new video card.

3. Select the A: drive by double-clicking on it (assuming A: is the drive holding the disk). Note that your setup may be different, thus your drive may be different.

4. In the file list to the right, look for the Setup file or whatever file the video board's manual tells you to execute to install video files. Double-click on this file to start the program, then follow the onscreen directions.

To Use Windows 95 My Computer

1. Double-click on the My Computer icon on the desktop.

2. Double-click on the A: folder. Note that your setup may be different, thus your drive may be different.

3. Look for the Setup file or whatever file the video board's manual tells you to execute to install the video files. Double-click on this file to start the program, then follow the onscreen directions.

To Use Windows 3.1 File Manager

1. Double-click on the File Manager icon. It probably will be in your Main Folder, which is the default.

2. Double-click on the A: folder. Note that your setup may be different, thus your drive may be different.

3. Look for the Setup file or whatever file the video board's manual tells you to execute to install the video files. Double-click on this file to start the program, then follow the onscreen directions.

Some of these installation programs will ask you what type monitor you have. Once the installation program loads the video driver, you will often find a new Windows setup program for the desktop that sets the display's resolution and number of colors.

You can use these setup programs to tell Windows how many colors you want to display on your screen (typically 16, 256, and so on), and at what resolution (640x480, 800x600, and so on). For more on resolutions and colors, please refer to Chapter 6, "Video Cards."

If you're running Windows 3.1, the utility may create its own folder and add its own setup utility or may install its utility in your Main folder. For this, you can check your video card's documentation.

If you're running Windows 95, you can set up the colors and resolutions using the Control Panel. To do this, simply click on Start, go to Settings and then to Control Panel, then Display. Click on the Settings tab, then on Change Display Type.

Problems & Solutions

This section contains some solutions to problems you may encounter.

If the Video Doesn't Display

1. Check your video card installation once again to be sure that the board is properly seated in its socket. (Be sure to shut off your PC and disconnect power before removing the cover to check it.)

2. Make sure that your motherboard doesn't already have built-in video. If it does, it may be conflicting with your new video board. Check the documentation for your motherboard to see how to disable the built-in video.

3. Make sure that the card is installed in the correct type of expansion slot (ISA, PCI, VESA, etc.).

4. Make sure that the monitor cable is fastened securely to the output port of the video card.

5. Some other card in your system may be using the same addressing spacing. For this, you'll have to consult the documentation for your various other cards to see if there might be conflicts.

6. If you're running Windows 3.1, you might try booting from your floppy disk, to see if your system is loading a TSR (terminate and stay resident) program or some other program that is conflicting with your card.

7. Consult with the motherboard's manufacturer to ensure that the bus is indeed a true PCI or VESA and to ask if there are any known problems with certain video cards. You also can check with the video card manufacturer for known problems or conflicts with certain systems.

8. Try moving the video card to a different slot.

If the Video Doesn't Display Correctly

1. If you are replacing an existing video card, you may want to see if you can uninstall its software drivers. It could be that Windows is still configuring for or looking for another card. If the previous card's menu still exists in Windows, you can check it to see if it has an "uninstall" option that removes it.

2. Check your system setup to make sure that you haven't set the software for a different video card or monitor.

3. If you're seeing flicker, the picture is scrambled, or the screen display is small, you may have to make adjustments to your monitor's horizontal and vertical frequencies. Be sure not to set your card to a frequency that exceeds that of your monitor.

4. Refer to the documentation that came with your video card for any troubleshooting suggestions and potential problems that are too specific to cover here.

Moving On

We have gone through the steps necessary to install a new video card. With a new video card, you should see much faster performance on your computer's screen. In the next chapter, I'll talk about how to add a new modem to cruise the Web and discover those online worlds.

Installing a Modem

This is it. Your new modem is your driver's license that lets you cruise the information superhighway. If you're ready to make this installation, read on.

If you've bought a new modem in order to send faxes, use your computer for an answering machine, or go online, you only have to install it and get it working with your system and software. I'll talk about how to install both external and internal modems, and I'll discuss the communications software that gets things working—usually the most complicated part of the installation. To install your modem, simply go to the appropriate section of this chapter, according to which you bought—an external or internal modem. If you're still not sure which type of modem to buy or whether you have chosen one that is right for your system and needs, please refer to Chapter 11, "Modems," for more information.

Installing an External Modem

An external modem—like a monitor—is one of the few upgrades that you can install without opening your computer's case. For the most part, the installation involves plugging in your modem, as follows:

1. Shut off your PC and connect a serial cable between the port on your computer (COM1 or COM2) and the similar port on your modem. It's important that you remember which port your modem is connected to. Your modem may include this serial cable or you may have to buy it separately. The serial port on the back of your PC will have either 9 or 25 pins, as shown in Figures 19-1 and 19-2.

Figure 19-1: A 9-pin serial port.

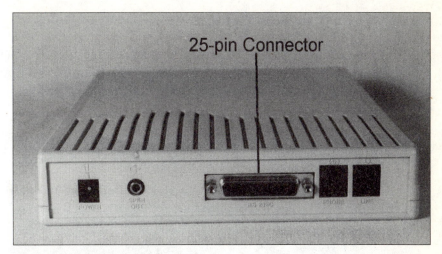

Figure 19-2: A 25-pin serial port.

Depending on the serial port that you have and want to use (you may have a mouse attached to one, usually the first 9-pin port, called COM1), you also may have to buy an adapter that connects between the different port sizes. You can buy one of these at any computer parts or Radio Shack store.

2. Hook up the modem to power. The external modem will come with its own power adapter.

3. Connect the modem to the telephone line: Plug one end of the telephone cord into one of the telephone ports on your modem, then plug the other end into the telephone wall jack. If you also would like to use a telephone with this jack, you can connect the telephone's cord to another port on your modem.

4. Turn on your modem and boot up your computer. If you are running Windows 95 and you have a modem that supports Plug and Play, the system will ask automatically for your driver disk. After that, you can reboot your computer, and your modem will be configured already and available for use by applications.

If you're running Windows 3.1 or are installing a non-Plug and Play modem in Windows 95, you'll want to install the drivers according to the instructions provided by the manufacturer. This will usually involve running a setup program on a floppy disk, which is described in the following sections:

To Install With Windows 95 Explorer

1. Right-click your mouse on the Start button on the left side of the task bar.

2. Select Explore to open the Windows 95 Explorer. (See Figure 19-3.)

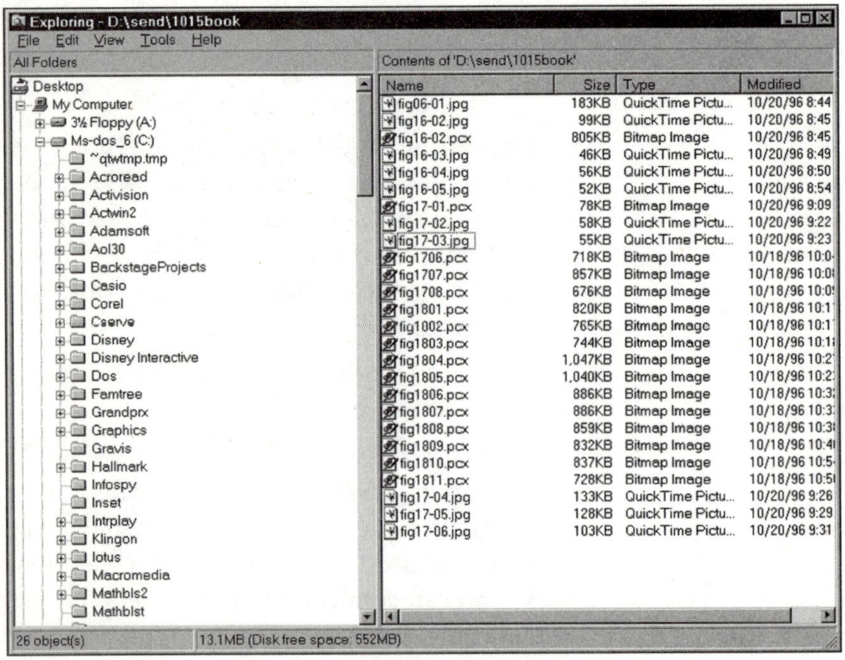

```
Exploring - D:\send\1015book                              _ □ ×
File   Edit   View   Tools   Help
All Folders                      Contents of 'D:\send\1015book'
Desktop                          Name          Size   Type              Modified
 My Computer                     fig06-01.jpg   183KB  QuickTime Pictu... 10/20/96 8:44
  3½ Floppy (A:)                 fig16-02.jpg    99KB  QuickTime Pictu... 10/20/96 8:45
  Ms-dos_6 (C:)                  fig16-02.pcx   805KB  Bitmap Image      10/20/96 8:45
   ~qtwtmp.tmp                   fig16-03.jpg    46KB  QuickTime Pictu... 10/20/96 8:49
   Acroread                      fig16-04.jpg    56KB  QuickTime Pictu... 10/20/96 8:50
   Activision                    fig16-05.jpg    52KB  QuickTime Pictu... 10/20/96 8:54
   Actwin2                       fig17-01.pcx    78KB  Bitmap Image      10/20/96 9:09
   Adamsoft                      fig17-02.jpg    58KB  QuickTime Pictu... 10/20/96 9:22
   Aol30                         fig17-03.jpg    55KB  QuickTime Pictu... 10/20/96 9:23
   BackstageProjects             fig1706.pcx    718KB  Bitmap Image      10/18/96 10:0
   Casio                         fig1707.pcx    857KB  Bitmap Image      10/18/96 10:0
   Corel                         fig1708.pcx    676KB  Bitmap Image      10/18/96 10:0
   Cserve                        fig1801.pcx    820KB  Bitmap Image      10/18/96 10:1
   Disney                        fig1002.pcx    765KB  Bitmap Image      10/18/96 10:1
   Disney Interactive            fig1803.pcx    744KB  Bitmap Image      10/18/96 10:1
   Dos                           fig1804.pcx  1,047KB  Bitmap Image      10/18/96 10:2
   Famtree                       fig1805.pcx  1,040KB  Bitmap Image      10/18/96 10:2
   Grandprx                      fig1806.pcx    886KB  Bitmap Image      10/18/96 10:3
   Graphics                      fig1807.pcx    886KB  Bitmap Image      10/18/96 10:3
   Gravis                        fig1808.pcx    859KB  Bitmap Image      10/18/96 10:3
   Hallmark                      fig1809.pcx    832KB  Bitmap Image      10/18/96 10:4
   Infospy                       fig1810.pcx    837KB  Bitmap Image      10/18/96 10:5
   Inset                         fig1811.pcx    728KB  Bitmap Image      10/18/96 10:5
   Intrplay                      fig17-04.jpg   133KB  QuickTime Pictu... 10/20/96 9:26
   Klingon                       fig17-05.jpg   128KB  QuickTime Pictu... 10/20/96 9:29
   lotus                         fig17-06.jpg   103KB  QuickTime Pictu... 10/20/96 9:31
   Macromedia
   Mathbls2
   Mathblst
26 object(s)      13.1MB (Disk free space: 552MB)
```

Figure 19-3: Use Windows Explorer to set up your new internal modem.

3. Select the A: drive by double-clicking on it (assuming A: is the drive holding the disk). Note that your setup may be different, thus your drive may be different.

4. Look for the Setup or Install file or whatever file the modem's manual tells you to execute to install the video files. Double-click on this file to start the program, then follow the onscreen directions.

To Use Windows 95 My Computer

1. Double-click on the My Computer icon on the desktop.

2. Double-click on the A: folder. Note that your setup may be different, thus your drive may be different.

3. Look for the Setup or Install file or whatever file the modem's manual tells you to execute to install the modem drivers. Double-click on this file to start the program, then follow the onscreen directions.

To Use Windows 3.1 File Manager

1. Double-click on the File Manager icon. (It probably is located in your Main folder, which is the default.)

2. Double-click on the A: folder. Note that your setup may be different, thus your drive may be different.

3. Look for the Setup file, or whatever file the modem's manual tells you to execute to install the modem drivers. Double-click on this file to start the program, then follow the onscreen directions.

4. Most of the software that you install—including communications programs, software that supports specific online services like CompuServe and America Online, as well as fax software—will ask for the type of modem that you have and the port that it's connected to. Just select your modem in each application's setup list. If your modem doesn't appear to be working when you use your software, refer to the "Troubleshooting" section later in this chapter.

Installing an Internal Modem

An internal modem is an expansion board that you install. The physical installation of the board usually is not difficult, but the setup can be a nuisance. If you purchase a modem that supports Plug and Play in Windows 95, this greatly simplifies things. But even if you don't, I'll offer suggestions for configuring your modem.

1. First, check your modem's documentation to see if there are any jumpers that you have to set. What you will be doing here is evaluating your system to see what ports you already are using and what port your new modem will have to use. Generally, you can install your modem at COM4. This, of course, will depend on your particular system.

> **Tip**
>
> With most systems, a good way to begin when first installing your modem is to try COM4. Also, if your system is configured already with four COM ports, you'll have to disable one to use with the modem. To disable a COM port, you will probably have to adjust some switches on your motherboard or reconfigure your system's CMOS setup. For more on this, check your system's documentation.

2. Turn off your PC and unplug it. Following the directions and cautionary notes in Chapter 13, open your PC's case. With the cover off, you're ready to begin.

> **Caution**
>
> Be sure that your PC is shut off. Also, if you aren't using a wrist strap, be sure to ground yourself before handling any components. To do this, simply touch the metal case of your PC.

3. Find an appropriate slot, unscrew the retaining screw, and remove the slot cover, as shown in Figure 19-4.

Figure 19-4: Unscrew the retaining screw and remove the slot cover to prepare a slot for the internal modem.

4. Slide the new internal modem into the slot and use a rocking, pushing motion to seat the board into the socket, as shown in Figure 19-5. Make sure that the board is well seated in the socket. Replace the board's retainer screw.

Figure 19-5: Push the board in with a rocking motion to seat it into its socket.

Tip
Always hold expansion cards by their edges and try not to touch the metal connectors that fit into the PC's slots. Your body can build up enough static electricity to fry an entire card or one of its components, rendering it useless. When inserting new cards, it makes sense to keep some room between them when you can. This way, more air can circulate between them and keep them cooler.

> ### *Caution*
> Be sure that the internal modem is not touching any other expansion board.

5. At this point, your modem is installed. You can put the cover back on your PC, reconnect power, and go to the configuration stage.

Configuring Your Internal Modem

The next step is to install the modem's software drivers. Look for the disks that usually come with a modem, and turn on your computer.

If You Are Running Windows 95 & Have Installed a Plug-&-Play Modem

Windows 95 should boot up and immediately recognize that your new modem is installed in your system. At this point, the program will ask for the disk that contains your modem drivers, and you can follow the onscreen instructions to load your drivers. With Plug and Play, Windows 95 will perform most of the modem configuration for you.

If You Have Installed a Non-Plug-&-Play Card With Windows 95

If you install a non-Plug-and-Play card, you'll have to manually enter the modem's driver. Here are instructions on how to do this for Windows 95 (both File Explorer and My Computer) and Windows 3.1:

To Use Windows 95 Explorer

1. Right-click your mouse on the Start button on the left side of the task bar.

2. Select Explore to open the Windows 95 Explorer. (See Figure 19-6.)

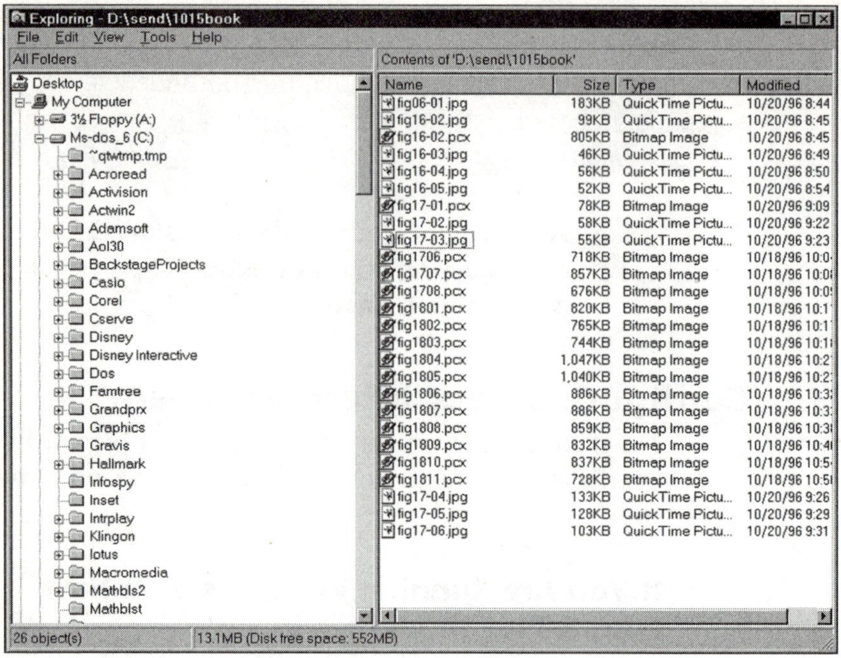

Figure 19-6: Use Windows Explorer to set up your new internal modem.

3. Select the A: drive by double-clicking on it (assuming A: is the drive holding the disk). Note that your setup may be different, thus your drive may be different.

4. Look for the Setup file or whatever file the modem's manual tells you to execute to install the drivers. Double-click this file to get it started, then follow the onscreen directions.

To Use Windows 95 My Computer

1. Double-click on the My Computer icon on the desktop.

2. Double-click on the A: folder.

3. Look for the Setup file or whatever file the manual tells you to execute to install the modem drivers. Double-click on this file to start the program, then follow the onscreen directions.

If You're Running Windows 3.1

1. Double-click the File Manager icon. It probably is located in your Main folder, which is the default.

2. Double-click on the A: folder.

3. Look for the Setup file or whatever file the modem's manual tells you to execute to install the video files. Double-click on this file to start the program, then follow the onscreen directions.

Setting Up Communications Software

After installing your modem's drivers, you'll want to set up your communications software so that it can run your modem (this also refers to fax, voice, and any software that supports a modem—for simplicity, we'll refer to any such software as communications software). The basics here are as follows:

1. First you'll need to use the setup feature in your communications software. Usually, the software will ask you to choose a modem from a list. Try to find your modem's brand and model number, and select it. If your exact model number isn't on the list, you can try another model by the same manufacturer and usually get good results. If your modem's brand isn't listed, check with your modem documentation to see what type of modem it emulates. More than likely, it will be a Hayes-compatible modem. The best programs on the market actually will search for your modem and suggest one to choose—a major convenience.

2. The software also will ask where your modem resides and want information such as the port (COM1, COM2, etc.) and the modem's speed. Enter this information, and you're usually ready to go.

Troubleshooting

If you use your software to dial a number and nothing happens (you should hear a dial tone and then the number dialing), there's probably something wrong with your configuration. In this case, what you have to do is examine your system with a utility to determine if two devices on your computer are trying to use the same port or system resources. You can find such diagnostic tools on this book's Companion CD-ROM.

When you can identify a setting that doesn't appear to be used by any other computer device, you'll have to reset your modem and your software. Unfortunately, troubleshooting your modem and getting it to work can be a lengthy trial-and-error process. Hang in there—it eventually will work. If you're having lots of trouble, you can call the modem manufacturer's representative, who is quite accustomed to dealing with these problems.

Moving On

We have gone through the steps necessary to install a new external or internal modem. With a new modem you can now send faxes, go online, and surf the Web. Welcome to the world of cyberspace! In the next chapter, I'll talk about how to add a hard drive so you can store all the programs that you'll probably be downloading with your new modem.

Installing an IDE Hard Drive & Floppy

When you move into a new house, it may feel as if there's lots of room, but soon you realize that you've filled every closet and cabinet and there's still stuff on the garage floor. I'm also reminded of those cowboy movies in which the two gunslingers meet in the middle of a hot dusty street and say, "This town ain't big enough for the two of us." Your computer is exactly the same way—there's never too much room, and before you know it, you're making choices as to which files get run out of town.

I'll show you how to increase your system's storage capacity by adding a new hard drive so you have more space to store your data and program files. I'll also talk about how to replace a floppy drive should you need to get a new one. If you want to see what it feels like to have lots of room on a hard drive (trust me, this feeling lasts for a week, at most, before your drive fills up), here's everything you need to know.

If you need some tips on buying a hard drive, please refer to Chapter 7, "Hard Drives." Otherwise, with your new integrated drive electronics (IDE) drive of 1 gigabyte (GB), 2GB, or even more in hand, you'll have room to burn. Temporarily, at least.

> **Tip**
>
> Most PCs have 200 watts of power and can adequately power two hard drives. However, 200 watts is probably a minimum. Check your system's power supply before adding a new hard drive.

Adding a New IDE Hard Drive

In principle, adding a new hard drive isn't difficult. The two things that tend to cause problems are first correctly configuring the hard drive and setting the jumpers and then properly configuring the system.

> **Tip**
>
> If you're adding a second drive, you may need a Y-cable that splits the power from one power connector and cable and ends up with two connectors—one for each of two drives. You can purchase a Y-cable from any computer store. Also, you may require a ribbon cable that has two connectors. While it isn't rocket science, it is trickier to route a two-connection ribbon cable around your system. For this, you may have to plan ahead.

1. The first step in installing your hard drive is to make sure that its settings are correct. Most of the time, your new hard drive will come with a booklet that lets you know about any particular settings or jumpers and how to set them. The documentation also should mention other secondary issues. For example, the BIOS (or CMOS) on an

older system may not be able to support a drive larger than 528 megabytes (MB). If this is the case with your BIOS, some manufacturers, such as Seagate, include a disk utility that can fool the BIOS into thinking that you have a smaller drive.

Probably the most important consideration to keep in mind is whether the drive that you're adding is the first or second drive in your PC. That's because you will have to configure the drive to be either a *master* or *slave,* as described in the following paragraphs:

If the hard drive is the first one that you're adding to your system, it should be set as the master. You'll need to check with your hard drive documentation, but most hard drives arrive already set as master drives. You shouldn't have to do anything. If your drive is not set as the master drive already, your documentation should give you advice on how to do this.

If the hard drive is the second one in your system, you'll have to set it as a slave drive. Please check your hard drive documentation for advice on how to do this. Keep in mind that when you add a second drive, you also have to consider the settings on your master drive. Again, check the hard drive documentation.

Caution

Be sure to back up all of your important data on your computer before beginning and take a minute to record information about your hard drive and system settings. If you're replacing a drive, you can use your backups to reinstall your applications and data. I've found that when it comes to important data, it doesn't hurt to do two backups of your data just in case one medium fails— that happened to me once.

2. Shut off your PC and unplug it. Following the directions and cautionary notes in Chapter 13, "The Tools & Work Area," open your PC's case. With the cover off, we can begin the actual installation.

> **Caution**
>
> Be sure that your PC is shut off. Also, if you aren't using a wrist strap, be sure to ground yourself before handling any components. To do this, simply touch the metal case of your PC.

3. If your system already has an IDE controller card, you can skip this step. If you are installing a new IDE controller card, I'll assume that you want to remove an older controller card and hard drive. To do this:

   a) Disconnect the cables that lead from your hard drive controller card to your floppy drives and to your existing hard drives (assuming that this is a single card; on some older systems, you may have multiple cards).

   b) With all connectors and cables removed from your hard drive controller, unscrew the retaining screw from the board as shown in Figure 20-1.

Figure 20-1: Remove the board's retaining screw.

c) Grasp the board by the edges and gently pull it from its socket, using a rocking motion as necessary, as shown in Figure 20-2.

Figure 20-2: Use a rocking motion to remove an old card.

Caution—Removing Expansion Cards

Always hold expansion cards by their edges and try not to touch the metal connectors that fit into the PC's slots. Your body can build up enough static electricity to fry an entire card or one of its components, rendering it useless.

d) With the socket clear (and assuming that you will be using the same socket, which may not be the case), you now can install your new hard drive controller board. Keep in mind that as with any other board, you must install a board into a like slot (PCI to PCI, ISA to ISA, etc.). For more information on expansion slots, please refer to

Chapter 4: "The CPU & the Mother of All Boards." Grasp the board by the edges and rest its contacts in the socket. Press down and gradually insert the board into the socket. Use a rocking motion if necessary to properly seat the board, as shown in Figure 20-3. Replace the retaining screw to secure your board to the case. With your IDE controller card in place, you're ready to install your hard drive.

Figure 20-3: Use a gentle rocking motion to insert a new controller card.

Removing the Old Hard Drive

When you open your computer and inspect the existing hard drive, you'll find that both the floppy and hard drives are mounted in a metal cradle or cage, as shown in Figure 20-4.

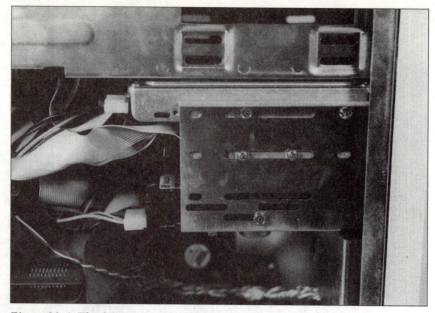

Figure 20-4: The drives are mounted in a metal cage.

To remove the hard drive, use a screwdriver to carefully loosen the screws that hold the hard drive to the cage, as shown in Figure 20-5. Most drives attach to the cradle with four screws—two on each side. Once you loosen these, you'll find that you can move the drive a bit.

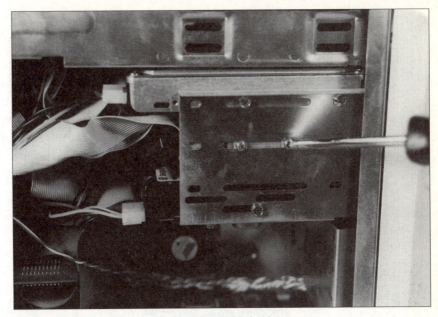

Figure 20-5: Removing the screws that hold the drives.

At this point, remove the connectors and cables from the drive, noting where they attach and to which drive (if you'll be using the same controller card). Even better, you can use adhesive labels to identify connectors. Then remove the screws and pull the drive out of the cage. You now have an empty drive bay space for your new hard drive. It's time to go out with the old and in with the new.

Tip
Be gentle when handling hard drives—they are fragile.

Installing Your New Drive

Now we're ready to perform the actual installation.

1. Hold your new drive in the drive bay. If you bought the hard drive with an installation kit (highly recommended), then all of the proper rails and screws should be readily available, as shown in Figures 20-6 and 20-7. Just use the hardware to mount the new board, similar to the way the old hard drive was mounted. There also should be documentation with your installation kit that explains some of the variations for installation.

Figure 20-6: You may need rails to fit your hard drive into your system's cradle.

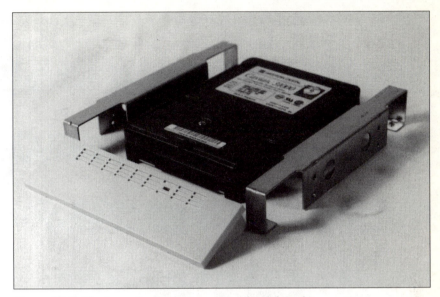

Figure 20-7: The type of rails that come in a hard drive kit.

2. With the rails in place (if they're necessary), attach the data cable to your controller card, as shown in Figure 20-8.

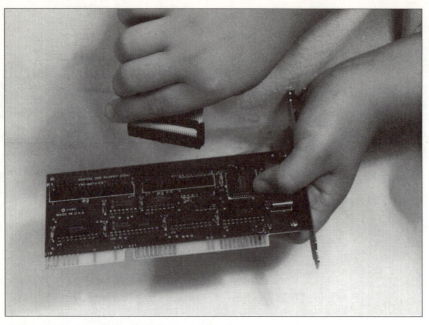

Figure 20-8: Attach the cable to the back of your controller card.

3. Attach the data cable to the connector on the back of your
   hard drive, as shown in Figure 20-9. Take extra care to
   check the orientation of the connector—look for the side of
   the ribbon cable that has a single wire of a different color.
   The side of the connector nearest the colored wire needs to
   be aligned with pin 1 on the hard drive connector and pin
   1 on the controller card—both of these usually have a
   diagram that shows you the connections.

Figure 20-9: Attach the cable to your hard drive. Look for the colored wire on the cable that will attach to the first pin of a connector.

4. Attach the power connector as shown in Figure 20-10. If you labeled these, they will be easy to find. These cables can be inserted only one way.

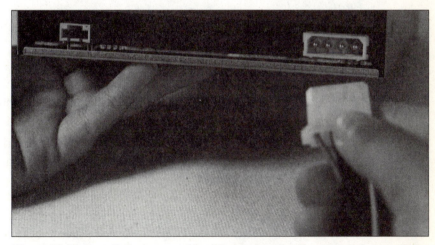

Figure 20-10: Install the power cable. (Please note that the previously installed data cable has been removed for picture clarity.)

5. Check all connections and screws to ensure that your installation is secure.

6. Before putting the cover back on, reconnect your video card, keyboard, and mouse, then reconnect the power to your PC and check to see that the computer boots up.

> **Caution**
> *Don't forget that you have a live machine.* Under no circumstance should you probe your PC or touch any components when your system is running. *Always* shut off power before doing any work on your PC or removing or adjusting any component. Not only can you get a dangerous shock, you also can fry system components.

> **Caution**
> When you are running the hard drive, be sure that the drive is stationary and can't move.

7. If everything looks OK, put the cover back on, and we're ready to move on to the configuration.

8. At this point you've physically installed your new hard drive, but your system still doesn't know it's there. So that your system and BIOS can recognize it, you have to set your system's CMOS. Check your hard drive's documentation first, as some drives come with very specific instructions. With most installations, you access your system's CMOS by booting the computer and holding down a key, but this varies from system to system. Check your PC's documentation for instructions on how to do this, and for

information about what settings (cylinders, heads, tracks, etc.) to enter for your drive. Access the CMOS screen and type in the hard drive settings.

9. Reboot your system using the bootable floppy disk that contains basic DOS commands (see Chapter 13). Most new drives come from the factory already low-level *formatted*. What you will have to do now is create a disk *partition*.

Definition, Please

Formatting refers to preparing your drive so that it's ready to be used. It's much like defining how it will use its space to store data.

Definition, Please

When you partition a hard drive, you define how the drive will appear in your system. For example, if you have a 1 gigabyte (GB) drive, you can have your system recognize and use this drive as a 1GB space or drive or you can partition the drive into two 500MB drives.

Drive partitioning has to do with making the most use of available space. Without going into a lot of detail, I can say that the way your system stores files, in smaller units called clusters, affects how efficiently your PC stores data and how much space on the hard drive it wastes. Generally, the larger the partition—say, 1GB and up—the more can be wasted, because the larger partitioned drives store clusters in larger units. If you have a small file, it will take up only part of that larger cluster, wasting the remaining space. Here's the bottom line—if you want to make the most efficient use of your hard drive space, you probably should not make any of the partitions greater than approximately 500MB.

To partition your drive, use a DOS utility called FDISK (fdisk.exe). Depending on how you want your system to recognize your drive, you can use FDISK as described in the following paragraphs:

FDISK will bring up a screen that lets you create a DOS partition or logical DOS drive. Look for the command that says "Create a DOS Partition or Logical Drive."

When the command asks you if you want to use the maximum size available for the partition, answer Y (yes) if you want to create one large disk or N (no) if you want to divide your new drive into smaller disks. You then will specify the size of the disks in terms of number of megabytes or percentage of capacity. After that, set the main drive as the active partition with the command, "Set Active Partition."

10. After partitioning your new drive, you must format it. For this, use a DOS utility called FORMAT (format.exe). If you've installed a main bootable C: hard drive, type:

format c:/s

For other drives, replace the letter **c** with the appropriate drive letter and remove the **/s,** which tells the computer to format a disk so that it can boot. For example, to format drive D:, you would type:

format d:

This also applies to those new disks you created when you partitioned the disk.

> **Caution**
>
> If you type the wrong drive letter while using the FORMAT utility, you can wipe out an entire disk. Be extra sure that you're typing in the number or letter of the drive that contains the disk that you want to format.

11. If your system boots up properly after the partition and format, you now will have what seems like a continent of hard drive space available. So far, so good. At this point, you can try to copy files to the hard drive. Turn off your system, disconnect the power, put the cover back on, reconnect everything, and you're done. On the other hand, if things aren't working, please refer to the following troubleshooting section.

Troubleshooting

If, at any point in the previous procedure, your system won't read your drive, the following suggestions might help:

○ If you're greeted with a message that says "Hard Disk Drive Controller Failure," double-check your connections and power. If these are in order, your problem is likely an incorrect system configuration or setting. Recheck your CMOS to see that you have the right settings and then go over the drive settings that you initially made.

○ If you see a message that says "No ROM Basic—System Halted," rerun FDISK and be sure that the hard drive used to boot the system is set as the active drive.

○ If your system boots up but doesn't seem to recognize the new drive, your master/slave settings may be incorrect. Check them.

○ If your screen comes up blank, check your video and monitor first for power and connections. You also can try removing your new host adapter (if you installed one) and then see if the system boots up normally. If it does, you may have a defective card.

○ If, after experimenting, you can't make your drive work, call technical support for the drive manufacturer, who can help you troubleshoot your setup.

Replacing Your Floppy Drive

This section covers the basics of installing a new floppy drive in case you want to upgrade an existing one (typically a 720 3.5 inch to a 1.44 3.5 inch) or if you want to replace a drive that has gone bad.

Removing the Existing Floppy Drive

1. Shut off your PC and unplug it. Following the directions and cautionary notes in Chapter 13, open your PC's case.

> **Caution**
> Back up all of the important data on your computer before beginning, and take a minute to record information about your hard drive and system settings.

> **Caution**
> Your floppy drive is a fragile mechanical device. Treat it gently.

Caution

Be sure that your PC is shut off. Also, if you aren't using a wrist strap, be sure to ground yourself before handling any components. To do this, simply touch the metal case of your PC.

With the cover off, you're ready to begin. As with hard drives, you'll find that floppy drives are mounted in drive cradles or cages, as shown in Figure 20-11. If you're installing a new drive, you'll need to look and see if you have room for another one.

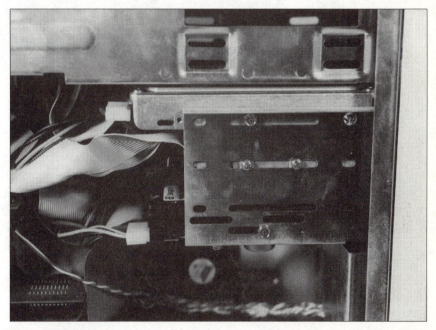

Figure 20-11: Like hard drives, floppy drives are mounted in a metal cradle or cage.

2. Loosen and remove the screws along the side of the drive that secure it to the cradle, as shown in Figure 20-12.

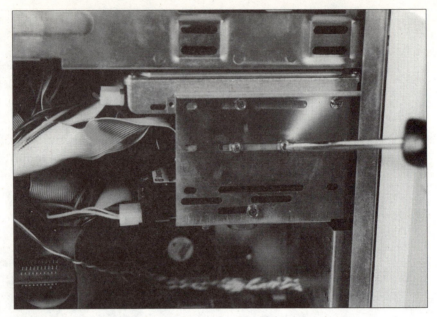

Figure 20-12: Loosen the screws along the side of the drive.

3. Remove the power and data connectors from the back of the floppy drive. Pay particular attention to the direction that the data connector is mounted (look for the colored stripe on one side of the ribbon cable—it goes with pin 1, as usually shown in a diagram on your controller card and the back of your drive). Don't worry too much about the power connector. It goes on in only one direction.

4. After removing the screws and the cables, pull the drive out of the front of the cage, as in Figure 20-13.

Figure 20-13: Pull the floppy drive out of the front of the drive.

You have successfully removed your old floppy drive.

Installing a New Floppy Drive

1. Different floppy drives require different setups. Most of the time, your floppy drive will come with a booklet that lets you know about any particular settings or jumpers. Follow these directions first.

2. Get ready to mount the drive in the drive bay. Take a look at the size of the cradle and select the appropriate rails to make the drive fit and install securely. You may or may not have to use these, depending on the size of your new drive and the size of the existing bay.

3. As you prepare to slide the drive into its bay, reconnect the power and data connections, referring to your notes or labels to make sure that the data cable connects correctly.

I've been assuming that you are replacing an existing drive. If you're adding a new drive, you need to consider how to add the drive to the flat ribbon cable. In Figure 20-14, the drive behind the twisted line is the first drive, A:, and the second drive, B,: is in front of the twisted line. Keep this in mind as you are changing your drives, and be sure to configure them if necessary.

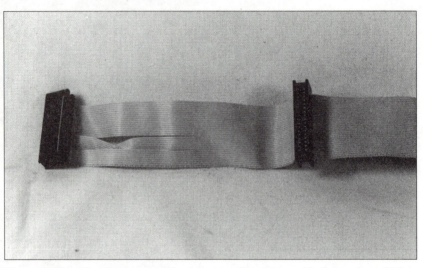

Figure 20-14: The placement of the drives on the ribbon cable determine which is the first drive (A:), and which is the second (B:).

4. Insert the screws to hold the drive in place in the cradle.

5. Recheck all connections and mounts to make sure everything is secure.

6. Configure your system so that it knows the drive exists. For this, you should be able to call up your CMOS setup by holding a key during boot-up. Check your motherboard's manual for more details. In the CMOS window, you'll be setting the type of drive (1.44MB, etc.) for each drive.

7. Before putting the cover back on, reconnect your monitor, keyboard, and mouse and see if the computer boots up.

> ### Caution
> *Don't forget that you have a live machine.* Under no circumstance should you probe your PC or touch any components when your system is running. *Always* shut off power before doing any work on your PC or removing or adjusting any component. Not only can you get a dangerous shock, you also can fry your components.

8. Try to read a disk in the floppy. If everything looks okay, try to format a floppy disk by typing **format a:** (replace the **a** with the appropriate designation for your drive), or you can use the commands in Windows to format a drive. Keep in mind that when you format a disk, you will lose any information on it. Do not format any disk that's storing important data.

9. If everything is in order, turn off your PC and disconnect the power. Put the cover back on and replace all of the screws. Reconnect the power, and you're ready to roll. If things aren't happening, please refer to the following troubleshooting section.

Floppy Troubleshooting

If your floppy drive doesn't work at all or if both floppy drives light up at the same time, recheck your CMOS configuration, and then recheck the power and data connections.

If you're sure of all your power and data connections but your drive still doesn't run, you can put your old floppy back in to see if it works. If it does, your new drive may be defective.

See Chapter 22, "You've Got Trouble My Friend," for some more floppy troubleshooting.

Moving On

If you've followed the instructions in this chapter, you now have a new installed hard drive, and you may have even added a new floppy drive. At this point, you're probably enjoying your new-found hard drive real estate, which lets you save data and install new programs at your beck and call—for a while, at least. In the next chapter, I'll show you how to install a new CD-ROM drive.

Installing Multimedia: The CD-ROM Drive & Sound Card

A CD-ROM drive and a sound card are the heart of your multimedia system. With these components, you'll be able to experience the latest multimedia titles, games, and educational programs. Without a doubt, this upgrade isn't about improving performance—it's about adding an entire new capability that opens a new world of computing.

You can choose to purchase a CD-ROM drive by itself, or you can buy it as part of a multimedia upgrade kit, which usually includes the CD-ROM drive, a sound card, and speakers. Regardless of how you buy your components, the installation is much the same.

If you're not sure what speed CD-ROM drive or what type of sound card you should purchase for your needs, please refer to Chapter 2, "What Do You Want to Do With Your System?" and Chapter 3, "What Upgrades Will You Need?" And for more information on CD-ROM drives and sound cards, please refer to Chapters 9 and 10 respectively, for more details and buying hints. For this chapter, I'll assume that you have your CD-ROM drive and a sound card in hand and can't wait to experience the joys of multi-media.

Before installing that CD-ROM drive, you have to consider what type of drive it is and what type of port or board you will need to connect with it and support it. As mentioned in the earlier chapters, CD-ROM drives come in three major kinds: those that need a SCSI, those that operate with a proprietary board, and those that require an ATAPI port.

If you buy a multimedia kit with a sound card and CD-ROM drive, you can be fairly sure that the port on the sound card connects with and supports the CD-ROM drive. Some CD-ROM drives—although this is getting rare—connect only with their own proprietary boards, and some sound cards offer a port for them. ATAPI CD-ROM drives connect with standard EIDE (enhanced integrated drive electronics) controllers. Just to make things interesting, some sound boards feature this connection, too.

So, depending on your setup, CD-ROM drive, and existing system boards, you might be installing a board as well as a CD-ROM drive. Therefore, I'm going to discuss a generic CD-ROM drive placement that includes a sound board. Your particular setup may be different, and you should check the documentation that comes with your CD-ROM drive and your sound board for details.

If you have a system with an existing SCSI interface or if you plan to install a CD-ROM drive to your existing EIDE controller, you can skip this next section—which deals with the sound card—and go directly to the installation of the CD-ROM drive. If you have to install a proprietary board, please refer to the documentation that comes with that board. You will find that some of the tips scattered throughout the following instructions for the sound board installation will apply to a proprietary board as well.

> **Tip**
>
> If you already have a joystick or game port on your PC (many computers have combo ports along with the parallel and COM), you should disable the joystick port on your sound card to make sure that there is no conflict. To do this, consult the board's documentation.

To Install the Sound Card

1. Shut off your PC and unplug it. Following the directions and cautionary notes in Chapter 13, "The Tools & Work Area," open your PC's case.

> **Caution**
>
> Be sure that your PC is shut off.

2. Check with your sound board documentation to see if there are any settings that you will have to make or jumpers to arrange on the board. If you buy a sound board that supports Plug and Play, Windows 95 can make most of the configurations for you and you can ignore this step. Also, there are sound boards that you can install and make changes later through a software utility.

3. Find a free slot in which to install your sound board. Remove the slot's retaining screw, as shown in Figure 21-1.

Figure 21-1: Find an open slot and remove the slot cover.

4. To install the board, grasp it by its edges and rest its contacts in the socket. Press down gently and gradually insert the board into the socket. Use a rocking motion, if necessary, to properly seat the board, as shown in Figure 21-2.

> **Caution**
> If you aren't using a wrist strap, be sure to ground yourself before handling any components. To do this, simply touch the metal case of your PC.

Figure 21-2: Use a gentle rocking motion to insert the sound card.

Caution
Be sure that the video board is not touching any other expansion board. In fact, it makes sense to keep some room between them when you can. This way, more air can circulate between them and keep the boards cooler.

5. Check your sound card documentation to see if you need to make any internal connections for the board. For example, sound cards come with input ports that support incoming CD audio. Replace the retaining screw to secure your board to your system. With your sound board in place, you're almost ready to install your CD-ROM drive, but there's one more step that you need to take first.

6. At this point, you need to install the sound card's drivers, which usually come on a floppy disk. Just put the disk into your system's drive. Using Microsoft Explorer or My Computer or Windows File Manager or the Run command, run the install file. In most cases, this will be named Setup, but check with your video card documentation. Note that if you purchase the CD-ROM and sound card together in a multimedia upgrade kit, you'll probably install these drivers later, after installing the CD-ROM drive.

If You Are Running Windows 95 & Have Installed a Plug-&-Play Video Card

Windows 95 should boot up and immediately recognize that a new component—a sound card—is installed in your system. At this point, the program will ask for a disk that contains your video card drivers. Follow the instructions on the screen to load your drivers. Windows 95 will perform most of the configuration for you.

Note: Check your documentation, particularly if you are installing a multimedia upgrade kit. It may ask you to perform this step at the same time you configure your CD-ROM drive. If so, skip the following section and go to the instructions for installing the CD-ROM drive.

Insert the driver disk into your floppy drive. Use Explorer or My Computer if you're running Windows 95, or use File Manager if you're running Windows 3.1.

If You Are Running Windows 95 & Have Installed a Non-Plug-&-Play Card

To Use Windows 95 Explorer

1. Right-click your mouse on the Start button on the left side of the task bar.

2. Select Explore, as shown in Figure 21-3, to open the Windows 95 Explorer.

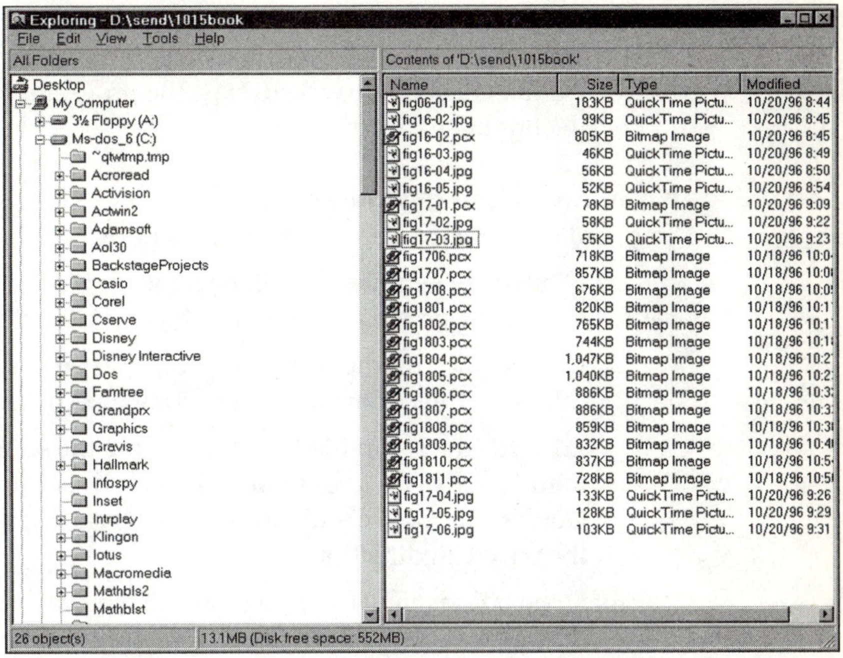

Figure 21-3: Use Windows Explorer to execute the Setup file.

3. Select the A: floppy drive by double-clicking on it (assuming A: is the drive holding the disk). Note that your setup may be different, thus your drive letter may be different.

4. Look for the Setup file or whatever file the sound board's manual tells you to execute in order to install the sound drivers. Double-click on this file to start the program, then follow the onscreen directions.

To Use Windows 95 My Computer

1. Double-click on the My Computer icon on the desktop.

2. Double-click on the A: folder. Note that your setup may be different, thus your drive letter may be different.

3. Look for the Setup file or whatever file the sound board's manual tells you to execute to install the sound drivers. Double-click on this file to start the program, then follow the onscreen directions.

If You Are Running Windows 3.1
To install by running a setup file, using Windows 3.1 File Manager:

1. Double-click on the File Manager icon. It probably is located in your Main folder, which is the default.

2. Double-click on the A: folder. Note that your setup may be different, thus your drive letter may be different.

3. Look for the setup file or whatever file the sound board's manual tells you to execute to install the sound drivers. Double-click on this file to start the program, then follow the onscreen directions.

4. Some boards may ask you to install a driver manually. To do this, double-click on Control in the Main Group window. When the dialog box opens up and displays information about your system, select Drivers. Click on the Add button and select Unlisted or Updated Driver. At this point, you can insert your floppy disk of drivers, and Windows will copy them and make them available to you. For more details, consult your sound board's documentation.

Installing the CD-ROM Drive

1. Examine your system's drive bays to determine whether you need to physically rearrange your existing hard and floppy drives to accommodate your new CD-ROM drive. Also consider how cables will have to run inside your computer so that your CD-ROM drive will connect easily with the board that supports it.

2. Connect the power, four-wire audio, and data cables, as in Figures 21-4 and 21-5. Please refer to the instructions that came with your CD-ROM drive. You may find that it's easier to install these cables before you install your CD-ROM drive in its bay.

Figure 21-4: Install the data cable into your CD-ROM drive.

Figure 21-5: Install the power cable into your CD-ROM drive.

3. Slide the CD-ROM drive into the bay that you have selected for it. Attach the screws to secure the drive in its bay.

4. Reconnect your monitor, mouse, power, and other cables.
At this point, you will have to install the CD-ROM drivers.
Just use the disks that came with your CD-ROM drive. The
disks will install the CD-ROM drivers and a file called
MSCDEX, which is essential for making your CD-ROM
drive work with Windows.

5. Power up your system. Insert the driver disk into your
floppy drive. After that, you can use Explorer or My Computer if you're running Windows 95 or File Manager if
you're running Windows 3.1, as in the following directions:

To Use Windows 95 Explorer

1. Right-click your mouse on the Start button on the left side
of the task bar.

2. Select Explore.

> ### Caution–Safety
> *Don't forget that you have a live machine.* Under no circumstance
> should you probe your PC or touch any components while your
> system is running. *Always* shut off power and unplug your com-
> puter before doing any work on your PC or before removing or
> adjusting any component. Not only can you get a dangerous
> shock, but you also can fry your components.

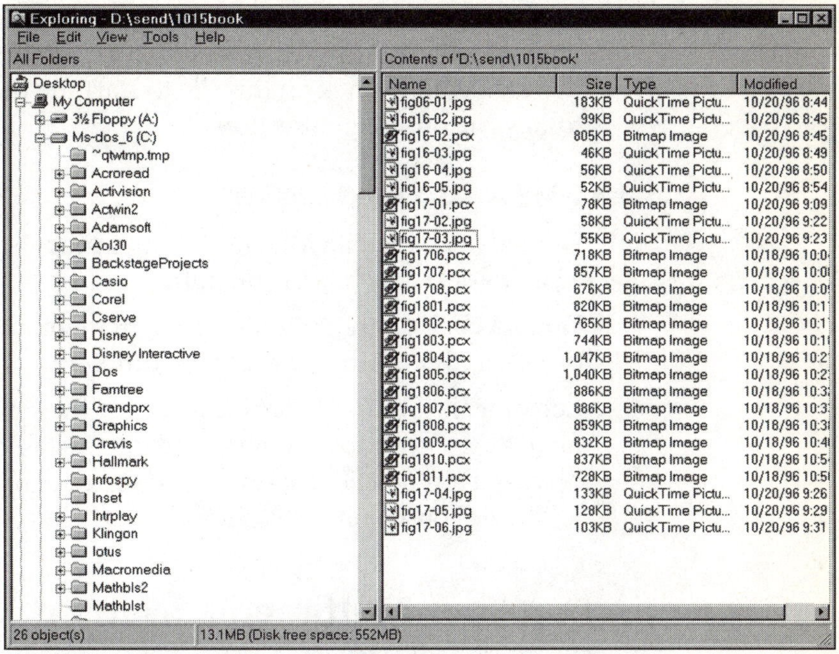

Figure 21-6: The Windows 95 Explorer window.

3. Select the A: drive by double-clicking on it (assuming A: is the drive holding the disk). Note that your setup may be different, thus your drive letter may be different.

4. Look for the Setup file or whatever file the sound board's manual tells you to execute in order to install the sound drivers. Double-click on this file to start the program, then follow the onscreen directions.

To Use Windows 95 My Computer

1. Double-click on the My Computer icon on the desktop.

2. Double-click on the A: folder. Note that your setup may be different, thus your drive may be different.

3. Look for the Setup file or whatever file the sound board's manual tells you to execute in order to install the sound drivers. Double-click on this file to start the program, then follow the onscreen directions.

To Use Windows 3.1 File Manager

1. Double-click the File Manager icon. It probably is in your Main folder, which is the default.

2. Double-click on the A: folder. Note that your setup may be different, thus your drive may be different.

3. Look for the Setup file or whatever file the sound board's manual tells you to execute in order to install the sound drivers. Double-click on this file to start the program, then follow the onscreen instructions.

Powering Up Your Multimedia System

With your multimedia system in place, now is a good time to finalize the installment. Plug your speakers into the sound card. Also, if appropriate, connect your speakers to power (some run off batteries). If you bought a multimedia upgrade kit, it usually will include speakers. Otherwise, you'll have to buy some separately, or you can connect your sound card to a stereo system, if you prefer.

Test Your New Multimedia System

If you got through the software installation, you should be in pretty good shape. At this point, you can reconnect power and turn on your computer to see if everything is running properly. Be sure to read some CD-ROMs, preferably a multimedia title with some sound and video that will put your new multimedia system through its paces. If everything appears to be in order and working, replace the system's cover. If something isn't working, check out "Troubleshooting," which follows.

Troubleshooting

If your CD-ROM can't read a CD, check your configurations. You can look at Explorer in Windows 95 or File Manager in Windows 3.1 to see if it recognizes that your drive exists. If not, try the following suggestions:

○ If your system doesn't know that you have a CD-ROM drive installed, check the software configurations and recheck your installation. (Be sure to disconnect power before again removing the cover of your PC.) You may have missed a cable. Make sure that all cables are attached securely. Also, check that your controller board is properly seated.

○ Check with your manual to see what suggestions it offers for the particular configuration of your CD-ROM. Ultimately, you may have to edit your config.sys or autoexec.bat files. Your documentation should have instructions on how to edit those DOS files.

○ Another possible problem is that you may have the wrong drivers or an incorrect version of these drivers (although this is unlikely). For this problem, you should contact the company to see what its latest drivers should be. Also, if you have a modem and Web access and the company has a Web page, you can check for information there.

○ You also should check your CD-ROM's controller card. Be sure that the port is active (you'll have to check the board's documentation for this), and be sure that you don't have two ports on at the same time that may be conflicting with each other. This can happen, for example, if you install a sound board with an active port, but also have a proprietary port installed to control your CD-ROM.

○ One other possibility is that your computer requires that you set up your CD-ROM drive in its CMOS. This is rather unusual. For more on how to do this, check your system's documentation.

○ When you've exhausted these possibilities, call the CD-ROM manufacturer for technical support.

○ If you're not hearing any sound (either through your speakers or through headphones), adjust the volume on your speakers to make sure that they are not set too low and make sure that your speakers are powered up. Another thing to check is whether your speakers are connected to the correct jack on the sound card. Look at your card's documentation for help here.

○ If you're not hearing any sound, you may have an internal system conflict caused by two devices trying to use the same system resources. For this problem, you can run the Device Manager in Windows 95 to see if it identifies any system conflicts. To access this function, click Start, then Settings, and then System. If you're not sure which boards may be causing a conflict, you can use a utility program to evaluate your system (some of these are on this book's Companion CD-ROM), or you can gradually remove boards from your system to identify the culprit board, in the process described in Chapter 22, "You've Got Trouble My Friend."

Moving On

In this chapter I've shown you how to install multimedia— a CD-ROM drive and a sound board—in your system. This is the last chapter that contains installation procedures. The next chapter talks about finding out what's wrong with your computer, should it not operate correctly. I hope that you will experience trouble-free operation with your PC, but the next chapter will help if you do have problems and need to find out what's wrong.

You've Got Trouble, My Friend: Repairing Your PC

In an ideal world, Santa Claus would actually exist, politicians would never lie, and our computers would never break down (particularly when we have critical deadlines to meet). I hope that you won't have to use this chapter, but if you need it, here it is.

This chapter presents a troubleshooting strategy and lists symptoms, possible problems, and suggestions for things to check, should something go wrong or your system begin to act up.

You'll find that, for the most part, my suggestions will take you down to the component level—a board, a hard drive, and so on. My intent is to help you determine which component is giving you problems so you can replace it. In that case, you once again can use this book to save money in making your selection and purchase and to install your new component with my step-by-step instructions.

You may have been surprised when I suggested simply replacing a faulty component instead of repairing it. The fact is, most of us don't have the sophisticated equipment necessary to test a component to its factory specifications. In fact, even most computer shops lack this capability.

Computer components aren't like car components. You can take an auto component apart, tinker with it, replace a broken part, and put it back together. In a computer, the components tend to be so tightly integrated, they're often not worth separating. Chips are soldered onto boards, and nothing is meant to be taken apart and put together again. This is why even many computer repair shops don't try to repair a faulty component. They find out which part is causing the trouble and just replace it.

So if something has gone wrong with your computer, here are some suggestions on finding the problems and fixing it.

General Troubleshooting

When something goes wrong with your system, your first inclination might be to open up the case immediately and start poking around—get under the hood, so to speak. But most of the time, you can trace problems to something that you just did, which has nothing to do with the computer's hardware. Many computer problems that I've seen are system conflicts—unexplained phenomena that seem to belong in the Twilight Zone.

When something goes wrong with a computer, it can be hard to determine exactly which component is faulty. Sometimes the culprit is something that appears to be unrelated to the apparent problem. I'll talk later in this chapter about strategies you can use to identify such problems. The key to troubleshooting is to try to re-create the problem. Once you can make the problem surface consistently, you can begin to see what components relate to it, home in on it, and solve it.

When something stops working, take a minute to think:

○ Did you recently add a new component?

○ Did you recently install a new software package?

○ Did you recently change any settings in your system or operating system?

If the answer to any of these questions is yes, chances are good that you just introduced a new system conflict or something isn't configured correctly. Also, be sure to check all of your PC's plugs and connectors. It's not unusual for someone to accidentally unplug a monitor connection, power cord, mouse, phone, printer, or anything else in the general vicinity. I can't tell you how many times I've unsuccessfully tried to print something and found that I had dislodged the printer cable accidentally.

Also, can you reproduce the error? Try to retrace everything that you did before the glitch appeared and see if it shows up again. If you can trace what software or hardware may be involved in the process, you'll have a valuable clue as to what's going on. You can also look at the LEDs (lighted electronic displays) on your modem, hard drive, or CD-ROM drive to see if they're trying to access the system when the lockup occurs. If so, they might be involved.

Software can cause internal conflicts. Newly installed software may be looking for hardware that doesn't exist, or it may be configured incorrectly. Try to identify the software that is causing the problem, then work on its configuration. Software problems usually recur in the same place while you're performing the same task.

One thing that's easy to do is to reinstall the suspect software package. It may configure itself correctly and solve the problem. If that doesn't work, you can uninstall the program completely to see if your computer now runs smoothly. If, after you remove the software, your computer runs smoothly, you can begin checking configurations of your hardware as they relate to the problem software.

Incorrect CMOS configurations also can cause problems, and these don't always immediately surface. When something goes wrong, you can check your system's CMOS to make sure that all configurations are correct and that they agree with those listed by each component's manufacturer. As I've mentioned in other chapters, it always helps to keep a written list of your existing CMOS settings so you can quickly re-enter them when you need to.

If you've checked everything from the outside and the problem persists, now it's time to open your computer and check the internal cables, board installations, and chips. Make sure all boards and connectors are seated where they should be and all cables are connected tightly (look for loose and dangling cables). Also, it's not unusual for cables to stop working because they've been nicked or pinched by boards, the case, or other parts. If so, a new cable will fix the problem. It's probably a good idea to replace any cable that has a nick in it; one with even a serious crimp can be suspect. Check that all expansion cards are seated properly in their slots and that anything connected to them is secure.

If you have just installed a new component, take it out and see if the system works. Also, you may have installed a board improperly so it wasn't making a good connection (sometimes a properly installed board shifts position when you put in the retaining screw). New components can conflict with existing ones, in which case your system should work immediately when you remove the culprit component. Then you can check the part's documentation to see how to configure it so that it will address system resources in a different way.

If you've tried all of these general troubleshooting suggestions and are still having a problem, you will need to do more specific diagnostic checks to try to determine which system component is the culprit. When you figure out which component is causing the problem, you're more than halfway to the solution.

Isolating a Faulty Component

After you check for and resolve system conflicts, most of the troubleshooting that you can do easily will involve looking for faulty components. When your computer won't run and you have no way of guessing which component is causing a conflict, it's best to remove components gradually from your system, one by one, until the problem clears up.

Set your computer on a workbench and boot it. When the problem occurs, turn off your computer, remove a nonessential expansion board—the sound card, for example—and reboot. If everything works correctly, then the problem or conflict is probably with the sound card. You can continue this process of systematic elimination until the computer operates properly. This method has worked well for me.

However, an even better way to locate suspect components is to use two similar computers and swap components between them. I realize this approach is not very practical for most of us, but it's what the pros often do. If you do have two systems, simply remove a component from the system that isn't working and place it in the system that is working correctly. When the working computer stops functioning or the newly installed component doesn't do what it's supposed to do, you've found the culprit.

When you think about it, replacing a component is really cost-effective. These days, with hard drives available for less than $200, floppy drives for less than $50, and IDE controller boards for less than $20, the labor charges for a technician's time would soon eat up the cost of a new board or component. Even if a technician determines which component on a board is faulty, there's no guarantee the part can be found and replaced or repaired. For example, a common capacitor may be available, but a specialized chip probably won't be. Buying a new component usually is best.

Also, don't forget about cables. When a printer, mouse, monitor, or hard drive fails, often the culprit isn't the component itself but rather the cable that connects it. Fortunately, a cable is a fairly low-cost item to buy and replace. (Sometimes cables come undone within a system. Just reconnect them.)

More Specific Troubleshooting

This section provides troubleshooting tips for specific problems you may be having. If you don't find your particular problem described here, the suggestions provided for a similar problem may prove to be useful.

If Your Computer Doesn't Turn on at All

Check all incoming power cords and the outlet. Unplug them, then plug them in again to make sure that they are connected and that they work. Plug something else into the outlet to be sure it's hot. If you're sure you're getting power but the monitor remains dark, the memory chips may have gone bad. If this is the case, you'll find that the computer may stop at the same number as it checks memory each time you boot up.

If you just added new RAM, you can remove your new RAM and reinstall the old RAM to see that everything is working correctly (if you completely replaced your existing RAM). If you installed additional RAM, you can check to see if the old RAM works without the new RAM.

If your old RAM works correctly, the problem is likely to be your new RAM installation. Either the RAM chips are not the proper ones for your system, your system isn't configured correctly to recognize them, or the RAM chips are faulty. Try installing the new RAM chips again. If they don't work, review your system's documentation to check what type of RAM you can add. You can contact your motherboard's manufacturer to double-check.

Don't forget that when you install new RAM, you must account for the RAM that you already have. Sometimes, if you're mixing SIMMs of different speeds, they will not configure unless you go into your system's CMOS setup to change something called *wait states*. For this, you'll have to check the manufacturer's instructions. Also, double-check how you can add new RAM—in many cases, motherboards require that you install SIMMs in pairs.

If everything appears to be in order, you may have a bad SIMM. Return the SIMM to the manufacturer and exchange it for another set.

You may get error messages that indicate memory parity problems. These are almost always a result of some software problem. Sometimes they can be caused by a virus, but unfortunately, memory parity problems are common because of all the variations in software and hardware. Still, it doesn't hurt to run a virus checker.

Also, you might open up your machine to see if the RAM chips are properly seated in their sockets. It's a rarity that a SIMM or RAM configuration should unseat, but I've heard of it happening.

If your computer doesn't work correctly after you replace your CPU with an OverDrive chip, something in the installation has caused a problem. After all, the computer worked fine before you made the upgrade.

Double-check your chip installation. Make sure that the chip is properly installed and seated in its socket. You also can check that in the process of replacing the chip, you didn't disconnect any other cables or components accidentally. After inspecting the connections, expansion boards, and chip, try booting again.

If you're absolutely sure that your connections look right and the computer won't boot, first see if the chip's manual has any other suggestions. As a last resort, you can reinstall your old CPU chip and see if the computer runs. If it does, there's probably something wrong with the new chip. However, if your old chip doesn't run anything, you've inadvertently changed something in your system. Check the connections again and try booting your computer.

If Your Hard Drive Is Failing

If you have hard drive problems, your primary task is to retrieve and save your data. If you have a recent backup, great. If you don't, try booting from a floppy; then access your hard drive and copy your data to floppies if you can. If you can succeed up to this point, you can troubleshoot without the risk of losing data. Once you have your data backed up, you're free to work with your drive.

Note that if you can boot from a floppy and access your hard drive, chances are that your hard drive is in working order but something has gone wrong with its configuration. If you see a message that says "No ROM Basic—System Halted," rerun FDISK and be sure that the hard drive that is used to boot the system is set as the active drive. (For more information on FDISK, see Chapter 20, "Installing an IDE Hard Drive & Floppy.")

Before you do anything with your drive, check your CMOS setup. Your drive may be configured incorrectly. Check the parameters listed in your hard drive's documentation to see if they match. Another thing you can do before you actually touch the drive is to run any software disk utilities you may have. Open up your computer and check the cables and connections to make sure everything is in order.

If these steps fail to yield results, you can move to more drastic steps. While there are ways to reconstruct the drive step by step, I recommend using a disk utility to do this, since many of the steps are very involved. You also can use the FDISK command to see if it acknowledges that the hard drive exists, then repartition and reformat your hard drive. Remember that when you do this, you will lose all of the data on your drive. Make sure that everything is backed up.

Caution
When you use FDISK to repartition your drive, you will lose all of the data on your drive.

If you just can't access the hard drive, you probably have a serious crash at hand. If the drive is still covered under warranty (some companies cover them for up to three years), you can contact the company to get a replacement. Otherwise, you may have to buy a new one.

A hard drive often will give some warning before it crashes, although it doesn't hold up a sign that says WARNING: CRASH IN PROGRESS. DRIVE CAREFULLY. However, you may notice that the drive is making funny noises or taking a lot longer than usual to access data. If you see your drive acting up in any way, run, don't walk, to your floppy disk drawer or tape drive and back up all your data.

Caution
When you copy data from a suspect hard drive that appears to be failing, don't copy the data onto your normal backup disks or media. If the drive is acting up, it might write corrupted data on top of your older backups, and then you'll lose everything.

By the way, there are specialized companies that can retrieve data from crashed drives, but this service is very expensive. In fact, it's really only for large companies that can afford such rates. Your best insurance for the data on a drive is to routinely back it up.

If You Can't Read a Floppy

Sometimes when you insert a floppy disk to be read by your computer, you'll hear an incessant grinding noise, which means that the drive just can't read the disk. Sometimes taking the floppy out and then putting it back in will work (it has to do with the alignment of the disk in the drive).

If your problem is serious, your system may tell you when you boot up that you have a bad floppy drive. In this case, either the controller card or the floppy drive has failed. To test them, you can swap components between machines, as described previously. Before you do that, you might open up your computer and check that all of the power connections and data cables are in place.

However, although floppy drives do get out of alignment now and then, it's more likely that the disk that you're trying to read has failed. The first thing I would try is to see if another computer can read the disk, preferably the computer that originally formatted the disk. If the other computer can read the disk, you can at least get to your data and copy it to a disk that's been formatted on your computer.

If your floppy drive is out of alignment, you usually can tell, because other machines will have a hard time reading a disk formatted with a misaligned drive. As with a hard drive, it's a good idea to try and salvage any important data that you can from the floppy, using a utility if necessary, and to check your floppy drive. If it looks as if your floppy drive is not functioning properly, you can have it repaired, but it's less expensive to buy a new floppy drive and install it yourself.

If Your System Locks Up

Periodic lockups are difficult to trace. A computer that's hard to boot when it's cold may indicate a hardware problem. While many lockups can be attributed to software conflicts, you can use the process of elimination to troubleshoot the hardware. Remember that if it's software, you might be able to re-create the problem.

If you get a "Parity Error" message, you'll have to use the process of elimination to see which component is causing the problem. While this message indicates that something has gone awry in memory, it doesn't tell which component is faulty.

If Screens Don't Look Right

Check your video card installation, CMOS settings, and board settings in Windows. Then, recheck your video card installation to be sure that the board is properly seated in its socket. Check your system setup to make sure that you haven't set the software for a different video card or monitor. See that the monitor cable is fastened securely to the output port of the video card.

If you've just installed a new video card, make sure that your motherboard doesn't already have built-in video. If it does, it may be conflicting with your new video board. Check the documentation for your motherboard to see how to disable it. Make sure that the card is installed in the correct type of bus (ISA, PCI, VESA, etc.). There's a chance that another card in your system may be using the same addressing spacing. If this is the case, you'll have to consult the documentation for your various cards to see if there might be conflicts. One simple step that sometimes works is to move the video card to a different slot. Another possibility is that driver remnants from your old video card may be interfering with the new one. You'll want to remove these.

With a new card, you can consult with the motherboard's manufacturer to ensure that the bus is indeed a true PCI or VESA and to learn if there are any known problems with certain video cards. You also can call the video card manufacturer to check on known problems or conflicts with certain systems.

If you've just installed some new software, you might try booting from your floppy disk to see if your system is loading a terminate and stay resident (TSR) program or some other program that is conflicting with your card.

If you're seeing flicker, the picture is scrambled, or the screen display is small, you may have to make adjustments to your monitor's horizontal and vertical frequencies. Be sure that you don't set your card to a frequency that exceeds that of your monitor.

Refer to the documentation that came with your video card for any troubleshooting suggestions and potential problems that are too specific to cover here.

If your screen comes up blank, check your video and monitor first for power and connections. If you can, try installing the video card in another system to see if it works—if it doesn't, it probably has gone bad.

If You're Having CD-ROM Problems

If your CD-ROM can't read a CD, check your configurations. You can look at Explorer in Windows 95 or File Manager in Windows 3.1 to see if it recognizes that your drive exists. If not, try the suggestions described in the following paragraphs:

If your system doesn't recognize that you have a CD-ROM drive installed, check to see if anything has changed in your software configurations. Consult the documentation for your CD-ROM drive to verify its correct configuration. You may have to edit your config.sys or autoexec.bat files.

Examine all cables to ensure that they are securely attached, and check that they are free from crimps and nicks. If you have a suspect cable, replace it. Also, be sure that your controller board is seated properly.

Be sure that the port is active (you'll have to check the board's documentation for this), and check to see that you don't have two ports on at the same time that may be conflicting with each other. This can happen, for example, if you install a new sound board with an active port but you also have a proprietary port on another card installed to control your CD-ROM.

If You're Hearing the Sounds of Silence

If you don't hear any sound from your sound board, adjust the volume on your speakers to make sure that they are not set too low, and make sure that your speakers are powered up. Also, see whether your speakers are connected to the correct jack on the sound card. You also can attach some headphones to your PC to see if you can hear anything that way.

If you still don't hear anything, you probably have an internal system conflict, which may be caused by two devices trying to use the same system resources. To find out, run the Device Manager in Windows 95 (click Start, Settings, and then System) or Configura-

CD-ROM

tion Manager in Windows 3.1, and look for conflicts. If you're not sure which boards may be causing a conflict, use a utility program to evaluate your system (some of those on this book's Companion CD-ROM can help) or gradually remove boards from your system to identify the culprit board. Most problems with sound cards are due to faulty configuration. For more suggestions, consult the documentation that came with your sound card.

If You Have Printing Problems

If your printer isn't printing, check first that it has paper (particularly if it's a laser printer—the paper tray isn't always easily visible). If your printer is on an A/B switch to share a printer, be sure that it's set to print from your current machine. Also, you can check the print cable to be sure that everything is connected properly.

If a printer has two paper trays, be sure that your software is configured to print from the correct one and that it has paper. See that your software is set properly to output to your printer. It's easy to accidentally change this, particularly if you regularly use more than one printer.

With paper in place, check that the printer is set to "Online," so it's ready to print. For more information on this, consult the documentation that came with your printer. If this doesn't help, reset the printer and try again. Shut the printer off and then back on, run the printer self-test (if it has one), and try yet again. If you know how, you can use the Print command from DOS to send data directly to the printer. If this works, you almost certainly have a configuration or driver problem.

If nothing seems to be out of place with the printer or its connections, you might test whether it will print from another PC. Two other suspect areas are the printer cable and the parallel port. Try swapping cables and see if that clears up the problem. If you recently extended your parallel cable, this could be a problem, as the PC isn't sending the data far enough. You might check with the cable's manufacturer to see how far you can extend a printer connection.

You also can open your computer and see if the I/O card is seated properly. If the printer works on another PC, you more than likely have a problem with your cable or parallel port. But before you replace the port, check to see if there is a conflict between it and any new cards you recently added.

Lack of Communications—Modem Problems

You probably won't find any problems with your modem until you try to use it with a communication, fax, or other software package. If you use your software to dial a number and nothing happens (with an external modem, you should hear a dial tone and then the number dialing), there's probably something wrong with your configuration. In this case, you'll want to recheck your modem installation with your software. Make sure that you have the correct port and baud rate set. Also, if you selected your modem from a list during the configuration, select another modem from the same manufacturer. If your problem is a driver, this might work.

If your modem isn't specifically listed in the program's installation, you may have to check and set parity, data bits, stop bits, and local echo on or off, according to the documentation. Just to make sure that the problem isn't a particular software program, you might try your modem with another piece of software. For example, if you're having problems with a fax program, you can set up and run America Online or a communications package. If the modem works, the problem's the software.

The easiest way to find a system conflict is to examine your system with a utility to determine if two devices on your computer are trying to use the same port or system resources. You'll find such diagnostic tools on the Companion CD-ROM.

When you identify a setting that doesn't appear to be used by any other computer device, you'll have to set your modem and your software. Unfortunately, troubleshooting your modem and correcting a problem can be a lengthy trial-and-error process. If you're having lots of trouble, you can call the modem manufacturer's representative, who is quite accustomed to dealing with such problems.

Keyboard Problems

If your system stops recognizing your keyboard, more than likely there's a problem with your keyboard. The first step is to try the keyboard on another system to see if it works there. If it doesn't, it's probably time to buy a new keyboard, a relatively inexpensive prospect.

If your system doesn't recognize your keyboard, it should tell you as it boots up. I've found that I can sometimes unplug and the replug the keyboard, and that sometimes fixes the problem (usually temporarily).

Mouse Traps

If your mouse should stop working suddenly, chances are good that you've changed something in your system that is conflicting with your mouse or something has gone wrong with your mouse's cable. If this continues, even after you reboot your computer a few times, here are some suggestions.

First, check your mouse's connections. Is its connector securely plugged into its port? Once you have this established, you can go into your system and check to see if your mouse settings are correct. Windows usually offers a mouse utility in your control panel (this varies with the type of mouse you have). You can refer to it to see if the system is recognizing your mouse. When your system doesn't see a mouse, it usually will tell you upon boot-up. You probably have a system conflict and will have to evaluate your system and change some settings. The system diagnostic utilities on the accompanying CD-ROM will help you with this.

To ensure that your mouse is functioning properly, you can install it on another PC to see if it works. If it does, then the problem lies in your system's configuration. If it doesn't work, it's probably time to take a close look at that mouse and possibly buy a new one.

Moving On

In this chapter, I talked about general strategies you can use to troubleshoot your system, should you run into problems. Using these, you should have a reasonable chance of identifying problems down to the component level so you can replace whatever is not working. If you will be purchasing new components, be sure to read the earlier chapters that tell you what to look for and how to find the best prices. So you can minimize your need for this chapter, Chapter 23, "Maintenance," will talk about things you can do to keep your system in great shape.

Maintenance

Service every three months or three thousand miles is great advice for keeping your automobile in good shape. Unfortunately, there's no mileage counter on your computer, but there are things you can do to help it work at peak performance for years. In Chapter 22, "You've Got Trouble, My Friend," I talked about troubleshooting and how to find out what's wrong when your computer isn't working properly. In this chapter, I'll discuss what you can do to help your computer work a good long time. If you follow some of the suggestions here, you may avoid having to take the computer to the shop (and put your money and energy into upgrading it instead).

Computer Placement

Where you keep and use your computer has a lot to do with how well it runs. Some environments will wreak havoc on a system eventually. For this reason, you should consider several issues when deciding where to set up your computer.

First, computers don't like high temperatures or rapid temperature changes. Therefore, you should try to keep your computer in a relatively cool area and never in a place that's hotter than 105 degrees Fahrenheit. Even if your house is fairly cool, a sunny spot by the window can get very hot on a summer day, so it's not a great place to put your computer (and it also makes it hard to read the screen).

Another mortal enemy of your computer is moisture. Excess humidity will cause a computer's metal parts to corrode, which can be particularly damaging to contacts on cables, boards, and other parts. As you read in Chapter 22, faulty cables and connectors are hard to diagnose and troubleshoot.

While there's not much you can do if you live in a high-humidity area, you can help your system out by installing a bag of silica gel in the case to absorb any excess moisture that might accumulate in there.

If your PC gets cold—if, for instance, you leave it in a cold garage or the trunk of your car overnight—be sure to let it warm up to room temperature before you turn it on. You'll save some of your mechanical parts that may be sluggish, and any moisture that may have accumulated near mechanical parts will have a chance to dry out.

Sometimes the interior of your system can get wet. This is usually due to a kid with a cup of juice or a careless grown-up with a cup of coffee. (I've seen people who actually set their coffee mugs on the PC.) If the inside of your computer gets wet, *don't* dry it with a hair dryer. The problem is that the dryer's heat can damage your components. It's best to disassemble your PC, gently dab the individual parts with a dry cloth, and let them air-dry over a few days. Of course, it's best to keep all drinks and fluids away from the PC.

Another environmental factor that seriously affects your computer is vibration. For those of you who live in California, there's not much you can do if there's an earthquake (although some manufacturers sell equipment specifically for attaching PCs and monitors to the desk so they don't fall over during a temblor). However, what I'm really talking about is constant vibration, not occasional severe shaking.

When your hard drive is operating, the disks are spinning rapidly on a microscopic cushion of air. Because of this, vibration is a killer. Even the slightest movement will cause the heads to slam into the drives and can cause you to lose data. Eventually, such damage could lead to a hard drive crash.

To avoid vibration, try to put your computer on a stable platform in an area that is free of high traffic, kids' playgrounds, and aerobics classes. If your computer's case is set on the floor, be careful that you don't tap your feet on it. The PC is just not meant for that kind of treatment.

Excessive dust and smoke are two more enemies. Smoke leaves a residue on parts, particularly on the heads on your floppy drive, where it can collect until the drive no longer can read a disk. Fortunately, your hard drive is sealed, so it's not as susceptible. Although your computer has a filtering system, it can't stop everything from coming in, and smoke tends to go everywhere. Don't allow smoke around your computer if you can help it. If you do choose to smoke, you might consider purchasing an electronic air filter and placing it near you, to help cut down on the amount of smoke that ends up in your computer.

Dust can collect in your computer, too. If it gets thick enough, it acts as an insulator, blocking air from circulating around the components, so they run hotter than they are designed to do. The excess heat eventually can cause a part to fail. It's probably a good idea to open up your computer periodically and check to see if you need to remove any dust that has accumulated. In particular, clean the exterior of your power supply, since the holes in its ventilation system can become clogged. If there's no ventilation, the unit can run hot and cause damage to itself and nearby components. It's not uncommon to open a PC and see a layer of dust. I've been guilty of letting my computer get that bad—but then, my lawn mower has a lot of dust on it, too.

You can use a can of compressed air (sold in electronics shops for this purpose) to occasionally blow dust out of the case. Although they can be expensive, small vacuum cleaners also are available for cleaning the inside of electronic equipment. A fine brush also works, although the compressed air will reach some of the places that the brush can't. **Caution:** When removing dust, never use a damp cloth inside your system, as this will introduce moisture that could harm components.

Magnetic fields also are bad for PCs. It's annoying when a nearby magnetic field causes a monitor's picture to blur, and sometimes such fields will cause transmissions through external cables to garble—for example, it may mess up a printout.

At their worst, magnetic fields actually can destroy PC data because all storage in your system is based on magnetic media. Potential sources of magnetic interference include any electric motor and speakers (unless they are the magnetically shielded types made for use with computers).

To be very conservative, it's probably best to keep any other electrical appliance away from your PC. This includes electric pencil sharpeners and fans. Even such seemingly innocuous items as refrigerator magnets can cause damage, so don't use them to stick papers and memos to file cabinets in your office. Telephones also can be a problem. Even some of your own computer peripherals, such as the printer and monitor, can throw off magnetic fields of their own (unless they're shielded). One more thing: Try not to run cables under or near fluorescent lights; they emit noise that can disrupt and alter signals.

Power

There's not much you can do if your office is struck by lightning, but you can take precautions against irregularities in your system's power supply. Unfortunately, this subject is muddled by lots of marketing hype and gray areas, and you can end up spending way too much money to protect your system.

Power surge protectors will help defend your system against spikes. Even more effective is an *uninterruptible power supply (UPS)*—a power supply that provides backup power during short-term electrical irregularities. UPSes can range in price from around a hundred dollars to several thousand dollars, depending on size and manufacturer.

For the most part, the protection that surge protectors provide is rather questionable, and it's difficult to tell if they are working. Most of us probably buy a surge protector because it's convenient to plug everything associated with the computer into it, but it's hard to say if they really do any good if there is a power problem. For instance, a recent power outage on the West Coast fried a lot of computers. I don't know if any statistics are available concerning who was or was not using a surge protector, but a lot of people use them, yet there were a lot of damaged cards.

There are also devices that can protect your system from surges that come through the telephone lines, which can occur when lightning strikes. If you have a modem connected to your system, you might consider buying such a protector.

My recommendation is to buy what you can afford comfortably. If you're in charge of a network, you probably need to have standby power supplies and uninterruptible power supplies. A surge protector may not be much protection, but it's probably better than nothing.

Periodic Maintenance

As I mentioned earlier, you can't change the oil every three thousand miles and get a tune-up each year, but there are things you can do to prolong the life of your computer system. I recommend that you do the following at least once a year.

❍ Check all of your system's cables, connectors, and boards to make sure that they are connected properly. Replace any that show signs of corrosion or breakage. Also, be sure that hard drives are secure in their mounts.

❍ Open the case and clean the interior of your system with a brush and compressed air. Never use moist cloths or spray cleaners inside your computer. Clean the ventilation ports of your power supply to make sure that air is free to circulate. It's also good to remove your floppy drive and blow out any collected debris with compressed air.

○ Since dirt, dust, and smoke particles can collect on disk drives, use compressed air to clean out the interior of each drive. Another precaution you can take is to use a cotton swab with a touch of rubbing alcohol on it to clean the read/write head.

○ Clean the mouse ball to remove the gunk that tends to collect on it. Most mice have a circular compartment on the bottom that you can turn to release the ball. When it's out, you can wipe it and also get at the roller contacts inside the mouse, using cotton swabs and a little rubbing alcohol.

   If you aren't using one, you'll probably find a mouse pad will mean a better performing and cleaner mouse. A pad costs only a couple of bucks, a small investment for better mouse performance. If you don't mind an advertisement sitting on your desk, you may even get one for free. I use a free mouse pad that sports an ad for a product that I don't even like. I'm not proud.

○ You can shoot compressed air from a can onto your keyboard to remove debris and help keep the keys from sticking. Sometimes, turning a keyboard upside down helps remove some larger chunks of stuff that have fallen and stuck under the keys.

Other Maintenance (or, Defending Your System From Children & Other Gremlins)

If your CD-ROM drive is dusty, you can wipe it off with a dry cloth. Gently wipe with a minimum of pressure from the center to the outside (don't use a circular motion). Also, always handle CD-ROM disks by the outside, and never touch the data surface. Never stack them or lay them about; always store them in an appropriate holder.

   If you have kids, your monitor probably looks a lot like mine—covered with tiny fingerprints and other grime. You can wash your screen with water and a cloth, but I don't recommend using a conventional window cleaner on it. According to my sources, monitor manufacturers spread a special coating on a monitor's screen to prevent glare, and you can damage this coating with window cleaner. Just use plain water. Some manufacturers market special spray-on monitor cleaners, similar to window cleaner, that work well.

If you have sticky keys, you may have to take more drastic measures. If you can open your keyboard or pop-off the culprit keys with a letter opener or screwdriver, you can try brushing out the interior. Keep in mind that you can't do this with all keyboards, so don't force it open if it doesn't look like it was meant to come apart—you might not get it back together. If you've allowed kids with dripping Popsicles near your keyboard (shame on you), you even can clean the interior with mild household detergent.

If it's really bad, though, it's probably best to buy a new keyboard. Some experts say that if your keyboard is unusable because its keys are sticking, go ahead and dunk the keyboard in water (it's probably useless anyway), let it dry, and see if that helps. You have to decide if you have anything to lose. I've never tried it and don't intend to try it on any keyboard I might want to keep, but you may be more adventurous than I am.

Other System Considerations

If your system has an older hard drive, you may have to park it. *Parking* means to place the drive's head in a particular position when you shut the system down so that you can move the drive safely without damaging it or the data it holds. Most of these older drives came with special parking programs or utilities. If yours did, you should follow its instructions each time you power down your system.

With newer drives, parking isn't an issue. However, with all drives, you must minimize the shock and movement around them as they operate. Shaking a moving drive is a sure way to drastically shorten its life and lose precious data.

If you're not using a cache program, you might consider it. As I mentioned in earlier chapters, a cache program is a chunk of memory that looks ahead for data that may be needed by the system, then reads and holds the data for use. A cache reduces the number of times that a drive has to perform a specific read. As a result, your system performs faster, your hard drive operates more efficiently, and you reduce the number of hard drive operations. This may increase the drive's life span, although it's rather difficult to measure how effective it is, and it does depend on the type of programs that you are running. Both Windows and DOS come with caches that you can readily use.

It also makes sense to perform periodic diagnostics on your hard drive, using software such as Norton Utilities to check for and correct minor drive problems. Periodic drive maintenance includes *defragging* (actually, *defragmenting*) the drive. This means that you reposition data on your drive, using a specific utility, so your drive runs optimally, resulting in faster performance. As explained in Chapter 7, "Hard Drives," a defragger arranges data on your drive so the heads have to move the least distance on the drive to find contiguous data (data in order), instead of skittering all over to find scattered bytes.

After a while, particularly if you add a lot of Windows programs, your system begins to accumulate extra files, many of which you may no longer need. These files take up valuable hard drive space and system resources, since they load each time you run Windows.

Periodically examine your Windows system files and check for excess files that you no longer need. For instructions, please refer to Appendix B, "Removing Unwanted Windows 3.x Files," where you'll find details on removing temporary (*.tmp) files and more. Be sure that you first move files to a temporary directory, then reboot and use your computer for a while to make sure that the files you moved aren't system essentials. If you delete them first and then find that you need them, you'll have problems.

You also need to protect your computer from viruses. Viruses, of course, are those infamous programs that surreptitiously alter your computer's operation. Their unwelcome effects range from obnoxious message displays to outright system crashes and loss of data.

Like their biological brethren and namesakes, computer viruses spread by latching onto files (like cells), usually programs, and modifying their codes. When you run an infected file, the virus activates itself in the memory of your computer and looks for other programs to affect. You can get viruses through shared floppies, networks, and files downloaded from the Internet.

Fortunately, there are virus detection programs on the market that can hunt down viruses and minimize their damage. These programs identify viruses by their signatures—combinations of bytes unique to each virus. Once the detection program locates a virus, it alerts you, destroys the virus, and tries to repair the file. Sometimes a file is too far gone, and in this case, it's best to delete the file and replace it from your backups. You do have backups, don't you?

To remain effective, a virus detection program has to be up-to-date so it can recognize the new viruses that are constantly pouring into circulation. For this reason, manufacturers offer update services—sometimes at extra cost—to keep your virus protection current. Popular virus utilities include McAfee's VirusScan and Norton AntiVirus.

Most people I know who compute have run into a virus at one time or another. It's a shame that we all have to be concerned with these mean-spirited pranks, but they are a reality. Virus detection software is an excellent addition to your digital toolbox, particularly if you have lots of crucial data.

Moving On

In this chapter I discussed maintenance that you can perform on your system to ensure that it operates a good long time. If you follow the steps here, you shouldn't have to refer to Chapter 22 *too* much.

At this point, I've concluded this discussion of what you want to do with your computer, what upgrades you'll need to do it, basics on hardware, installation steps, troubleshooting, and computer maintenance. I hope that this book has helped you effectively upgrade your PC. May your system run forever troublefree and with the latest cost-cutting and cutting-edge components.

SECTION IV

Appendices

About the Companion CD-ROM

The Companion CD-ROM included with your copy of *Upgrade & Repair Your PC on a Shoestring* contains valuable software programs for inexpensive PC maintenance.

To view the CD-ROM, double-click on the LAUNCHME.EXE file from your Windows Explorer or File Manager. You'll see a menu screen offering several choices. (See "Navigating the CD-ROM" below for your option choices.) If the viewer does not run properly on your machine, follow these instructions for optimum performance:

1. Copy the LAUNCHME.EXE and LAUNCHME.INI files to the same directory on your hard drive.

2. Open the LAUNCHME.INI file in a text editor such as Notepad.

3. Find the section in the .INI file that reads:

```
[Memory]
;ExtraMemory=400
; Amount of kBytes over and above physical memory
for use by a projector.
```

4. If your computer has enough memory to do so, delete the semicolon from the ExtraMemory line and change the ExtraMemory setting to a higher number.

5. Save the changes to the LAUNCHME.INI file and close the text editor.

6. With the CD-ROM still inserted, launch the viewer from the hard drive.

If the viewer still does not run properly on your machine, you can access the material on the CD-ROM directly through the File Manager (Windows 3.x) or Windows Explorer (Windows 95).

Navigating the CD-ROM

Your choices for navigating the CD-ROM appear on the opening screen. You can read about and install the Software, browse the Hot Picks, learn more about Ventana, or quit the CD. A complete listing of the programs follows.

Program	Description
SYSCHK version 2.43	SYSCHK is a system information diagnostic utility that provides valuable details on devices installed in your system. Clean, easy-to-use menus show CPU, IRQ, BIOS, Bus Type, Mouse info, Serial and Parallel Port info, Modem, IDE and SCSI, CD-ROM, TSR, Novell Network, Video, CMOS, Memory, benchmark speed, Windows, and lots more. Print out a complete configuration report on your system!
SNOOPER version 3.44	System information utility. Ideal for tech support, HW inventory, etc. Snooper is shareware and purchase of this book and Companion CD-ROM does not satisfy the user's obligation to the author.

Program	Description
CTS IRQ Info version 1.6	IRQInfo is the most accurate software IRQ mapping utility available anywhere. It tests for drives, networks, sound cards, COM ports, printers, modems, scanners, SCSI...just about anything that uses an IRQ. IRQInfo is simple to use and presents an easy-to-read chart showing how each IRQ is used in the computer. IRQInfo PRO includes additional tests and a TSR module to detect more devices.
Space Hound version 1.79b	Space Hound is a professionally designed and developed multipurpose Windows utility program. The overall mission of the program is to "sniff out" wasted space on your hard disk that is duplicated, obsolete, or simply forgotten. Five primary displays guide you in identifying files that are duplicated, obsolete, and even files that may have been forgotten. Space Hound provides the tools to assist you in determining which files fall into these categories. In addition to helping you "sniff out" wasted and nonproductive disk space, the program provides excellent reporting capabilities to aid you in managing your data.
6th Sense version 2.2	Handy menu-driven "front ends" for DOS 6 DIR/FORMAT commands.
Integrity Master version 3.02a	A high-performance (100% assembly language) program offering virus protection, security, and change logging all in one easy-to-use package. It detects damage caused by hardware glitches, software bugs, and even deliberate sabotage to your data. If a virus strikes, Integrity Master identifies it by name and (unlike its competition) identifies any damage caused by the virus. Integrity Master offers full assurance that your PC is OK by fully checking all files, boot

Program	Description
	sectors, and even the CMOS. Integrity Master is a top-rated virus scanner. Unlike other products, Integrity Master detects not just viruses but also any damage caused by a virus.
Info Spy version 2.57	A highly rated tool to diagnose, spy, and investigate your Windows environment. Also integrated Resource/Memory monitor and alarms, System Scheduler, Screen Capture, Terminal Security, Monitoring, File Manager, AutoReboot, CMOS saver, and much more. Includes over 100 menu options that empower you to take back control of your system. Any user with a fax/modem can easily and quickly fax all InfoSpy information to any fax. Awarded best Windows Resource Monitor Ziff-Net December 1995. http://ourworld.compuserve.com/homepages/DeanSoft
PC-Doctor 2.0 for Windows	This software package, developed by Watergate Software, can test your computer, determine its configuration, and perform low-level DOS testing. PC-Doctor 2.0 for Windows by Watergate Software is a dynamic system information and diagnostic tool that provides more than 250 professional-level hardware diagnostic tests in a modular, easy-to-use format. These extensive tests detect failures in system components from the CPU to SCSI devices, CD-ROM drives, and PCMCIA cards, as well as providing complete system hardware information. Plus, handy help screens and an online manual keep you well informed of the diagnostic process. PC-Doctor and Watergate Software are registered trade marks and the property of Watergate Software. Watergate Software, Inc. 200 Powell Street, Suite 1200 Emeryville, CA 94608

Program	Description
SysInfo version 6.4	A simple DOS utility that determines system components (e.g., RAM, XMS and EMS memory, if SHARE driver is loaded, type of COM ports (and number), etc.). (Limited when determining drives greater than 1 gigabyte.)
FaxMail for Windows version 5.12	A 16-bit program that adds a <Fax> button to all your Windows Programs giving any program that has the capability to print, the capability to fax.
FaxMail Network for Windows	Also version 5.12, this is a 32-bit program that basically differs from FaxMail for Windows only in that it can run either on a single PC or on a network.
MEG	MEG graphs PC disk space and memory plus system information. Shows any drive as large easy-to-read pie and 3D bar graphs.

Technical Support

Technical support is available for installation-related problems only. The technical support office is open from 8:00 A.M. to 6:00 P.M. Monday through Friday and can be reached via the following methods:

> Phone: (919) 544-9404 extension 81
> Faxback Answer System: (919) 544-9404 extension 85
> E-mail: help@vmedia.com
> FAX: (919) 544-9472
> World Wide Web: **http://www.vmedia.com/support**
> America Online: keyword *Ventana*

Limits of Liability & Disclaimer of Warranty

The author and publisher of this book have used their best efforts in preparing the CD-ROM and the programs contained in it. These efforts include the development, research, and testing of the theories and programs to determine their effectiveness. The author and publisher make no warranty of any kind expressed or implied, with regard to these programs or the documentation contained in this book.

The author and publisher shall not be liable in the event of incidental or consequential damages in connection with, or arising out of, the furnishing, performance, or use of the programs, associated instructions, and/or claims of productivity gains.

Some of the software on this CD-ROM is shareware; there may be additional charges (owed to the software authors/makers) incurred for their registration and continued use. See individual program's README or VREADME.TXT files for more information.

Removing Unwanted Windows 3.x Files

After a while, particularly after you add lots of Windows programs, your system begins to accumulate extra files, many of which you may no longer need. Even after you delete a Windows program, there's a good chance that it has left some files on your drive that are just taking up space. These files take up valuable hard drive real estate and system resources, since they load every time you run Windows.

For this reason, you should examine your Windows system files periodically and check for excess files. One warning though: The techniques listed here are for more advanced users and for those who tend to add and use lots of programs. If you aren't using a lot of Windows programs, you probably can skip this process.

Almost every time you install a Windows application, it makes some change to your system files, such as the Windows initialization file—called WIN.INI—and sometimes your SYSTEM.INI files.

Definition, Please

The WIN.INI file tells Windows how to operate. It controls screen colors, display, program groups, and everything else. If you look at WIN.INI using a text editor, you'll notice that it's made up of a series of statements with equal signs that define Windows settings. Unlike the DOS configuration files—config.sys and autoexec.bat. The WIN.INI file can weigh in at around ten lines, and spread itself over ten full pages.

SYSTEM.INI, on the other hand, provides information on your hardware. Adding a new application is far less likely to make changes to this file.

The other factor that causes Windows to bloat has something to do with what are called *dynamic link library* (DLL) files.

Definition, Please

Dynamic link library (DLL) files serve a function in Windows. For example, many CD-ROM programs that show video will install a run-time DLL for Apple's QuickTime for Windows. If you take a look at your Windows and System directories, you'll probably see lots of cryptic looking *.DLL files.

Removing excess Windows files isn't as simple as locating and deleting suspect files, because Windows shares resources between its applications. If you delete a file that is shared between applications, you can cause programs to crash. When cleaning out your hard drive, you have to make careful backups before you delete anything. Backups provide you with a way to restore your original parameters in the event you delete something that causes the system to crash. From here, proceed with caution.

To make a backup, you should create a boot disk that contains your Autoexec.bat and Config.sys files (found in your C: root directory) and WIN.INI, and SYSTEM.INI files from your Windows directory. I usually copy these files into a temporary directory on my hard drive. This way, they're always available should something go wrong, and I can simply copy them back to the Windows directory. You also might want to print these files out, so you have an additional backup on paper.

> ### Caution
> Be sure to back up all of your system files before making any changes. Without a backup, it's easy to create problems with system configurations that can be hard to reconstruct.

Some programs come with their own uninstall routines. If you no longer need a program on your drive, and it came with an uninstall routine, by all means use it. By using these routines, most programs will delete their own associated files.

If a program didn't come with an uninstaller or if you have remnants left from lots of other programs on your drive, you'll have to use a text editor to do some serious cutting. Once again, be sure you have your key files, the WIN.INI and SYSTEM.INI files, backed up and in a safe place.

Using the text editor, open up WIN.INI, look for lines that relate to applications that are no longer on your hard drive, and delete them. What you're looking for are lines that name a removed application. Sometimes these are obvious, and sometimes they're not. If you're not sure, be conservative and leave it alone.

After paring the files down, restart Windows, then run your current applications to ensure that the changes haven't affected them. Only after you are sure that your changes don't affect any other programs (you may want to use your system for a few days to be sure), delete the old version of the WIN.INI. But if your system crashes, reinstate your backup by copying your original WIN.INI (the backup copy you saved) into the Windows directory.

Sometimes you can recognize DLL files by their names. You also can find them by searching through an application's *.EXE and *.INI files (something for advanced users). Another type of file to look for are Windows *.tmp files. I periodically remove these, and sometimes they can amount to some fifty files. Again, when you find a file that you think you want to remove, don't delete it—move it to another directory. That way, you always can bring it back if you realize that you do need it after all.

One last solution is to use a commercial uninstall program that reviews your system and removes duplicate and unneeded files.

In any event, these file removal techniques can keep your system lean, and save valuable hard drive space.

Those Pesky General Protection Faults

You know how three simple letters can instill fear in just about anybody—just think of IRS. For Windows users, equally dreaded are GPF, or General Protection Fault, which tells you that something has gone haywire in Windows. As I said before, because computers are especially susceptible to Murphy's Law, these GPFs usually strike when you least expect them, when you can least afford to lose data, and only when you have neglected for the last three hours to save your work.

Anyone who has used Windows undoubtedly has encountered a GPF at one time or another. What usually happens is that you are computing routinely when a box suddenly appears to tell you that there's been a General Protection Fault. At this point, your keyboard's locked out, and your only alternative is to click the Close button to get out. Usually, the dialog box goes away, and your application closes, taking your unsaved data to never-never land.

Why do GPFs occur, and what can you do to protect yourself against them? Besides constantly saving your data, there are some steps you can take.

For the most part, GPFs occur when you're pushing Windows to its limits by running lots of applications at the same time or when you're using memory-intensive applications. As an operating environment, Windows does its best to manage the various applications and distribute memory among them, but sometimes applications try to use memory that isn't available to them. This is a common GPF-triggering situation.

Another situation that generates GPFs is when your system isn't configured properly. For example, your config.sys may not have enough file handles to support a certain program. If the program runs and finds that it doesn't have enough file handles, you'll probably see a GPF. Still other situations involve hardware drivers that are interacting incorrectly with the operating system, add-on memory managers that map memory in a way that is incompatible with Windows, and even bad memory chips. There are undoubtedly more situations that trigger GPFs, but these problems are responsible for a good chunk of them.

When You Encounter a GPF

When Windows displays a GPF, your top priority is to retain your unsaved data. For the most part, a GPF will wipe out all of the work you've done since your last save. However, some applications do provide a way to try to recover data. If these are available, you'll definitely want to make use of them.

If you do, though, here's something to remember: If your application helps you recover from a GPF and lets you save your file, be sure to use the Save As command and rename the file; don't use Save. This way, you don't write potentially corrupt data over your good data file. After you finish dealing with your data, you should assume that Windows isn't in any shape to continue, and reboot. The possibility of a GPF is just one more reason to always save your data at regular intervals.

Solving the GPF Problem

You can reduce your chances of triggering a GPF if you monitor your system resources to be sure that you don't let them get under 15 or 20 percent. If Windows isn't running any applications, you'll probably find that it lists between 70 and 80 percent of your system resources as being free.

To view your system resources, click on the Help menu of the Windows 3.x Program Manager, and you'll see an option listed at the bottom of the menu called System Resources. Click on this option to display a window showing the system resources, expressed as a percentage. In Windows 95, you can click Start, Settings, Control Panel, and then System, then select the Performance tab to see this percentage.

Sometimes you might experience GPFs after you install a new application or piece of hardware. If you should begin encountering GPFs when you haven't seen any before, sit back and try to remember if there's anything new that you added to your computer or if you've changed the way you're doing things. If you can identify something new in your system, you can check the installation, and if necessary, reinstall the application or hardware and its drivers and see if the problem clears up.

Another strategy is to try to re-create the GPF by running the same applications that caused it in the first place. At this point, you can write down the GPF message, and then call the publisher or manufacturer of the suspect software or hardware to see if they might be able to help you clear up the problem.

Of course, if GPFs become unbearable, Windows may just have too many remnants from past installations and various applications, in which case your only real option is to reinstall Windows and all of your applications. This is a last resort. But before you go to this measure, be sure to read some of the tips in Appendix B on removing unneeded files. You can try to perform some file housecleaning first and see if this helps.

We may not like seeing those GPF messages in our Windows computing, but with a little caution and some troubleshooting, there's no reason that they have to bring our work to a stop.

Upgrade-Related Vendors

Associations

The Association of Shareware Professionals
545 Grover Rd.
Muskegon, MI 49442-9427
616-788-2765

Hardware Manufacturers

Acer America Corp.
2641 Orchard Pkwy.
San Jose, CA 95134
800-733-2237, 408-432-6200
www.acer.com
Hardware—Systems

ACS Computer Group
100 San Lucar Ct.
Sunnyvale, CA 94086
408-481-9988
Hardware—Multimedia

Adaptec
691 S. Milpitas Blvd.
Milpitas, CA 95035
408-945-8600
Hardware—Peripherals

Advance Integration Research, Inc.
2188 Del Franco St.
San Jose, CA 95131
800-866-1945, 408-428-0800
Hardware—Motherboards

Advance Micro Research, Inc.
245 Corporate Ct.
San Jose, CA 95131
408-456-9430
Hardware—Systems

Advanced Digital Systems
13909 Bettencourt St.
Cerritos, CA 90703
800-888-5244
Hardware—Multimedia

Advanced Gravis Computer
101-3750 N. Fraser Way
Burnaby, BC V5J 5E9 Canada
604-431-5020
www.gravis.com
Hardware—Entertainment

Advanced Micro Devices
25A Technology Dr,. Bldg. 2
Irvine, CA 92718
800-266-0488
www.amd.com
Hardware—CPUs

Aiwa America, Inc.
800 Corporate Dr.
Mahwah, NJ 07430
800-920-2673
Hardware—Backup

Allsop Computer Accessories
4201 Meridian
Bellingham, WA 98226
800-426-4303
Hardware—Mouse Pads, Glare Filters, Peripherals

Alps America
3553 N. First St.
San Jose, CA 95134
800-950-2577, 408-432-6000
Hardware—Printers, Pointing Devices, CD-ROM Drives

Altec Lansing Multimedia
Rts. 6 and 209
Milford, PA 18337-0277
717-296-2818
Hardware—Multimedia

American Megatrends, Inc.
6145-F Northbelt Pkwy.
Norcross, GA 30071
800-828-9264, 404-263-8181
www.megatrends.com
Hardware—Motherboards

Apple Computer
1 Infinite Loop
Cupertino, CA 95014
800-776-2333
www.apple.com
Hardware—Systems

AST Research
16215 Alton Pkwy.
Irvine, CA 92718
800-876-4278, 714-727-4141
www.bravo.ast.com
Hardware—Systems

ATI Technologies
33 Commerce Valley Dr. E
Thornhill, ON L3T 7N6 Canada
905-882-2600
www.atitech.com
Hardware—Video Cards

Aztech Labs, Inc.
47811 Warm Springs Blvd.
Fremont, CA 94539
510-623-8988
Hardware—Multimedia, CD-ROM Drives

Bose Corp.
The Mountain
Framingham, MA 01701
508-879-7330
Hardware—Speakers

Brother International Corp.
200 Cottontail La.
Sumerset, NJ 08875
909-356-8880
brother.com.jp/brother2e
Hardware—Printers

C. Itoh Electronics
2701 Dow Ave.
Tustin, CA 92680
800-877-1421
Hardware—Printers

Calcomp, Inc.
14555 N. 82nd St.
Scottsdale, AZ 85260
800-451-7568
www.calcomp.com
Hardware—Printers, Pointing Devices

Canon USA, Inc.
1 Canon Plaza
Lake Success, NY 11042
516-488-6700
www.usa.canon.com
Hardware—Printers

Cardinal Technologies
1827 Freedom Rd.
Lancaster, PA 17601
717-293-3000
Hardware—Modems

CH Products
970 Park Center Dr.
Vista, CA 92083
619-598-2518
Hardware—Entertainment

Chinon America Inc.
660 Maple Ave.
Torrance, CA 90503
800-441-0222, 310-441-0222
Hardware—Storage

Citizen America Corporation
2450 Broadway, #600
Santa Monica, CA 90411-4003
800-556-1234, 310-453-0614
Hardware—Printers

Colorado Memory Systems, Inc.
800 Taft Ave.
Loveland, CO 80537
303-669-8000
Hardware—Storage

Compaq Computer Corporation
20555 State Hwy. 249
Houston, TX 77070
800-231-0900
www.compaq.com
Hardware—Systems

Computer Peripherals, Inc.
667 Rancho Conejo Blvd.
Newbury Park, CA 91320
800-854-7600
Hardware—Modems

Conner Peripherals
3081 Zanker Rd.
San Jose, CA 95134
800-421-1879, 408-456-4500
www.conner.com
Hardware—Storage

Creative Labs
1901 McCGraphicshy Blvd.
Milpitas, CA 95035
408-428-6600
www.creativelabs.com
**Hardware—Multimedia Upgrade Kits, Multimedia,
Sound Cards**

Curtis by Rolodex
225 Secaucus Rd.
Secaucus, NJ 07094
201-422-0240
Hardware—Peripherals

Cyrix Corp.
P.O. Box 850118
Richardson, TX 75085-0118
800-848-2979
www.cyrix.com
Hardware—Chips

Dell Computer Corporation
9505 Arboretum Blvd.
Austin, TX 78759
800-426-5150, 512-338-4400
www.dell.com
Hardware—Systems

Diamond Multimedia Systems
2880 Junction Ave.
San Jose, CA 95134-1922
408-325-7000
www.diamondmm.com
Hardware—Video Cards, Multimedia Upgrade Kits

Digital Equipment Corp.
Digital Dr.
Merrimack, NH 03054
800-722-9332
Hardware—Systems

Eizo Corp.
23535 Telo Ave.
Torrance, CA 90505
310-325-5202
www.traveller.com/nanao/
Hardware—Monitors

Epson America, Inc.
20770 Madrona Ave.
Torrance, CA 90503
800-BUY-EPSON
Hardware—Printers, Scanners

Fujitsu America, Inc.
3545 North First St.
San Jose, CA 95134
800-642-7617, 408-432-1300
www.fujitsu.com
Hardware—Printers

Future Domain Corp.
2801 McGaw Ave.
Irvine, CA 92714-5835
714-253-0400
Hardware—Peripherals

Gateway 2000
610 Gateway Dr., N.
Sioux City, SD 57049
605-232-2000
www.gw2k.com
Hardware—Systems

Goldstar Technology, Inc.
1000 Sylvan Ave.
Englewood Cliff, NJ 07632
201-816-2000
www.goldstar.co.kr
Hardware—Monitors

Hard Drives International
1912 W. Fourth St.
Tempe, AZ 85281
800-766-3475
Hardware—Storage

Hauppauge Computer Works, Inc.
91 Cabot Ct.
Happauge, NY 11788-3706
800-443-6284, 516-434-1600
Hardware—Motherboards

Hayes Microcomputer Products, Inc.
5835 Peachtree Corners, E
Norcross, GA 30092
800-377-4377
www.hayes.com
Hardware—Modems, Software, Communications

Hercules Computer Technology, Inc.
3839 Spinnaker Ct.
Fremont, CA 94538
510-623-6030
www.hercules.com
Hardware—Video Cards

Hewlett Packard Co.
16399 W. Bernardo Dr.
San Diego, CA 92127
800-752-0990
www.hp.com
Hardware—Printers

Hitachi America, Ltd.
50 Prospect Ave.
Tarrytown, NY 10591-4698
800-448-2244
www.hitachipc.com
Hardware—Peripherals

IBM Corp.
Rt. 100, Box 100
Somers, NY 10589
800-IBM-3333
www.ibm.watson.com
Hardware—Systems

Intel Corp.
2200 Mission College Blvd.
Santa Clara, CA 95052
408-765-1703
Hardware—CPU

Iomega Corp.
1821 W. Iomega Way
Roy, UT 84067
801-778-1000
www.iomega.com
Hardware—Storage

Irwin Magnetic Systems, Inc.
2101 Commonwealth Blvd.
Ann Arbor, MI 48105
800-421-1879
Hardware—Storage

Kensington Microware, Ltd.
2855 Campus Dr.
San Mateo, CA 94403
800-535-4242, 415-572-2700
Hardware—Peripherals

Key Tronic Corp.
P.O. Box 14687
Spokane, WA 99214
509-928-8000
Hardware—Keyboards

Kingston Technology
17600 Newhope St.
Fountain Valley, CA 92708
714-435-2600
www.kingston.com
Hardware—Memory

Kyocera Electronics
100 Randolph Road
Sumerset, NJ 08875-6727
908-563-3400
Hardware—Printers

Logitech, Inc.
6505 Kaiser Dr.
Fremont, CA 94555
510-795-8500
Hardware—Peripherals Hardware, Pointing Devices

Matrox Graphics Inc.
1025 ST. Regis
Dorval, PQ H9P 2T4 Canada
514-685-2630
www.matrox.com
Hardware—Video Cards

Maxell Corp. of America
22-08 Rt. 208
Fair Lawn, NJ 07410
800-533-2836
Hardware—Storage

Maxtor
211 River Oaks Pkwy.
San Jose, CA 95134
408-432-1700
www.maxtor.com
Hardware—Storage

Media Vision
47900 Bayside Pkwy.
Fremont, CA 94538
510-770-8600
mediavis.com/mainmenu
Hardware—Multimedia Upgrade Kits

MicroClean, Inc.
2050 S. Tenth St.
San Jose, CA 95112
408-995-5062
Hardware—Peripherals

Micropolis Corporation
21211 Nordoff St.
Chatworth, CA 91311
800-395-3000, 818-709-3300
www.microp.com
Hardware—Storage

Minden Group
236 N. Santa Cruz Blvd., Ste. 237A
Los Gatos, CA 95030
408-399-6645
Hardware—Memory

Minolta
101 Williams Dr.
Ramsey, NJ 07446
201-825-4000
Hardware—Printers

Mitsuba Corporation
1925 Wright Ave.
La Verne, CA 91750
800-648-7822
Hardware—Systems

Mitsubishi Electronics America
5665 Plaza Dr.
Cypress, CA 90630
800-843-2515, 714-220-2500
www.mela-itg.com
Hardware—Monitors

Mitsumi Electronics Corp.
6210 N. Beltline Rd., Ste. 170
Irving, TX 75063
214-550-7300
Hardware—Peripherals, Storage

Mustek, Inc
1702 McGaw Ave.
Irvine, CA 92714
800-468-7835
www.mustek.com
Hardware—Scanners

NEC
475 Ellis St.
Mountain View, CA 94039
800-366-9782
www.nec.co.jp/index_e
Hardware—Monitors

Nokia Display Products
3000 Bridgeway Blvd.
Sausalito, CA 94965
415-331-6622
Hardware—Monitors

Number Nine Visual Technology Corp.
18 H Graphicswell Ave.
Lexington, MA 02173
800-GET-NINE
www.nine.com
Hardware—Video Cards

Okidata
532 Fellowship Rd.
Mt. Laurel, NJ 08054
800-654-3282, 609-273-0300
www.okidata.com
Hardware—Printers

Orchid Technology, Inc.
45365 North Port Loop W.
Fremont, CA 94538
800-767-2443, 510-683-0300
www.orchid.com
Hardware—Video Cards

Panasonic
Two Panasonic Way
Secaucus, NJ 07094
201-348-9090
Hardware—Printers Hardware, Scanners

Pinnacle Micro, Inc.
19 Technology
Irvine, CA 92718
800-553-7070
www.pinnaclemicro.com
Hardware—Storage

Pioneer New Media Technologies, Inc.
2265 E. 220th St.
Long Beach, CA 90810
800-444-6784
Hardware—Storage

Plextor
4255 Burton Dr.
Santa Clara, CA 95054
408-980-1838
Hardware—Storage

Plustek USA, Inc.
1362 Bordeaux Dr.
Sunnyvale, CA 94089
408-745-7111
Hardware—Scanners

Practical Peripherals Inc.
31245 La Baya Dr.
Westlake Village, CA 91362
800-442-4774
www.practinet.com
Hardware—Modems

Princeton Technology, Inc.
2552 White Rd.
Irvine, CA 92714
714-851-7776
Hardware—Memory

Prometheus Products, Inc.
9524 S.W. Tualatin-Sherwood Rd.
Tualatin, OR 97062
503-452-0948
Hardware—Modems

Quickshot Technology, Inc.
950 Yosemite Dr.
Milpitas, CA 95035
408-263-4163
Hardware—Entertainment

Ricoh
547 Perimeter Center, Ste. 550
Atlanta, GA 30350
770-395-9800
Hardware—Printers

Samsung Electronics America
105 Challenger Rd.
Ridgefield Park, NJ 07660
201-229-4000
Hardware—Monitors, Printers

Samtron
18600 Broadwick St.
Rancho Dominguez, CA 90220
310-537-7000
Hardware—Monitors

Sceptre Technologies, Inc.
16800 E. Gale Ave.
City of Industry, CA 91745
818-369-3698
Hardware—Monitors

Seagate Technology
920 Disc Dr.
Scotts Valley, CA 95066
408-438-6550
www.seagate.com
Hardware—Storage

Sharp Electronics Corp.
Sharp Plaza
Mahwah, NJ 07430
201-529-8200
Hardware—Printers

SimmSaver Technology, Inc.
228 North Pennsylvania
Wichita, KS 69083
316-264-2244
Hardware—Memory

Sony Corp.
1 Sony Dr.
Park Ridge, NJ 07645
201-930-1000
www.sony.com
Hardware—Monitors, Systems

Star Micronics America
70 Ethel Rd., W
Piscataway, NJ 08854
908-572-5550
www.smc.com
Hardware—Printers

Summagraphics Corporation
60 Silvermine Road
Seymour, CT 06483
800-729-7866
www.sumagraphics.com
Hardware—Pointing Devices

Supra Corp.
312 S.E. Stonemill Dr., Ste. 150
Vancouver, WA 98684
360-604-1481
www.supra.com
Hardware—Modems

SyQuest Technology
47071 Bayside Pky.
Fremont, CA 94538
510-226-4137
www.syquest.com
Hardware—Storage

Teac America
7733 Telegraph Rd.
Montebello, CA 90640
213-726-0303
Hardware—Storage

Tektronix Inc.
26600 S.W. Parkway Ave.
Wilsonville, OR 97070
800-835-6100
Hardware—Printers

Toshiba
9740 Irvine Blvd.
Irvine, CA 92718
714-583-3000
Hardware—Printers

U.S. Robotics, Inc.
8100 N. McCormick Blvd.
Skokie, IL 60076-2920
800-342-5877
www.usr.com
Hardware—Modems

Verbatim Corp.
1200 W.T. Harris Blvd.
Charlotte, NC 28262
704-547-6500
Hardware—Storage

ViewSonic Corp.
20480 Business Pkwy.
Walnut, CA 91789
909-869-7976
www.viewsonic.com
Hardware—Monitors

Viking Components
11 Columbia
Laguna Hills, CA 92656
714-643-7255
Hardware—Memory

Wacom Technology Corp.
501 S.E. Columbiz Shores Blvd. , Ste. 300
Vancouver, WA 98661
360-750-8882
Hardware—Pointing Devices

Western Digital
8105 Irvine Center Dr.
Costa Mesa, CA 92718
714-932-5000
www.wdc.com
Hardware—Storage

Wyse Technology
3471 N. First St.
San Jose, CA 95134
408-473-1200
Hardware—Monitors

Yamaha Systems Technology, Inc.
100 Century Center Court
San Jose, CA 95112
408-467-2300
Hardware—Speakers

Zoom Telephonics, Inc.
207 South St.
Boston, MA 02111
617-423-1072
www.zoomtel.com
Hardware—Modems

Mail Order Companies

ABC Computer Technologies, Inc.
1295 Johnson Dr.
City of Industry, CA 91745
800-876-8088
www.abscomputers.com
Hardware—Systems

APZ Computers
800-983-8889
Hardware—Systems, Peripherals

CDW Computer Centers, Inc.
1020 E. Lake Cook Rd.
Buffalo Grove, IL 60089
800-726-4239
www.cdw.com
Hardware—Peripherals, Software, Memory

CTX
20470 Walnut Dr.
Walnut, CA 91789
909-595-6293
www.ctxintl.com
Hardware—Systems

Complete Systems -N- More
1740 N. Greenville Ave.
Richardson, TX 75081
800-705-9596, 972-705-9668
Hardware—Peripherals, Systems

Computability
P.O. Box 17882
Milwaukee, WI 53217
800-741-7752
www.computability.com
Hardware—Peripherals, Software

Computer Discount Warehouse
1020 E. Lake Cook Rd.
Buffalo Grove, IL 60089
708-465-6000
Hardware—Systems, Peripherals, Software

Computer Gate International
408-730-0673
www.computergate.com
Hardware—Peripherals

CyberMax Computer, Inc.
133 N. 5th St.
Allentown, PA 18102
899-443-9868
www.cybmax.com
Hardware—Systems

Global Computer Supplies
11 Harbor Park Drive
Port Washington, NY 11050
800-829-0785
Hardware—Systems, Peripherals

Hi-Tech USA
15c62 Centre Pointe Dr.
Milpitas, CA 95035
800-831-2888
Hardware—Peripherals

Insight
800-INSIGHT
www.insight.com
Hardware—Peripherals

Kenosha Computer Center
2133 91st St.
Kenosha, WI 53143
800-255-2989
www.kcc-online.com
Hardware—Peripherals

Memory 4 Less
2622 W. Lincoln, Ste. 104
Anaheim, CA 92801
888-821-3354
Hardware—Memory

Memory Express
800-877-8188
Hardware—Memory

Micro Mall Direct
16812 Hale Ave.
Irvine, CA 92606
800-347-1273
Hardware—Peripherals

Micro X-Press
800-875-9737
www.microxpress.com
Hardware—Systems, Peripherals

Micron Electronics
900 Karcher Road
Nampa, ID 83687
800-214-6674
www.mei.micron
Hardware—Systems

MicroWareHouse
1720 Oak St.
Lakewood, NJ 08701-3014
800-243-5622
Hardware—Peripherals

Midland ComputerGraphics
5699 W. Howard
Niles, IL 60714
800-407-0700
www.midlandcmGraphics.com
Hardware—Peripherals

Midwest Computer Works
600 Bunker Ct.
Vernon Hills, IL 60061
800-869-6757
Hardware—Systems, Peripherals

Midwest Memory Works
600 Bunker Ct.
Vernon Hills, IL 60061
800-770-4341
www.mcworks.com
Hardware—Memory

Midwest Micro
800-728-8590
www.mwmicro.com
Hardware—Peripherals

NECX Direct
800-961-9208
www.necx.com
Hardware—Peripherals

O.S. Computers
58 Second St., 5th Floor
San Francisco, CA 94105
800-938-6722
Hardware—Peripherals

PC Mall
800-681-3282
Hardware—Peripherals

PCs Compleat
PC Mall
800-598-5601
www.pcscompleat.com
Hardware—Systems, Peripherals

The PC Zone
800-252-0286
www.pczone.com
Hardware—Systems, Peripherals

Programmer's Paradise, Inc.
1163 Shrewsbury Ave.
Shrewsbury, NJ 07702
908-389-8950
Software—Developers' Tools

Publishing Perfection
800-716-5000
Hardware—Peripherals

Quantex
800-836-0566
www.quantex.com
Hardware—Systems

Royal Computer
1208 John Reed Ct.
Industry, CA 91745
800-486-0008
Hardware—Systems

Storage USA
101 Reighard Ave.
Williamsport, PA 17701
800-538-DISK, 717-327-9200
Hardware—Storage

TC Computers
5005 Bloomfield St.
Jefferson, LA 70121
800-723-8282
www.tccomputers.com
Hardware—Systems

Treasure Chest Peripherals
800-677-9781, 504-733-2527
Hardware—Motherboards, Peripherals

Tri State Computer
650 6th Ave.
New York, NY 10011
800-433-5199, 212-633-2530
Hardware—Peripherals

USA Flex, Inc.
444 Scott Dr.
Bloomingdale, IL 60108
800-678-4394, 630-582-6206
Hardware—Systems, Peripherals

Worldwide Technologies
437 Chestnut St.
Philadelphia, PA 19106
800-457-6937
www.worldwidetechnolgies.com
Hardware—Memory, Motherboards, Storage

Retail

CompUSA
14951 N. Dallas Pkwy.
Dallas, TX 75240
214-982-4451
Hardware—Systems, Peripherals, Software

MegaHaus Hard Drives
2201 Pine Drive
Dickinson, TX 77539
800-786-1185, 713-534-3919
Hardware—Storage

Software Publishers

Activision, Inc.
11601 Wilshire Blvd. Ste. 1000
Los Angeles, CA 90025
516-431-0589
www.activision.com
Software—Entertainment

Adobe Systems Inc.
1585 Charleston Rd.
Mountain View, CA 94043
415-961-4400
www.adobe.com
Software—Graphics/DTP

Alpha Software Corp.
1 North Avenue
Burlington, MA 01803
800-451-1018, 617-272-3680
Software—Database

Apogee Software, Ltd.
P.O. Box 496389
Garland, TX 75049
800-276-4331
www.swcbbs.com/apogee/agogee.htm
Software—Entertainment

Arabesque Software, Inc.
P.O. Box 3098
Bellevue, WA 98009-3098
800-457-4272
Software—Business

Asymetrix Corp.
110 110th Ave. NE Ste. 700
Bellevue, WA 98004
206-637-1673
www.asymetrix.com
Software—Multimedia

Autodesk, Inc.
111 McInnis Pkwy.
San Rafael, CA 94903
800-445-5415, 415-517-5000
www.autodesk.com
Software—Technical

Avalan Technology
7 October Hill Rd.
Holliston, MA 01746
800-441-2281
www.avalan.com/~avalan
Software—Communications

Award Software International
777 E. Middlefield Rd.
Mountain View, CA 944043
415-968-4433
Software—Communications

Berkeley Systems, Inc.
2095 Rose St.
Berkeley, CA 94709
510-540-5535
www.berksys.com
Software—Entertainment

Borland International
100 Borland Way
Scotts Valley, CA 95066
408-431-1000
www.borland.com
Developers' Software

Broderbund Software
500 Redwood Blvd.
Novato, CA 94948-6121
415-382-4400
Software—Educational, Entertainment

Caere Corp.
100 Cooper Ct.
Los Gatos, CA 95030
408-395-7000
www.caere.com
Software—Business

Caligari Corp.
1955 Landings Dr.
Mountain View, CA 94043
800-351-7620
Software—Graphics/DTP

Claris Corporation
5201 Patrick Henry Dr.
Box 58168, Santa Clara, CA 95052
800-544-8554
www.claris.com
Software—Business

Computer Associates International, Inc.
1 Computer Associates Plaza
Islandia, NY 11788-7000
800-225-5224
www.cai.com
Software—Business

Corel Corp.
1600 Carling Ave.
Ottawa, ON K1Z 8R7 Canada
613-728-8200
www.corel.com
**Software—Graphics/DTP, Educational,
Entertainment, Business**

DacEasy, Inc.
17950 Preston Rd., Ste. 800
Dallas, TX 75252
800-322-3279
www.daceasy.com
Software—Accounting

Datastorm Technologies, Inc.
3212 Lemone Blvd.
Columbia, MO 65201
800-474-1547, 314-443-3282
www.datastorm.com
Software—Modem

DataViz
55 Corporate Dr.
Trumbull, CT 06611
800-733-0030
www.dataviz.com
Software—Utilities

Davidson & Associates, Inc.
P.O. Box 2961
Torrance, CA 90509
800-545-7677
www.davd.com
Software—Educational, Entertainment

DeLorme Mapping
P.O. Box 298, Lower Main St.
Freeport, ME 04032
207-865-4171
Software—Mapping

Discovery Channel Multimedia
7700 Wisonson Ave
Bethesda, MD 20814
301-986-0444
Software—Educational, Multimedia

Disney Interactive
500 South Buena Vista St.
Burbank, CA 91521-8404
800441-1243
www.disney.com
Software—Entertainment, Educational

Dragon Systems, Inc.
320 Nevada St.
Newton, MA 02160
617-965-5200
Software—Voice Recognition

EdMark Corp.
6727 185th Ave. NE
Redmond, WA 98052
206-556-8400
Software—Educational

Franklin Quest Co.
2550 S. Decker Lake Blvd.
Salt Lake City, UT 84119
801-975-9992
Software—Business

Global Village Communication
1144 E. Arques Ave.
Sunnyvale, CA 94086
408-523-1000
www.globalcenter.net
Software—Communications

Gold Disk, Inc.
P.O. Box 789, Streetsville
Mississauga, ON L5M 2C2 Canada
Software—Multimedia

GoldMine Software
17383 Sunset Blvd.
Pacific Palisades, CA 90272
310-454-6800
Software—Business

Graphix Zone
42 Corporate Pk., Ste. 200
Irvine, CA 92714
714-883-3838
Software—Entertainment

Great Plains Software
1701 S.W. 38th St.
Fargo, ND 58103
800-456-0025
www.gps.com
Software—Accounting

Hilgraeve
111 Conant Ave., Ste A
Monroe, MI 48161
313-243-0576
Software—Communications

Individual Software
5870 Stoneridge Drive #1
Pleasonton, CA 94560
510-734-6767
Software—Business

Interplay Productions
17922 Fitch Ave.
Irvine, CA 92714
714-553-6655
www.interplay.com
Software—Entertainment

Intuit
P.O. Box 3014
Menlo Park, CA 94026
800-624-8742
www.intuit.com
Software—Home, Accounting

Janna Systems, Inc.
3080 Yonge St. Ste. 6060
Toronto, ON M4N 3N1 Canada
800-268-6107
Software—Business

Jian
1975 W. El Camino Real, Ste. 301
Mountain View, CA 94040
415-254-5600
Software—Business

Kurzweil Technology Group
1432 Main St.
Waltham, MA 02154
617-890-2929
Software—Voice Recognition

Learning Company
314 Erin Dr.
Knoxville, TN 37919
615-558-8270
Software—Educational

Living Books
160 Pacific Avenue. Mall, Ste. 201
San Francisco, CA 94111
415-352-5200
Software—Educational

Lotus Development Corp.
55 Cambridge Pky.
Cambridge, MA 02142
617-577-8500
www.lotus.com
Software—Business

LucasArts Entertainment Co.
P.O. Box 9367
Canoga Park, CA 91309-0367
800-98-LUCAS
http://www.lucasarts.com
Software—Entertainment

Macromedia
600 Townsend St.
San Francisco, CA 94103
415-252-2000
Software—Multimedia

MapInfo
1 Global View
Troy, NY 12180
518-285-6000
Software—Business

MapLinx Corp.
5720 LBJ Fwy., Ste. 180
Dallas, TX 75240
214-231-1400
Software—Business

Maxis
2 Theatre Square
Orinda, CA 94563-3346
510-254-9700
Software—Entertainment

McAfee Associates
4423 Cheney St.
Santa Clara, CA 95054
800-332-9966, 408-988-3832
www.mcafee.com
Software—Utilities

MECA Software
56677 Sunset Ave.
Yucca Valley, CA 92284
619-365-7686
Software—Educational

MetaTools Digital Theater
6303 Carpinteria Ave.
Carpinteria, CA 93013
805-566-6200
Software—Graphics/DTP

Micro Logic Corporation
P.O. Box 70
Hackensack, NJ 07602
800-342-5930
Software—Business

Microcom, Inc.
500 River Ridge Dr.
Norwood, MA 02062
800-822-8224, 617-822-8224
Software—Communications, Hardware, Modems

Micrografx
1303 E. Araphao Rd.
Richardson, TX 75081
800-371-7783
www.micrografx.com
Software—Graphics/DTP

Microsoft Corp.
1 Microsoft Way
Redmond, WA 98052
206-882-8080
Software—Business, Operating System, Developers' Tools, Entertainment, Education

Microtax Software
4655 Cass St., #214
San Diego, CA 92109
800-366-4170
Software—Educational

Mindscape, Inc.
88 Rowland Way
Novato, CA 94945
415-897-9900
Software—Entertainment, Educational

Multicom Publishing
100 First St., Ste. 2420
San Francisco, CA 94105
415-777-5300
Software—Educational, Entertainment

Mustang Software, Inc.
6200 Lake Ming Rd.
Bakersfield, CA 93306
805-873-2500
www.mustang.com
Software—Communications

Netscape
501 E. Middlefield Rd.
Mountain View, CA 94043
415-254-1900
Software—Internet

Nolo Press, Inc.
950 Parker St., #4
Berkeley, CA 94704
510-548-5902
Software—Business

Now Software
921 S.W. Washington St., Ste. 500
Portland, OR 97205
503-274-2810
Software—Business

Palo Alto Software, Inc.
144 E. 14th, #8
Eugene, OR 97401
503-683-6162
Software—Business

Parsons Technology, Inc.
1 Parsons Dr.
Hiawatha, IA 52233-0100
800-223-6925
www.parsonstech.com
Software—Home

Peachtree Software, Inc.
1505 Pavilion Pl.
Norcross, GA 30093
404-564-5700
www.peach.com
Software—Accounting

PKWare, Inc.
9025 N. Deerwood Dr.
Brown Deer, WI 53226
414-354-8699
Software—Utilities

Pro CD Inc.
222 Rosewood Dr.
Danvers, MA 01923
508-750-0000
Software—Business

Quark, Inc.
300 S. Jackson, #100
Denver, CO 80209
303-934-2211
www.quark.com
Software—Graphics/DTP

Quarterdeck Corp.
13160 Mindanao Way, Fl. 3
Marina Del Rey, CA 90292-9705
310-309-3700
Software—Utilities

Recognita Corp. of America
1156 Aster Ave., Ste. F
Sunnyvale, CA 94086
408-241-5772
Software—Business

7th Level —Software Publisher
1110 E. Collins Blvd. Ste. 122
Richardson, TX 75081
214-498-8100
www.7thlevel.com
Software—Entertainment

Sierra On-Line
P.O. Box 85006
Bellevue, WA 98015-8506
800-757-7707, 408-644-2018
www.sierra.com
Software—Educational, Entertainment

Sirius Publishing, Inc.
7320 E. Butherus Dr., Ste. 100
Scottsdale, AZ 85260
602-951-3288
Software—Entertainment

Smith Micro Software, Inc.
51 Columbia
Aliso Viejo, CA 92656
714-362-5800
Software—Communications

SoftKey International
1121 S. Orem Blvd.
Orem, UT 84058
801-221-9400
Software—Education, Entertainment, Business, Reference

Software Publishing Corp.
P.O. Box 54983
Santa Clara, CA 95056-0983
408-986-8000
Software—Business, Multimedia

Sonic Foundry
100 S. Baldwin, Ste. 204
Madison, WI 53703
608-256-3133
Software—Multimedia

Starfish Software
1700 Green Hills Rd.
Scotts Valley, CA 95066
408-461-5899
Software—Business

Symantec Corp.
10201 Torre Ave.
Cupertino, CA 95014
408-253-9600
www.symantec.com
Software—Utilities, Communications

Timeslips Corp.
17950 Preston Rd., Ste. 800
Dallas, TX 75252
800-285-0999
Software—Business

Ulead Systems, Inc.
970 W. 190th St., Ste. 520
Torrance, CA 90502
310-523-9393
Software—Graphics/DTP

Vertisoft Systems, Inc.
600 Montgomery, 4th Floor
San Francisco, CA 94188
800-548-8115
Software—Utilities

01 Communique Laboratory
1450 Meyerside Dr.
Mississauga, ON L5T 2N5 Canada
905-795-2888
Software—Business, Communications

Online Services

America Online
8619 Westwood Ctr. Dr.
Vienna, VA 22182
703-448-8700

CompuServe Inc.
5000 Arlington Centre Blvd.
Columbus, OH 43220
614-457-8600

Netcom On-Line Communications Services
3031 Tisch Way
San Jose, CA 95128
800-353-6600

Prodigy Services Co.
445 Hamilton Ave.
White Plains, NY 10601
800-Prodigy

Upgrade Vendors by Category

This appendix provides a listing of hardware manufacturers, software publishers, and retailers broken down by category. You can use this list when you're searching for a manufacturer of a particular component, need to find a place to order or buy a certain part or program, or want to see what software is available in a category. When you locate a company in this listing, please refer to Appendix D, "Upgrade-Related Vendors," for the name, address, telephone number, and Web URL to contact it.

BIOS
Award Software International

Glare Filters
Allsop Computer Accessories

Mouse Pads
Allsop Computer Accessories

Cleaning
MicroClean, Inc.

CD-ROM Drives

ALPS

Aztech Labs, Inc.

Creative Labs

Mitsumi

NEC

Plextor

Sony

Toshiba

CPUs

Advanced Micro Devices

Cyrix Corp.

Intel Corp.

Entertainment Hardware

Advanced Gravis Computer

CH Products

Quickshot Technology, Inc.

Keyboards

Key Tronic Corp.

Memory

Manufacturers

Kingston Technology

Princeton Technology, Inc.

SimmSaver Technology, Inc.

Viking Components

Mail Order

Hi-Tech USA

Kenosha Computer Center

Memory Express

Memory 4 Less

Midwest Memory Works

Micro Mall Direct
PCs Compleat
Worldwide Technologies

Modems

Manufacturer

Hayes Microcomputer Products, Inc.
Cardinal Technologies
Computer Peripherals, Inc.
Practical Peripherals Inc.
Prometheus Products, Inc.
Supra Corp.
US Robotics, Inc.
Zoom Telephonics, Inc.

Mail Order

Hi-Tech USA
Kenosha Computer Center
PCs Compleat

Monitors

Manufacturers

Eizo Corp.
Goldstar Technology, Inc.
Mitsubishi Electronics America
NEC
Nokia Display Products
Samsung Electronics America
Samtron
Sceptre Technologies, Inc.
Sony Corp.
ViewSonic Corp.
Wyse Technology

Mail Order

PCs Compleat

Motherboards

Manufacturers

    Advance Integration Research, Inc.

    American Megatrends, Inc.

    Hauppauge Computer Works, Inc.

Mail Order

    Hi-Tech USA

    Treasure Chest Peripherals

    Worldwide Technologies

Multimedia

Hardware Manufacturers

    ACS Computer Group

    Advanced Digital Systems

    Altec Lansing Multimedia

    Aztech Labs, Inc.

    Creative Labs

    Diamond Multimedia Systems

    Media Vision

Peripherals

Manufacturers

    Adaptec

    Curtis by Rolodex

    Future Domain Corp.

    Hewlett Packard

    Hitachi America, Ltd.

    Iomega Corp.

    Kensington Microware, Ltd.

    Logitech, Inc.

    Mitsumi Electronics Corp.

Mail Order

    APZ Computers

    CDW Computer Centers, Inc.

    Complete Systems-N-More

Computability
Computer Discount Warehouse
Computer Gate
Global Computer Supplies
Insight
Kenosha Computer Center
MicroWareHouse
Micro X-Press
Midland Computermart
Midwest Computer Works
Midwest Micro
NECX Direct
O.S. Computers
PC Mall
The PC Zone
Publishing Perfection
Treasure Chest Peripherals
Tri State Computer
USA Flex, Inc.

Pointing Devices

Manufacturers
ALPS
Logitech, Inc.
Summagraphics Corporation
Wacom Technology Corp.

Printers

Manufacturers
Alps America
Brother International Corp.
C. Itoh Electronics

Calcomp, Inc.
Canon USA, Inc.
Citizen America Corp.
Epson America, Inc.
Fujitsu America, Inc.
Hewlett Packard Co.
Kyocera Electronics
Minolta
Okidata
Panasonic
Ricoh
Samsung Electronics America
Sharp
Star Micronics America
Tektronics
Toshiba

Scanners

Manufacturers
Epson America, Inc.
Mustek, Inc.
Panasonic
Plustek USA, Inc.
Mail Order
Kenosha Computer Center

Speakers

Manufacturers
Bose Corp.
Yamaha

Storage

Manufacturers
Chinon America Inc.
Colorado Memory Systems, Inc.

Conner Peripherals
Hard Drives International
Iomega
Irwin Magnetic Systems, Inc.
Maxell Corp. of America
Maxtor
Micropolis Corporation
Mitsumi Electronics Corp.
Pinnacle Micro, Inc.
Pioneer New Media Technologies, Inc.
Plextor
Seagate Technology
SyQuest Technology
Teac America
Verbatim Corp.
Western Digital
Mail Order
MegaHaus Hard Drives
Storage USA

Systems

Manufacturers
AST Research
Acer America Corp.
Advance Micro Research, Inc.
Apple Computer
Compaq Computer Corporation
Dell Computer Corporation
Digital Equipment Corp.
Gateway 2000
IBM Corp.
Mitsuba Corporation
Sony Corp.

Mail Order
    ABC Computer Technologies, Inc.
    APZ Computers
    CTX
    Complete Systems -N- More
    Computer Discount Warehouse
    CyberMax Computer, Inc.
    Global Computer Supplies
    Micro X-Press
    Micron Electronics
    Midwest Computer Works
    The PC Zone
    PCs Compleat
    Quantex
    Royal Computer
    TC Computers
    USA Flex, Inc.

Video Cards

Manufacturers
    ATI Technologies
    Diamond Multimedia Systems
    Hercules Computer Technology, Inc.
    Matrox Graphics Inc.
    Number Nine Visual Technology Corp.
    Orchid Technology, Inc.

Internet Service Providers

Internet Software
Microsoft
Netcom On-Line Communications Services
Netscape

Online Services

CompuServe Inc.

America Online

Juno Online Services (e-mail only)

Prodigy Services Co.

Software—Accounting

DacEasy, Inc.

Great Plains Software

Intuit

Peachtree Software, Inc.

Software—Business

Adobe Systems, Inc.

Alpha Software Corp.

Arabesque Software, Inc.

Claris Corporation

Computer Associates International, Inc.

Corel Corp.

Franklin Quest Co.

GoldMine Software

Individual Software

Janna Systems, Inc.

Jian

Lotus Development Corp.

MapInfo

MapLinx Corp.

Micro Logic Corporation

Microsoft Corp.

Now Software

Pro CD Inc.

Recognita Corp. of America

Software Publishing Corp.

Starfish Software
Timeslips Corp.
Palo Alto Software, Inc.

Software—CAD

Autodesk, Inc.

Software—Communications

O1 Communique Laboratory
Avalan Technology
Datastorm Technologies, Inc.
Global Village Communication
Hilgraeve
Microcom, Inc.
Mustang Software, Inc.
Smith Micro Software, Inc.
Symantec Corp.

Software—Developers' Tools

Publishers
      Borland International
      Microsoft Corporation
Mail Order
      Programmer's Paradise, Inc.

Software—Educational

Broderbund Software
Corel Corp.
Davidson & Associates, Inc.
Discovery Channel Multimedia
Disney Interactive
EdMark Corp.
Learning Company
MECA Software
Microsoft Corp.

Microtax Software
Mindscape, Inc.
Multicom Publishing
Sierra On-Line
SoftKey International

Software—Entertainment

Activision, Inc.
Apogee Software, Ltd.
Berkeley Systems, Inc.
Broderbund Software
Disney Interactive
Graphix Zone
Interplay Productions
LucasArts Entertainment
Maxis
Microsoft Corp.
Mindscape, Inc.
Multicom Publishing
7th Level
Sierra On-Line
Sirius Publishing, Inc.
SoftKey

Software—Graphics/DTP

Adobe Systems Inc.
Caligari Corp.
Corel Corp.
MetaTools Digital Theater
Micrografx
Microsoft
Quark, Inc.
Ulead Systems, Inc.

Software—Home Finances

Intuit

Parsons Technology, Inc.

Software—Mapping

DeLorme Mapping

MapInfo

MapLynx

Software—Multimedia Development

Asymetrix Corp.

Gold Disk, Inc.

Macromedia

Sonic Foundry

Software—Utilities

DataViz

McAfee Associates

PKWare, Inc.

Quarterdeck Corp.

Seagate (Arcada)

Symantec Corp.

Vertisoft Systems, Inc.

Software—Voice Recognition

Dragon Systems, Inc.

Kurzweil Technology Group

Glossary

AT—An IBM computer that featured the 80286 processor and supplanted the original IBM PC and XT computers.

Autoexec.bat—A DOS file that executes a series of commands each time you turn on and boot your PC.

Average Access Time—The average amount of time that it takes for a hard drive's heads (the devices that read and write information to the drive) to move to the different tracks on a disk.

Average Seek Time—The average amount of time it takes for a hard drive's read/write head to move between two adjacent tracks.

Backup—A duplicate copy of a file or disk. This may be stored on a different medium such as tape.

Baud—A rate of data transmission that is approximately 1 bit per second.

BIOS—Internal built-in software that determines the compatibility of your system. BIOS stands for Basic Input Output System.

BPS—The amount of information bits that a modem can send and receive in a second. The more bits it can send, the better. BPS stands for bits per second.

Bus—Internal data highways between key computer components that define how fast data may travel. The larger or wider the bus, the more data that can pass.

Cache—A memory system that works closely with the processor to read ahead and hold data so that it's immediately available—thus speeding up the performance of your system.

CD-ROM drive—A device much like the one on your stereo that plays music CDs, but reads CDs that hold computer data. In many ways, a CD-ROM drive has the same basic function as a floppy drive, but runs CD-ROMs instead.

CGA—An older industry standard for computer graphics that could show 4 colors in a resolution of 320x200 pixels. CGA stands for Color Graphics Array.

Clone—A computer that works and responds just like any IBM computer, but is not manufactured by IBM. *See* IBM Compatible.

Cluster—Units that a computer uses to store information on a hard drive.

CMOS—A medium that stores data. As it relates to a PC, CMOS stores system information that defines some of the hardware and is also referred to as the BIOS. CMOS stands for complementary metal-oxide semiconductor.

Config.sys—A DOS file that configures the PC each time it's booted.

CPU—The main processor or chip in your PC. Sometimes, people use CPU to refer to your main PC case. CPU stands for Central Processing Unit.

Data Transfer Rate—A parameter that tells you how fast data can move from the hard drive to the CPU.

Defragger—A software program that rearranges and organizes a hard drive's clusters so a drive can read them as quickly as possible.

DMA—A circuit that transfers data between a device and memory. DMA stands for Direct Memory Access.

DOS—The operating system of the IBM PC and compatibles. This is a text-based operating system that makes users type in commands to perform basic system functions. DOS stands for Disk Operating System.

DOS boot disk—A floppy disk that contains the necessary information to boot, or start, a computer.

Dot pitch—The size of the pixel or dot that a monitor displays.

DRAM—A memory chip that must have power applied to it periodically to store data.

Driver—A set of instructions that tell software how to work with an external device, such as a printer.

EGA—An older industry standard for computer graphics that could display up to 16 colors in a resolution of 640x250 pixels. EGA stands for Enhanced Graphics Array.

EIDE—A hard drive standard that supports large drives, tape drives, and CD-ROM drives, and transfers data at a higher rate than IDE. EIDE stands for Enhanced IDE.

EISA—A bus standard. EISA stands for Extended Industry Standard Architecture.

E-mail—A means to communicate through computers that's similar to writing a letter or fax, but you don't send any paper. The message appears electronically on the recipient's computer screen.

Expanded memory—Additional memory beyond 640K RAM that may be used by applications that specifically support it.

Expansion cards—Specialized computer boards that let you add new functions to your computer. Some expansion cards are essential to a computer's operation—like the board to control your hard and floppy drives, or a video card that sends video to your monitor. Other expansion cards include internal modems and sound cards.

Expansion slot—A slot in your PC that accepts an expansion board so it may connect to the motherboard.

Extended memory—Memory beyond 1MB that a 386 or higher processor can access and use.

FAT—Part of a DOS disk that stores information on the location of files and available space. FAT stands for File Allocation Table.

File—The unit in which data is stored on a PC. Data files can contain any type of information that includes graphics, text, or programs.

File Allocation Table—A part of a DOS disk that stores information on the locations of files and available space. Also known as the FAT.

Format—A process where the PC prepares a disk to receive and store data.

Hard drive—An internal disk medium that acts as your computer's file cabinet to stores application (software) and data.

IBM compatible—Computers that act like IBM computers. Also known as a "clone."

IDE—A hard drive standard. IDE stands for Integrated Drive Electronics.

Interlace Monitor—A monitor that draws each screen in a way that results in a slight flicker.

IRQ—A parameter that connects hardware devices and a system's interrupt controller. IRQ stands for Interrupt ReQuest.

Jumpers—Board switches that let you apply settings and configure boards.

Kilobyte—1,024 bytes. Also referred to as KB or K.

Math coprocessor—A special chip that crunches numbers. If you're working with lots of mathematical functions—spreadsheets, for example—a math coprocessor will speed up your performance. Also referred to as a numeric coprocessor.

MCA—A bus standard created by IBM. MCA stands for MicroChannel Architecture.

MDA—An older display standard that only displays text in a single color. MDA stands for Monochrome Display Adaptor.

Meg—1,024 K bytes. Also referred to as MB.

Megahertz—1 million cycles per second. Also referred to as MH.

Memory—Your computer's workspace, where it loads applications and processes data.

MH—1 million cycles per second. Stands for megahertz.

Modem—A device that lets a PC talk with another PC or computer over telephone lines. A modem converts signals from your PC into a form that can be sent across a telephone line. At the other end of the phone line, a modem converts the signal back to its original form so that a computer can read and use the information. Modem stands for *mo*dulator/*dem*odulator.

Motherboard—A PC's main printed circuit board that holds the CPU, expansion cards, and memory.

MPEG—A compression standard for displaying video on a PC.

Multimedia—The convergence of sound, text, video, and graphics in a computer application.

Multimedia Upgrade Kit—Kits that include everything that you need to upgrade your computer to handle multimedia. These kits typically include a CD-ROM drive, sound board, speakers, and some software.

Nanosecond—One billionth of a second.

Non-interlaced Monitor—A non-interlaced monitor draws data to the screen in such as way that it reduces flicker.

Numeric coprocessor—A special chip that crunches numbers. If you're working with lots of mathematical functions—spreadsheets, for example—a numeric coprocessor will speed up your performance. Also referred to as a math coprocessor.

Operating system—A specialized program that lets a computer perform file, disk, and memory tasks, and accepts input from a mouse and keyboard.

OS/2—An operating system originally developed by Microsoft and IBM that was introduced after DOS. IBM continues to support and sell OS/2.

OS/2 Warp—A graphical operating system that was introduced by IBM.

Parallel port—Known also as LPT1 and LPT2, parallel ports are used most for connecting with a printer.

Pixel—The smallest unit or dot of color that a computer monitor displays.

Power supply—An electrical device in a PC that takes household current and prepares it for use by the computer.

Processor—The chip at the center of your computer's operations that controls everything the system does. The processor is what you're referring to when you call a computer a 386, 486, or Pentium. Also referred to as the CPU.

RAM—The memory in your computer where applications and data are loaded so the computer may work with them. RAM stands for Random Access Memory.

Refresh rate—Indicates how often a video card redraws the picture on your screen. The slower the rate, the more chance that you'll see in-between flicker.

Resolution—The number of physical dots on a computer screen. The more dots that appear, the higher the resolution, and the better the image looks.

RLL—An older hard drive standard. RLL stands for Run-Length Limited procedure.

ROM—Permanent memory that stores information. ROM stands for Read Only Memory.

RS-232—The PC's serial interface that connects with a mouse and external modem, and transfers data.

Sampling rate—Refers to how often your sound card samples or records sounds. The more times a sound card samples a sound, the higher the quality of the recording.

SCSI—A popular standard for connecting peripherals such as hard drives and CD-ROM drives. SCSI stands for Small Computer System Interface.

Sector—A portion of a disk where the computer can store data.

SIMM—A standard arrangement of memory that may be plugged into motherboards. SIMM stands for Single In-line Memory Module.

Software—Computer programs or applications that run on a computer.

Sound card—An expansion board that makes it possible for your PC to play sounds and music.

Utilities—Programs that assist you in diagnosing or fixing your system's problems.

VGA—An industry standard for displaying computer graphics. VGA stands for Video Graphics Array.

Video Card—A card in your computer that translates (outputs) video from your computer onto your computer's screen or monitor.

Voice modem—A special modem that supports voice capabilities.

World Wide Web—A portion of the Internet that features a graphical interface.

XT—A variation of the original 8088-based IBM PC that could work with a hard drive.

Index

A

accelerated video cards, described   77–78
adapters, hard drives   88
adhesive labels   165
AdLib sound cards   121
all-around system, described   26
America Online   16, 130–132
answering machines, voice modems
    135–137
anti-static bags, memory storage   205
anti-static wrist strap   165
AT bus   50
ATAPI (AT attachment packet interface)
    standard, CD-ROM drives   116
audio CD sound format   125
average access time, described   85–86
average seek time, described   85–86

B

background processing, Windows 95   135
backups
    CPU upgrades   185
    hard drive data   91–98
    hard drive installation   243
    hardware upgrades   174
    memory upgrade   205
    motherboard replacement   192
    opening computer case   174
    saving data   285
    video card replacement   214
bargain basement   147–158
    buying tips   154–157
    computer superstores   150–151
    computer swap meets   152–154
    mail order   151–152
    specialty computer stores   148–149
    warehouse stores   149–150
    where to buy   154

BIOS (basic input/output system)
    described   53
    528MB hard drive limitations   243
boards, expansion   177–182
boot disk   164
bps (bits per second), modems   139
bus
    described   43
    styles   50–53
    video cards   77

C

cables
    check for problems   282–283
    floppy drives   262
    hard drives   88
    length considerations when replacing
        expansion cards/motherboard   193
    pin one indicator   252–253
    pin one stripe indicator   194
    printer   290
    y-cable connectors   242
cache programs   54, 301–302
caddies, CD-ROM   118
Carbon Copy program   139
cards, game   267
CAS (Communications Application
    Specifications) support, modems   141
cases
    motherboard size limitations   55
    opening   173–177
    unplugging before opening   174
categories, vendors   363–374
caveat emptor, computer swap meets   153
CCITT (Consultative Committee of
    International Telephone and Tele-
    graph)   141
CD-ROM drives   111–118
    ATAPI (AT attachment packet interface)
        standard   116

controller types   115–116, 265–266
cost considerations   114–115
data transfer rates   113–115
described   20–21, 112
disk caddy   118
IDE vs. SCSI   115–116
installation   272–278
internal vs. external   117–118
kits vs. stand-alone   116–117
Kodak PhotoCD capable   114–115
kps (kilobytes per second)   113
MSCDEX file   274
multisession capability   114–115
troubleshooting   289
unable to read a CD   289
Windows 3.1 setup   276
Windows 95 setup   274–276
CDs
    companion, information   307–312
    games, hard drive storage
        requirements   81
    multimedia   112–113
    storage capacity   112
    unable to read   289
CGA (color graphics adapter)   71, 101
checklist, system component   6
chip puller   168
chips, processor speed development
    history   2
clockspeed, CPU   40–41
clones, described   29–30
clusters
    file   86–87
    hard drive file size   255–256
CMOS (complementary metal-oxide
    semiconductor)   201
    check wait states   284
    configurations, problems   281
    floppy drives settings   262

hard drive configuration settings 254–255, 285

information, recording before opening computer case   174

Codecs (compression/decompression schemes), described   25–26

colors, video cards display capability 75–76

COM ports, modems   234

commands
  FDISK, DOS   256
  Help | About (Windows)   61
  Mem (DOS)   61
  Print, DOS   290

communications software   239

communications, modem   129–146

components
  checklist   6
  isolating faulty   282–283

CompuServe   16, 131–132

Computer Shopper magazine   151

computers
  cleaning peripherals   301
  failure to turn on   282–283
  locking up   287–288
  placement   295–298
  superstores   150–151
  swap meets   152–154

connections, checking   284–285

connectors
  hard drive power   253
  Molex power   195
  y-cable   242

containers, parts   169

controller cards
  CD-ROM drives   115–116, 265–266
  hard drives   82–83
  IDE   244–247

conversion cards, memory   64–65

CPU (central processing unit)   39–56
  286 (80286) chips   45–46
  386 (80386) chips   46
  486 (80486) chips   46–48
  8088 chips   44–45
  backup before upgrading   185
  chip speed history   2
  clockspeed ratings   40–41
  described   32
  memory addressing   58
  non-ZIF-socketed replacement   187
  overdrive chips   43–44
  Pentium chips   48–50
  testing without replacing cover   188
  troubleshooting   188–189
  upgrade options   43–44
  upgrade socket   184
  upgrading   183–190
  ZIF (Zero Insertion Force) socket 185–187

Creative Labs, SoundBlaster sound cards   121

CRT (cathode ray tube)   99

D

data
  backing up   91–98, 285
  CPU upgrade   185
  hard drive installation   243
  memory upgrade   205
  opening computer case   174
  removing motherboard   192
  video card replacement   214

data pathway, video cards   78

data transfer rates
  CD-ROM drives   113–115
  described   85–86

daughterboards   54

defragging hard drives   302
defragmenter software   87
DIP (dual in-line package) memory
    63–64
dip switches, expansion boards   177
disk compression software, hard
    drives   84
disks, DOS boot   164
display resolutions, video cards   72–75
DOS boot disk   164
DOS, 640K memory limitation   58
dot pitch, described   105–107
DRAM memory, video cards   62, 76–77
drinks, spilled in computer   296
drive maintenance   301–302
drivers
    fax printing   134
    modems   232–233
    video cards   221–225
drives
    CD-ROM   20–21, 111–118
    floppy   90–91
    hard   81–98
    MO (magneto optical)   97–98
    recordable CD-ROM   95–96
    removable hard/floppy   96–97
    re-writable optical disk   97–98
    tape backup   94–95
DriveSpace program   84
DTP (desktop publishing)
    described   22–23
    hardware requirements   22–23
dust, effect on computer   297–298

E

EDO RAM memory, video cards   62,
    76–77
EGA (enhanced graphics adapter)   71, 101
EIDE (enhanced IDE)   82

8088 (IBM PC/XT) systems
    memory addressing limitations   58
    upgrade considerations   30, 44–45
EISA (Extended Industry Standard
    Architecture) bus   51
electrical power, disconnecting before
    opening case   174
electromagnetic emissions, monitors   107
e-mail, described   15
error messages, No ROM Basic-System
    Halted   285
errors, reproducing   281
expanded memory   59–60
expansion boards
    described   41–42
    dip switch settings   177
    IDE controller   244–247
    installing   177–182
    jumper settings   177
    removal from motherboard   193
    retaining screws   178
    static electricity concerns   179
expansion slots
    motherboards   53
    video cards   218
extended memory   60–61
external CD-ROM drives   117–118
external modems   142–144
    installation   230–234
    serial port connections   230–231
EZFlyer drive   97

F

faults, General Protection   317–320
fax/modem   132–135, 141
FDISK utility, DOS   256, 285
file formats, sounds   121–125

files
    clusters 86–87
    MIDI (musical instrument digital
    interface) 124–125
    MSCDEX 274
    removing unwanted Windows
    3.x 313–316
    swap 85
    wave (wav) 121–123
fine-point permanent marker 164
flashlight 163–164
flat ribbon cables, pin one stripe
    indicator 194
floppy disks, trouble reading 287
floppy drives 90–91
    CMOS settings 262
    installing new 261–263
    misalignment 287
    placement order on ribbon cable 262
    removing existing 258–261
    replacing 258–263
    testing before replacing cover 263
    troubleshooting installation 263
fluorescent lights, interrupt/alter
    signals 298
FM synthesis, sound cards 124–125
foam padding 164
formats
    hard drives 255–257
    sound file 121–125
forms, component checklist 6
forums, online 130
486 systems, upgrade considerations
    33–34, 46–48
Fujitsu DynaMO 230 drive 98

G
game cards, disabling when installing
    sound cards 267
games
    CD-ROM storage capacity 112
    hard drive storage requirements 81
    multimedia requirements 21
    sound cards compatibility
        standards 121–126
GB (gigabyte) 60
General Protection Faults 317–320
glossary 375–382
graphical operating systems, Windows
    95 11

H
hard drives 81–98
    528MB BIOS limitations 243
    adapters 88
    adding new 242–258
    average access time 85–86
    average seek time 85–86
    backups 91–98, 185
    cables 88
    clusters 255–256
    CMOS settings 254–255
    controller types 82–83
    data cable pin one indicator 252–253
    data transfer rates 85–86
    defragmenting 87, 302
    described 10
    disk compression software 84
    faulty 285–286
    FDISK to repartition 286
    file clusters 86–87
    formatting 255–257
    IDE controller card installation
        244–247

installation   241–258
kit vs. bare   88–89
low-level formatted   255
master vs. slave   243
mounting components   88–89
paddle board (card)   87
parking   301
partitioning   255–257
power connectors   253
power supply requirements   242
purchasing tips   88–90
reconstructing   285–286
recording setup information before
   opening computer case   174
removing old   196–197, 247–249
speed ratings   85–87
standard sizes   81
testing before replacing cover   254
troubleshooting installation   257–258
virtual memory   85
vs. RAM   81
y-cable connectors   242
hardware
accelerated video cards   77–78
CD-ROM drives   111–118
controllers   82–83
CPU   39–56, 183–190
expansion boards   41–42, 177–182
floppy drives   258–263
hard drives   81–98, 241–258
headphones   289
IDE controller card   244–247
memory   57–66, 203–212
MIDI instruments   124
modems   129–146, 229–240
monitors   99–110
motherboards   41–56, 191–202
multimedia   265–278
sound cards   119–128
tools   159–170

video cards   67–80, 213–228
hardware requirements
all-around system   26
DTP (desktop publishing)   22–23
image-editing   24
multimedia   21
online connections   15–17
video editing   25
Windows 3.1   14–15
Windows 95   13
headphones, sound card jack   289
high graphics
286 (AT) system upgrade
   requirements   31
386SX/386DX system upgrade
   requirements   33
486SX/486DX system upgrade
   requirements   34
horizontal scan rate, monitors   106
humidity, effect on computers   296

I

I/O (input/output) ports   53
IBM-compatible clones, described   29–30
IDE (integrated drive electronics)   82
IDE controller cards, installation   244–247
image-editing, described   23–24
instruments, MIDI   124–125
interlaced monitors   106
internal CD-ROM drives   117–118
internal data pathway, video cards   78
internal modems   142–144
configuration settings   237–239
installation   234–237
Internet
286 (AT) system upgrade
   requirements   31
386SX/386DX system upgrade
   requirements   33

486SX/486DX system upgrade
    requirements   34
  modem access   131–132
  online providers   131–132
  overview   15–17
Iomega Zip Drive   96–97
ISA bus   50, 77
ISP (Internet Service Provider)   132

J

joystick ports, disabling when installing
  sound cards   267
jumpers, expansion boards   177

K

keyboards
  cleaning keys   301
  troubleshooting   292
keys, cleaning   301
kilobytes   54
kits
  CD-ROM drives   116–117
  hard drives   88–89
  multimedia   116–117, 266
Kodak PhotoCD, CD-ROM drives compatibility   114–115
kps (kilobytes per second)   113

L

laser printers, paper trays   290
LCD (liquid crystal display)   100
LEDs (lighted electronic displays)   281
liquids, spilled in computer   296
low-level format, hard drives   255

M

magnetic fields, effect on computers   298
mail order   151–152
maintenance, 295–303
  computer placement   295–298
  hard drives   301
  periodic   299–300
  power   298–299
  system considerations   301–303
  system defense   300–301
master hard drive   243
MCA (MicroChannel Architecture)
  bus   51
MDA (monochrome display adapter)   71
media, backups   91–98
memory   57–66
  4GB limitation   60
  640K limitations   58
  adding/replacing   203–212
  addressing   58
  anti-static bags   205
  backing up data before upgrading   205
  bad chips   283–284
  conversion cards   64–65
  daughterboards   54
  described   10
  DIPs (dual in-line packages)   63–64
  DRAM   62
  EDO   62
  expanded   59–60
  extended   60–61
  inserting new SIMMs   208–211
  installation troubleshooting   211–212
  matching   204
  mixing/matching speeds   62
  motherboard sockets   64, 192, 206
  ns (nanoseconds) ratings   61
  removing existing SIMMs   207–208
  reusing old   54
  selling old   64

SIMM (single in-line memory
module)   54, 62–63
speed ratings   61
synchronous DRAM   62
testing before replacing cover   210–211
types   62–64
upgrade cost considerations   65
video cards   72, 76–77
virtual   85
vs. hard drive storage   81
wait states   212
Windows 95 guidelines   61
MFM (Modified Frequency Modulation
procedure) controller   82
MHZ (megahertz), described   40–41
MIDI (musical instrument digital interface) files, sound cards   124–125
MIDI instruments   124–125
MO (magneto optical) drives   97–98
modems   129–146, 229–240
16550A UART   144
bps (bits per second)   139
CAS (Communications Application
Specifications) support   141
CITT standards   141
COM port settings   234
commercial service connect speed cost
considerations   140
communications software   239
described   16–17, 129
downloading programs   130
driver settings   232–233, 237–239
external installation   230–234
fax capability   132–135, 141
forums   130
going online   130–132
installing   229–240
internal installation   234–237
internal vs. external   142–144
Internet access   131–132

modulator/demodulator   129
purchasing considerations   139–144
remote computing   137–139
speed ratings   139–141
troubleshooting   291
UART (universal asynchronous
receiver/transmitter) chip   144
V standard levels   140–141
voice capability   135–137, 141
Molex power connectors   195
monitors   99–110
adjustment controls   108
cleaning the screen   300–301
cost considerations   107
CRT (cathode ray tube)   99
dot pitch   105–107
flat screens   106
horizontal scan rate   106
interlaced vs. non-interlaced   106
LCD (liquid crystal display)   100
MPR II standard   107
pixels   99
purchasing guidelines   109
refresh rates   106
resolution   101–105
scanning frequency   106
size considerations   103–105
styles   101–103
upgrade issues   102
vertical scan rate   106
video card matching   72, 103
motherboards   41–56
alignment holes   198–199
BIOS (basic input/output system)   53
built-in I/O (input/output) ports   53
built-in VGA disabling   214
bus   42–43
bus styles   50–53
cable connections   194–195
cable lengths   193

caches 54
case size limitations 55
CPU upgrades 183–190
data backup before replacing 192
daughterboards 54
described 32
expansion card removal 193
expansion card slots 42, 53
hard drive connections 196–198
memory sockets 64, 206
Molex power connectors 195
paddle board (card) 87
PnP (Plug and Play) 52
purchasing tip summary 55–56
RAM installation 192
reassembling 198–201
replacing 191–202
SIMM slot considerations 54
standoffs 197–199
testing before replacing case 200–201
troubleshooting installation 201–202
upgrading 32
video card expansion slots 218
mounting components, hard drives 88
mouse, troubleshooting 292
MPEG video, video card add-ons 79
MPR II standards, monitors 107
MSCDEX file 274
multimedia 265–278
286 (AT) system upgrade
requirements 31
386SX/386DX system upgrade
requirements 33
486SX/486DX system upgrade
requirements 34
CD-ROM drives 20–21
CD-ROM kits 116–117
CD-ROM storage capacity 112

described 17–21
hardware requirements 21
kits 266
sound board (cards) 20–21
system testing 276
multisession, described 114–115
multitasking 12, 43

N
needle-nose pliers 161–162
non-interlaced monitors 106
ns (nanoseconds) 61
number of bits, sound cards 123
numeric coprocessor, described 47
nut drivers 166

O
Olympus Sys.230 drive 98
online
connections, hardware
requirements 15–17
described 130–132
services, modem connect speed cost
considerations 140
operating systems
described 11
graphical 11
hard drive storage requirements 81
Windows 3.1 14–15
Windows 95 10–13
overdrive chips
CPU upgrades 43–44, 183–190
Pentium systems 49
problems after installation 284

P

paddle board (card) 87
Panasonic PD/CD drive 98
paper trays, laser printers 290
partitions, hard drive 255–257
pcANYWHERE program 139
PCI bus 50, 52, 77
Pentium Pro, upgrade issues 34
Pentium systems, upgrade consider-
    ations 34, 48–50
periodic maintenance 299–300
pin one stripe indicator, flat ribbon
    cables 194, 252–253
pixels 69, 99
placement, computer 295–298
Plug & Play
    video card setup 221–222
    Windows 95 52
ports
    COM 234
    I/O (input/output) 53
    joystick (game card) 367
    serial 230–231
power connectors 195, 253
power supply
    disconnecting before opening case 174
    hard drives requirements 242
printers
    Online setting 290
    paper out message 290
    resetting 290
    self-test 290
    troubleshooting 290–291
printing, troubleshooting 290–291
processors, described 10
Prodigy 16, 131–132
programs
    cache 301–302
    downloading 130
    DriveSpace 84
    fax 135

FDISK, DOS 256
    remote computing 139
    Sound Recorder, Windows 122
    voice modem 137
publications, *Computer Shopper* 151

Q

questions
    upgrade expertise needed 5
    when to upgrade 4

R

RAM (random access memory) 39, 57–66
    adding/replacing 203–212
    motherboards installation 192
    problems with 284
    vs. hard drive storage 81
recordable CD-ROM drives 95–96
refresh rates
    described 79
    monitors 106
remote computing 137–139
Remotely Possible program 139
removable drives 96–97
requirements
    all-around system 26
    DTP (desktop publishing) 22–23
    image-editing 24
    multimedia 21
    online connections 15–17
    video editing 25
    Windows 3.1 14–15
    Windows 95 13
resolution
    monitors 101–105
    video cards 68–69, 72–78
re-writable optical disk drives 97–98
RLL (Run-Length limited procedure)
    controller 82

S

sampling rate, sound cards   123
scanning frequency, monitors   106
screens, troubleshooting   288–289
screwdrivers   160–161
screws
 expansion board retainers   178, 216, 220
 motherboard   197–199
 removing from computer case   174–175
SCSI (small computer system interface) controller   83
seek times, CD-ROM drives   114
self-test, printers   290
serial ports, external modem connections   230–231
SIMM (single in-line memory module)   62–63
 adding/replacing   203–212
 conversion cards   64–65
 described   54, 204
 inserting new   208–211
 removing existing   207–208
 problems   284
slave hard drive   243
smoke, effect on computer   297
sockets
 memory chips (SIMMs)   206
 ZIF (Zero Insertion Force)   185–187
software
 checking for conflicts   281
 communications   239
 defragger   87
 disk compression   84
 DTP (desktop publishing)   22–23
 fax   132–135
 hard drive storage requirements   81
 image-editing   23–24
 voice recognition   125–126

sound cards   119–128
 8-bit vs. 16-bit   123
 AdLib compatible   121
 audio CD sound format   125
 described   20–21
 file formats   121–125
 FM synthesis   124–125
 game compatibility   121–126
 game port/joystick disabling   267
 installation   267–272, 277–278
 MIDI (musical instrument digital interface) files   124–125
 no sound from speakers   289–290
 non-Plug & Play Windows 95 setup   270–272
 number of bits   123
 purchasing considerations   126–128
 sampling rate   123
 SoundBlaster compatibility   121
 speaker jack   289
 troubleshooting   289–290
 voice recognition   125–126
 volume knob   289
 wave (wav) files   121–123
 wavetable   125
 Windows 3.1 setup   272
 Windows 95 Plug & Play setup   270
Sound Recorder utility, Windows   122
SoundBlaster sound cards   121
speakers, no sound   289–290
specialty computer stores   148–149
standoffs, motherboard   197–199
static electricity, expansion board handling concerns   179
sticky keys   301
super VGA   75, 101
surge protectors   299
swap file   85
swap meets   152–154
SyJet drive   97

synchronous DRAM memory 62
Syquest drives 96–97
systems
    286 (AT) 30–31
    386SX/386DX 31–33
    486SX/486DX 33–34
    8088 (IBM PC/XT) 30
    component checklist 6
    IBM-compatible clones 29–30
    locking up 287–288
    Pentium 34
    Pentium Pro 34
    reasons to upgrade 1–8
    upgrade advantages/disadvantages 3
    uses for 9–28
    when to upgrade 4

T

tape drives 94–95
telephones, voice modem answering
    machines 135–137
temperature, effect on computers 296
terms 375–382
3D accelerators, video card add-ons 79
386 systems
    RLL/MFM hard drives 82
    UART chip upgrade 144
    upgrade considerations 31–33, 46
three-prong extractor 162–163
tools 160–169
    adhesive labels 165
    antistatic wrist strap 165
    chip puller 168
    containers 169
    DOS boot disk 164
    fine-point permanent marker 164
    flashlight 163–164
    foam padding 164
    needle-nose pliers 161–162
    nut/hex drivers 166

    screwdrivers 160–161
    three-prong extractor 162–163
    Torx screwdriver 167
    tweezers 162
    work space 165–166
Torx screwdriver 167
troubleshooting 279–293
    bad memory chips 283–284
    can't read a floppy 287
    CD-ROM drive installation 277–278
    CD-ROM drives 289
    check software 281
    CMOS configurations 281
    computer does not turn on 283–285
    CPU upgrade 188–189
    faulty hard drive 285–286
    floppy drive 287–288
    floppy drive installation 263
    general 280–282
    hard drive installation 257–258
    isolating a faulty component 282–283
    keyboards 292
    memory installation 211–212
    modem installation 240
    modems 291
    motherboards installation 201–202
    mouse 292
    no sound from speakers 289–290
    printer problems 290–291
    screen does not look right 288–289
    sound card installation 277–278
    sound cards 289–290
    system conflicts 281
    system lock up 287–288
    video cards installation 225–226
TV tuners, video card add-ons 70
tweezers 162
286 (AT) systems
    RLL/MFM hard drives 82
    UART chip upgrade 144
    upgrade considerations 30–31, 45–46

U

UART (universal asynchronous receiver/
    transmitter) chip, modems   144
uninterruptible power supply (UPS)   298
unwanted files, removing   313–316
upgrade socket, CPU   184
upgrade-related vendors   321–362
upgrades
    286 (AT) systems   30–31
    386SX/386DX systems   31–33
    486SX/486DX systems   33–34
    8088 (IBM PC/XT) systems   30
    advantages/disadvantages   3
    CD-ROM drives   111–118
    CPU   43–44, 183–190
    expertise needed   5
    floppy drives   258–263
    hard drives   81–98, 241–258
    IDE controller card   244–247
    memory   57–66, 203–212
    modems   129–146, 229–240
    monitors   99–110
    motherboards   32, 191–202
    multimedia   265–278
    Pentium Pro systems   34
    Pentium systems   34
    reasons for   1–8
    sound cards   119–128
    tools/work area   159–170
    video cards   67–80, 213–228
    when to   4
utilities
    defraggers   87
    disk compression   84
    FDISK, DOS   256
    Sound Recorder, Windows   122

V

vendors
    by category   363–374
    upgrade-related   321–362
vertical scan rate, monitors   106
VESA (local) bus   50, 52, 77
VGA (video graphics array)   70–71, 101
vibration, effect on computers   296–297
video capture board   25
video cards   67–80
    3D accelerators   79
    64-bit vs. 128-bit   78
    accelerators   77–78
    add-ons   79
    built-in VGA disabling   214
    bus styles   77
    color palettes   75–76
    described   10
    display resolutions   72–75
    drivers   221–225
    expansion slots   218
    installation   218–226, 288–289
    internal data pathway   78
    memory cost considerations   76
    memory types   76–77
    memory upgrades   72
    monitor matching   72
    MPEG video   79
    non-Plug & Play Windows 95
    setup   222–225
    pixels   69
    Plug & Play setup   221–222
    refresh rates   79
    removing existing   214–218
    replacing   213–228
    resolution   68–69, 72–78
    retaining screw   216, 220
    standard VGA Windows settings
        214–215
    standards   70–71
    testing before replacing cover   221

troubleshooting installation   225–226
TV tuners   79
upgrade considerations   69
upgrading   213–228
Windows 3.1 setup   222
video editing
   Codecs (compression/decompression
     schemes)   25–26
   described   25–26
   video capture board   25
virtual memory   85
viruses   302–303
voice modems   135–137, 141
voice recognition, sound cards   125–126
volume, speakers   289
VRAM, video cards   76–77

W

wait states
   checking in CMOS   284
   memory   212
warehouse stores   149–150
wave (wav) files   121–123
wavetables, sound cards   125
Windows
   DriveSpace program   84
   SCSI CD-ROM compatibility   115
   Sound Recorder   122
   swap file   85
   virtual memory   85
   wave (wav) files   121–123
Windows 3.1   14–15
   286 (AT) system upgrade
     requirements   31
   386SX/386DX system upgrade
     requirements   33
   486SX/486DX system upgrade
     requirements   34
   CD-ROM drives setup   276
   modem settings   232, 239
   no sound from speakers   289–290

removing unwanted files   313–316
sound card setup   272
standard VGA settings   214–215
unable to read a CD   289
video card setup   222
Windows 95
   286 (AT) system upgrade
     requirements   31
   386SX/386DX system upgrade
     requirements   33
   486SX/486DX system upgrade
     requirements   34
   background processing   135
   CD-ROM drives setup   274–276
   described   10–13
   graphical operating system   10
   hard drive storage requirements   81
   hardware requirements   13
   memory considerations   61
   modem settings   232–233, 237–239
   multitasking   12
   no sound from speakers   289–290
   non-Plug & Play sound card
     setup   222–225, 270–272
   Plug & Play sound card setup   270
   Plug & Play video card setup   221–222
   Plug and Play architecture   52
   standard VGA settings   215
   unable to read a CD   289
work space   165–166
WWW (World Wide Web)
   modem access   131–132
   overview   15–16

Y

y-cable connectors   242

Z

ZIF (Zero Insertion Force) socket   185–187
ZIP drives   96–97